MINORITIES IN EUROPE

CROATIA, ESTONIA AND SLOVAKIA

Centre for Migration Law
Law Faculty
University of Nijmegen

T.M.C. Asser Instituut
The Hague

MINORITIES IN EUROPE

CROATIA, ESTONIA AND SLOVAKIA

edited by

Snežana Trifunovska

T•M•C•Asser Press
The Hague

Published by T.M.C. ASSER PRESS,
P.O.Box 16163, 2500 BD The Hague, The Netherlands

Sold and distributed in North, Central and South America
by Kluwer Law International,
675 Massachusetts Avenue, Cambridge, MA 02139, U.S.A.

In all other countries, sold and distributed
by Kluwer Law International, Distribution Centre,
P.O.Box 322, 3300 AH Dordrecht, The Netherlands

ISBN 978-90-6704-117-1

Lay-out and cover: Oasis Productions, Nieuwerkerk a/d IJssel, The Netherlands
Printing and binding: Koninklijke Wöhrmann BV, Zutphen, The Netherlands

FOREWORD

A group of international experts in the field of minority protection, as well as ambassadors and diplomatic representatives from a number of Central and Eastern European countries, met for a two-day conference in Berg en Dal near Nijmegen, The Netherlands, on 30-31 October 1998.

It was the first conference organised jointly by the T.M.C. Asser Institute, The Hague, and the Centre for Migration Law of the Law Faculty of the University of Nijmegen. The intention was to discuss three aspects of the minority situation in the Republic of Croatia, the Republic of Estonia and the Slovak Republic: (a) political/security, (b) internal legal, and (c) economic aspects. This book is a collection of the papers presented at that conference.

One could rightly inquire as to the reasons which led the Organising Committee of the Conference to choose exactly these three countries. It was certainly not because the situation in these countries is very much different from other minority situations. Of course, all three countries have their own specific features, but the same could also be safely said of any other European State: each minority situation is unique and deserves attention. In this sense, a comparative analysis can be equally valuable for all other countries in which minorities live. Being aware of that, the Organising Committee looked at the criteria of resemblance rather than at the criteria of distinctiveness.

It is a matter of fact, indeed, that all three countries achieved independence as a result of the post-Cold War dissolution of their predecessor States: Croatia from the dissolution of the former Socialist Federal Republic of Yugoslavia; Estonia from the former Soviet Union; and Slovakia from the dissolution of the Czech and Slovak Federation. In Croatia it led to violent inter-ethnic conflict, whereas in the other two countries the dissolution was peacefully completed. Therefore, within all of these countries there is a relatively complex minority situation which is, *inter alia*, also due to the change of State borders.

Besides, all of them are relatively young democracies established in the post-Cold War period. In this sense they have in the recent past undergone a transformation of their political system - from one party communist to multiparty democracy, of their economic system - from centrally-planned State-ownership to a free-market economy, and are at this moment in the process of integrating in the West European political, security and economic structures.

In addition, the Organising Committee also took into consideration the fact that these countries revealed problems typical of the regions to which they belong. This is especially true for Croatia which insists on being a more Central

European than Balkan country; however, the events and the inter-ethnic war which took place in Croatia in the period 1991-1995, in this respect results in it being considered as part of the 'powder-keg' Balkan region. Similarly, Estonia shares the history of the other two Baltic States, Latvia and Lithuania, and in respect to minorities, it shares similar problems also partly created by the forced (im)migration of the ethnic Russians, once a dominant group, which after the dissolution of USSR remained as a minority in these countries.

Notwithstanding the choice which the Organising Committee made in selecting these three countries, it remained aware of the fact that a similar - threefold - analysis would be equally worthy and interesting for other European countries. It would contribute to the pinpointing of those minority aspects where real problems lie and to the means and mechanisms for an adequate protection afforded to minority groups, rather than to the general on-going discussion about minorities. Of course, the first and most important task of the countries which have minorities is to avoid by all means situations similar to those which occurred in the Federal Republic of Yugoslavia with respect to the Kosovo Albanians, from developing and escalating on their territories. But, beyond that bottom line, States have a duty to develop principles, norms and guarantee systems which go hand in hand with the current international standards safeguarding human rights, multiculturalism and pluralism.

Needless to say, none of the three aspects discussed can be considered exclusively and separately from each other: as pointed out in some articles which follow, national politics and security are closely inter-related with the general economic situation of the country as well as with the concrete economic position of minorities, and the same is true for the legal aspects in relation to the political and economic sphere. As a consequence of this, authors dealing with one of the aspects concerning a selected country have not been able to keep the discussion strictly within the bounds of their topics but have often touched upon the other two aspects by way of elaboration, explanation and/or comparison. Therefore readers will sometimes find the same points and facts being discussed with respect to one of the countries in more than one article, but in a different context. Of course, the views and opinions presented are the personal views of the authors and do not present, in any way whatsoever, the views of any of the organisations with which they are affiliated, or indeed any official views.

Both the T.M.C. Asser Institute and the Centre for Migration Law found a common interest in the field of minorities: the T.M.C. Asser Institute has already for some time been carrying out different academic projects dealing with the situation in Central and Eastern European States, and within the Centre for Migration Law minorities present one of the two major fields of interest and activity. As a result of this common field of interest they undertook the endeavour of organising the conference and jointly publishing this book. However, it should be pointed out that, while the effort to gather prominent experts on minority issues was undertaken by the Centre, it was the T.M.C. Asser Institute and its Director, Dr. Gerard Tanja, who, by providing the actual organisation and financial means, made the Conference a practical possibility.

At the end, in every project there are persons who cannot and should not be forgotten because of their contribution in its realisation. I would here mention with gratitude the members of the Organising Committee, Dr. Arie Bloed, Director of the the Constitutional and Legislative Policy Institute (COLPI), Budapest; Prof. Dr. Willem van Genugten, Professor of the Tilburg and Nijmegen Law Faculties; Dr. John Packer, Legal Advisor of the OSCE High Commissioner on National Minorities; and Dr. Gerard Tanja, who were not sparing in their time and energy in thinking over and extending concrete assistance in the realisation of the Conference.

As the editor I am especially grateful to the authors who with great enthusiasm cooperated in preparing the book and without whom this book would not be possible.

Nijmegen, September 1999

DR. SNEŽANA TRIFUNOVSKA
Centre for Migration Law
University of Nijmegen
The Netherlands

TABLE OF CONTENTS

Conclusion

Introduction

MINORITY RIGHTS AND PEACE: AVAILABLE STANDARDS, PROCEDURES AND INSTITUTIONS

by Gudmundur Alfredsson

1. INTRODUCTION

In 1948, at the time of the adoption of the Universal Declaration of Human Rights, the General Assembly decided that the United Nations could not remain indifferent to the 'fate of minorities'.[1] Regional and international organizations have subsequently undertaken to formulate standards and to monitor respect for minority rights, but these efforts often seem slow and otherwise inadequate in the face of continued violent conflicts or the threats thereof.

Widespread economic, political and social discrimination against minorities is a common phenomenon. It is combined with the denial of dignity, identities and cultures. Even genocide takes place in this modern age. Rights violations of this kind often lead to violent conflicts, with the minorities rising in rebellion against tyranny and oppression. Much of the new attention to minority rights is accordingly security-oriented, even more so as internal conflicts have a tendency to spill across international borders.

Respect for human rights is one method of conflict prevention, and preventive action is certainly less costly than reaction after violence erupts for both the state concerned and the international community. Democracy is generally conducive to human rights, but majority rule is not necessarily friendly to or understanding of the needs of a minority. Minority rights must therefore be enshrined in constitutional and legislative guarantees with available and accessible remedies, consistent with international standards. This approach also requires that the rights of individuals and groups be respected.

As a result of frequent rights violations and the ensuing violent conflicts, minority issues have become regular features on international human rights and peace agendas. Minorities have also gained a better knowledge of their rights and have learned to expect equality and justice, and they are increasingly presenting their demands to international and regional organizations.

---

[1] GA Resolution 217 (III) C of 10 December 1948. The Universal Declaration was adopted by the same resolution, in part A.

S. Trifunovska (Ed.), Minorities in Europe – Croatia, Estonia and Slovakia

The Organization for Security and Co-operation in Europe (OSCE) has taken the lead in recognizing and dealing with the link between minority rights and security questions. The new attitude was nicely summarized a few years ago in a report by the UN Secretary-General entitled *An Agenda for Peace* which comments on ethnic conflicts:

> 'One requirement for solutions to these problems lies in commitment to human rights with a special sensitivity to those of minorities, whether ethnic, religious, social or linguistic . . . (T)he increasingly effective machinery of the United Nations dealing with human rights, should enhance the situation of minorities as well as the stability of States.'[2]

The fundamental rules of human rights law concerning the equal enjoyment of all human rights and non-discrimination in that enjoyment apply, of course, to minorities and persons belonging to them. In response to the General Assembly reference to the fate of minorities, minority-specific provisions in a number of human rights instruments[3] aim to achieve equal rights for all by way of special measures.

The international and regional minority-specific standards and the corresponding monitoring methods are not perfect when measured against the basic rules concerning equal rights and non-discrimination. With an increased awareness of these deficiencies, important steps have been taken over the last few decades. Additional international and regional organizations have entered the arena, and new instruments and procedures, together with important case-law, have come into being.

Among the highlights of these developments are the quasi-judicial decisions of an international treaty body and efforts to engage governments and groups in dialogue. The Human Rights Committee under the International Covenant on Civil and Political Rights, mainly with reference to its Article 27, has adopted some far-reaching case-law with a strong reaffirmation in its General Comment No. 23 of 1994. In 1992, the OSCE established the post of High Commissioner on National Minorities. The United Nations in 1995 created a Working Group on Minorities (hereinafter WGM) with a mandate to review and encourage state compliance with the standards contained in the 1992 Declaration on the Rights of Persons belonging to National or Ethnic, Religious and Linguistic Minorities (hereinafter the 1992 Declaration).

---

[2] UN Doc. A/47/277 – S/24111, 17 June 1992, para. 18.

[3] For compilations of instruments with minority-specific language, see: Gudmundur Alfredsson and Göran Melander, *A Compilation of Minority Rights Standards. A Selection of Texts from International and Regional Human Rights Instruments and Other Documents*, Raoul Wallenberg Institute, Report No. 24, Lund (1997); Patrick Thornberry, 'Basic Documents on Minorities and Indigenous Peoples', in *World Directory of Minorities*, Minority Rights Group, London (1997) pp. 706-810; and Hurst Hannum, *Documents on Autonomy and Minority Rights*, Martinus Nijhoff Publishers (1993).

Beginning with a definition of beneficiaries, this article[4] describes the main rules of human rights law concerning the equal enjoyment of all human rights, non-discrimination and the special measures considered necessary for achieving equal enjoyment in fact. An overview of the institutions and procedures used by international and regional organizations to monitor State compliance follows. Finally, the article outlines the interaction between individual and group rights and offers a few concluding observations.

2. DEFINITION OF THE BENEFICIARIES

There is no universally accepted definition of the term 'minority'. Such a definition has long been sought in order to establish international standards and to apply them.[5] After all, it is useful to know to whom the standards apply and lawyers, of course, thrive on definitions. Nevertheless, much of the time it is self-evident which groups constitute minorities. Most of the proposed definitions have common components. Add national and international practice, and the elements of a definition will clearly emerge. The necessary components of the definition are certain objective characteristics, self-identification, the numbers involved, and long-term presence on the territory concerned.

The objective characteristics relate to the joint affiliation or affinity of the members of a minority as far as national or ethnic origin, culture, language and/or religion are concerned. The requirement appears in many instruments, even in the title of the 1992 Declaration. The reliance in European instruments on the term 'national minorities' does not change or limit this element; while different interpretations have been attached to this term, it should and is indeed likely to cover the same groups as the international standards.

The definition must also have a subjective element, as is acknowledged in some instruments and recommended by UN Special Rapporteurs. The element presumably comes in two layers, that is an individual decides whether he/she is a member of a minority, and the group must accept the individual concerned on the basis of the facts and in a non-arbitrary fashion.[6]

---

[4] The article draws on my contribution 'Minority Rights: Minority Rights and Monitoring Procedures', in *Minority Rights Handbook* of the *Latvian Human Rights Quarterly*, Issue 5/6, Riga (1998) pp. 9-28.

[5] The UN Secretariat has issued a compilation of definition proposals over a 40-year period, in Document E/CN.4/1997/WG.5.WP.1. For a demonstration of the variety of groups, see: Rudolfo Stavenhagen (Ed.), *World Guide of Ethnic Minorities and Indigenous Peoples*, UN University and El Colegio de Mexico, Vol. I (1998), and the Minority Rights Group's *World Directory of Minorities* (1997).

[6] ILO Convention No. 169 concerning Indigenous and Tribal Peoples in Independent Countries thus refers in Art. 1, para. 2, to self-identification. See also the Report of the Special Rapporteur to the Sub-Commission entitled 'Study on the Rights of persons belonging to Ethnic, Religious and Linguistic Minorities', in UN Doc. E/CN.4/Sub.2/384/Rev.1 (also available as a UN publication with sales numbers E.78.XIV.1 and E.91.XIV.2), paras. 567-568.

It is inherent in the term and almost unnecessary to state for the purposes of the definition, but a minority group must constitute less than one half of the state population, hence the reference to numbers. An actual minority cannot designate and treat the majority as a minority, as occurred in South Africa during the apartheid regime. A country may be composed of only minorities if no group makes up more than 50% of the population; as a result, all groups would be entitled to minority protection.

Perhaps the most difficult component of the definition is the requirement that a minority must have a long-term presence in the territory concerned. Refugees, migrant workers, immigrants and other aliens are entitled to human rights, without discrimination (with the exception of certain political rights). Several separate instruments have been adopted to protect aliens, but they do not immediately achieve minority status.[7] At some point, however, the newcomers become minorities. The likely turning point is when the individuals concerned identify more closely with the new territory or country (where they now live) than the old territory or country (where they came from). In other words, we are talking more or less about the time it takes for the offspring to go through the school system of the new country, that is one or two generations.

If groups in a given country meet the definition elements, states do not and should not have a say on the recognition of groups. The acceptance or non-acceptance by governments is simply irrelevant and non-acceptance should automatically be considered suspect. A state will not be relieved of its responsibilities by denying citizenship to members of a group on an arbitrary or discriminatory basis. Calling groups by other names, such as cohabiting nations or nationalities, is likewise insufficient for depriving them of minority protection. In grey areas, delimitation can be left to the practice of States, as with the implementation of human rights in general, but such practice should be subject to supervision by international organizations in accordance with existing standards and monitoring procedures.

In the context of the definition, it is important to distinguish 'minorities' from 'peoples'. As with the term 'minority', there is no universally accepted definition of the term 'people'. In practice, the latter term, for the purposes of self-determination and development, has been applied to the populations of territorial or administrative entities, within some sort of acknowledged borders, more often than not without regard to the ethnic composition and cultural characteristics of the inhabitants.

Minorities, on the other hand, are not entitled to the right of self-determination (at least not in an external sense, see the discussion on minority autonomy below). The very idea of minority rights, as regulated and pursued by the international community, implies continued sovereignty and territorial integrity of

---

[7] For a different and broader point of view, see General Comment No. 23 of the Human Rights Committee of 1994.

States. By guaranteeing equal rights and non-discrimination to everyone within a State, the intention is to improve the quality of life, to avoid tensions and thus to reduce the likelihood of State dismemberment.

3. EQUAL ENJOYMENT AND NON-DISCRIMINATION

Universally applicable rules of international human rights law establish equal enjoyment of all human rights and the prohibition of discrimination. Repeated stipulations in the UN Charter (Articles 1 and 55), the Universal Declaration of Human Rights (Articles 1, 2, 7, 10, 16, 21, 23 and 26) and a large number of other treaties and declarations demonstrate clearly that the rules on equal enjoyment and on non-discrimination are fundamental to international, as well as regional, human rights law.

Some of these instruments are of a general character while others focus on particular issues, such as discrimination in employment and education and racial discrimination. Many of the latter instruments contain minority rights. They include the International Convention on the Elimination of All Forms of Racial Discrimination, the Declaration on the Elimination of All Forms of Intolerance and of Discrimination Based on Religion or Belief, the Convention on the Rights of the Child, the Convention concerning Discrimination in respect of Employment and Occupation (ILO Convention No. 111), and UNESCO's Convention against Discrimination in Education.

The grounds on which discrimination is prohibited may differ from one instrument to another, but repeated references to race, culture, colour, language, religion and national and ethnic origins clearly cover situations normally faced by minorities. The non-discrimination clauses, and the equal enjoyment rule on which they rest, extend to every sphere of human rights, from political and economic rights to civil, cultural and social rights, including obviously education, language, democracy and the administration of justice.

In 1989, the Human Rights Committee observed in General Comment No. 18 'that the term "discrimination" as used in the Covenant should be understood to imply any distinction, exclusion, restriction or preference . . . which has the purpose or effect of nullifying or impairing the recognition, enjoyment or exercise by all persons, on an equal footing, of all rights and freedoms'. The Committee added that 'equality' does not necessarily mean identical treatment. In certain instances, groups may be treated differently for purposes which are legitimate under the Covenant, such as achieving equal rights, if the action is reasonable and objective.

In addition, members of minorities are guaranteed equality before the law and equal protection by the law (extending equally to civil and political rights and economic, social and cultural rights), equality before the courts, equal access to public service, the prohibition of incitement to discrimination, and language guarantees in the administration of criminal justice.

4. SPECIAL MEASURES

Special measures are intended to place minorities, as well as their members, in a position equal to the State's majority population. In the face of historical and continued discrimination against minorities, the rules in the international human rights instruments about equal enjoyment and non-discrimination have frequently been complemented by what the UN instruments usually call special measures. The label does not matter, however, and the measures can also be referred to as preferential treatment, reverse discrimination or affirmative action.

By instituting special measures, many human rights instruments recognize that equal enjoyment under the law and the prohibition of discrimination are not enough; equal enjoyment in fact must also be achieved. Special measures are needed to realize equal enjoyment and to place the groups, as well as their members, in a position comparable to the majority population.

The special measures do not constitute privileges; like non-discrimination they are rooted in the rule of equal rights. A group and its members cannot be really equal to the majority population unless and until equal conditions prevail; even then the group may continue to be disadvantaged because of the majority's dominance in national life.

Special measures allowing minorities to use their native languages, to run their own schools, to benefit from access to other services provided by the group for the group, and to participate in the political and economic affairs of States are intended to approximate circumstances which the majority takes for granted. The State must not only allow but also fund and otherwise support such activities on a basis proportional to the services provided to the majority population; the test is whether equal enjoyment of the rights concerned, to the degree possible, has been achieved in actual fact (the aim and result).

The International Covenant on Civil and Political Rights,[8] the International Convention on the Elimination of All Forms of Racial Discrimination, the Convention on the Rights of the Child, the Convention against Discrimination in Education, the Convention against Genocide, the 1992 Declaration and many regional texts establish special measures from which minorities stand to benefit. The special measures exist primarily in the fields of education, culture, language and religion, areas particularly relevant to the identity and existence of a group.

---

[8] Notwithstanding the negative formulation of Art. 27 of the Covenant, it should be read to imply the obligation of States to provide special measures of protection; to this effect, see paras. 6.1, 6.2, 7 and 9 of General Comment No. 23 of the Human Rights Committee.

However, the measures are also used in the political, economic and social spheres.

Article 27 of the International Covenant on Civil and Political Rights is the best known of the minority-specific provisions. In protecting cultural, religious and linguistic activities, Article 27 reaffirms, strengthens and adds to the equal enjoyment of the rights enumerated in the other articles of the two Covenants, such as the rights of individuals to take part in cultural life and to profess and practise a religion. While addressing 'persons belonging to minorities', Article 27 goes beyond mere individual rights and recognizes the necessity of a group element by using the phrase 'in community with the other members of their group'.

The Covenant and its first Optional Protocol are particularly important because the Human Rights Committee has made major contributions to the jurisprudence on minority rights. The Committee has thus found that traditional economic activities and land rights, if they are essential for the cultural life of an ethnic community, may fall under Article 27.[9] The case-law is reinforced by two General Comments (already quoted above) on non-discrimination and Article 27.

The Convention against Discrimination in Education, in Article 2(b), declares that the 'establishment or maintenance, for religious or linguistic reasons, of separate educational systems or institutions' shall not be deemed to constitute discrimination. The logical continuation, in Article 5(c), calls for the recognition of 'the right of members of national minorities to carry on their own educational activities, including the maintenance of schools and, depending on the educational policy of each state, the use or the teaching of their own language'. Special measures relating to minority education are as a rule qualified by references to the necessity of learning majority languages, awareness of majority cultures and the quality of the education offered.

Article 2(2) of the International Convention on the Elimination of All Forms of Racial Discrimination provides that, when necessary, States shall take 'special and concrete measures to ensure the adequate development and protection of certain racial groups or individuals belonging to them' in order to guarantee the full and equal enjoyment of all human rights. The Convention also states, in Article 1(4), that such measures are not to be considered discriminatory.

In addition to special measures, minorities are also guaranteed other rights. The instruments provide for the right to physical existence; the right to identity and characteristics which distinguish them from the majority; the right to protect and promote cultural heritage and cultural activities; the right to promote and use minority languages in private and business settings and for certain official purposes; and the right to communicate and maintain contacts with fellow kith and kin in different parts of their own country and across State borders.

---

[9] See paras. 3.2 and 7 of General Comment No. 23 of the Human Rights Committee and the *Lubicon Lake Band* and *Kitok* cases quoted there.

Generally, special measures for the groups and their members are to be abandoned when discrimination has been eliminated and equal rights have been realized. Some special measures, however, such as the maintenance of educational institutions, political participation in State affairs, autonomy and land rights, will require prolonged or permanent measures.

Regional organizations also protect minority rights. Many regional instruments spell out equal enjoyment and non-discrimination. Regional organizations such as the OSCE and the Council of Europe have also adopted instruments calling for special measures, when necessary, in order to achieve equal enjoyment in fact. This is true for several reports and documents adopted by the OSCE, as well as the European Charter on Regional or Minority Languages and the Framework Convention for the Protection of National Minorities which were completed by the Council of Europe in 1992 and 1994, respectively.

The two Council of Europe instruments are something of a disappointment. One would have expected more from an organization with an excellent human rights record and a strong emphasis on the rule of law and an advanced system of monitoring institutions, which have brought about impressive and respected case-law. Instead, the two recent Council of Europe texts focus on State actions to recognize and promote minority rights rather than on the rights of minorities and their members. The texts even partly foresee State shopping for rights and areas of protection. The monitoring is left to weak institutions which rely on State information reports instead of group complaints.

The bottom line is that international instruments and procedures seem to offer more direct and more effective protection of minority rights than the regional counterparts under the auspices of the Council of Europe and the OSCE. The notable exception is the dialogue functions of the OSCE High Commissioner on National Minorities (see below).

5. SPECIAL MEASURES IN THE FIELD OF POLITICAL RIGHTS

Respect for the political rights and representation of minorities is an essential aspect of their rights. The political and legislative process also has a significant bearing on the respect for other minority rights, including those relating to culture, language and education. Special measures are necessary to guarantee minority participation in national politics, particularly when decisions may affect the destiny of the group. States have a choice between a variety of measures, but the aim and result must be equal enjoyment of political rights. The measures may include giving groups power disproportionate to their size, in order to ensure fair influence and consultation on political issues.

Special political measures can include the requirement that governments obtain consent from or engage in meaningful consultations with groups about matters affecting them; constitutional or legislative recognition of minority laws and customs and their application by the group; guaranteed seats for minorities in legislative and other political organs; and the appointment of officials chosen by the group to either specific positions or to a fixed percentage of general posts.

Paragraph 35 of Part IV of the Document from the 1990 Copenhagen Meeting of the OSCE Conference on the Human Dimension says that the participating States must give persons belonging to minorities sufficient opportunity to participate in public affairs and to protect and promote their identity. Furthermore, in the same paragraph, States:

> 'note the efforts undertaken to protect and create conditions for the promotion of the ethnic, cultural, linguistic and religious identity of certain national minorities by establishing, as one of the possible means to achieve these aims, appropriate local or autonomous administrations corresponding to the specific historical and territorial circumstances of such minorities in accordance with the policies of the State concerned.'

Autonomy can be referred to as self-government, self-management, home rule, the delegation of powers to a municipal authority with expanded functions, or even internal self-determination (as distinct from external, see above). The label does not matter as long as the central government agrees to share power and leave local matters in the hands of group representatives. The most effective way to protect group dignity, identity and diverse customs and thus to place minorities on an equal footing with other parts of society is to allow group control of local affairs, including those affected by special measures. Autonomy is one of the best guarantees a minority could wish for and it has been successfully implemented in many countries, although other governments have resisted.[10]

Autonomy can be both territorial and personal. If the group is concentrated in one area, a minority administration can be territorial. If the group's members, however, are spread over a larger area and/or intermixed with other population groups, personal autonomy, meaning membership of and participation in the group's activities regardless of residence, is a legitimate and workable solution.

Autonomy is by its very nature a group right. The collective entity claims the right, enjoys it and through its membership determines the form and structures of administration. In exercising its powers, the group regime must respect democratic principles and other universally recognized human rights. The group must thus protect the rights of its own members and of other population groups, and it must guarantee representative leadership and equality of the sexes. Group rights must also be exercised in a manner consistent with other principles of international law relating to, for example, the sovereignty, territorial integrity and national unity of States and the maintenance of international peace and security.

---

[10] See Louis B. Sohn, 'The Concept of Autonomy in International Law and the Practice of the United Nations', in 15 *Israeli Law Review* (1980) pp. 180-190; and Markku Suksi (Ed.), *Autonomy: Applications and Implications*, Kluwer Law International (1998).

6. INTERNATIONAL MONITORING PROCEDURES

States carry the primary responsibility for implementing the human rights standards to which they have subscribed. In pushing States towards compliance (and persuasion is indeed often needed), international and regional organizations employ a variety of institutions and methods. The methods include complaints procedures under both treaties and resolutions, investigative and fact-finding mandates, State reporting obligations, good offices undertaken by high officials of international organizations, public debates with the consequent political and diplomatic pressure, and technical assistance. All of these procedures have been used on behalf of minorities, but the focus below is on procedures which have been created specifically for minorities or are most likely to be used by minorities.

Some expert committees set up by treaties can receive complaints concerning alleged violations of minority rights. The Human Rights Committee has delivered significant decisions lending additional meaning to the right to culture as spelled out in Article 27 of the Covenant on Civil and Political Rights. Under one petition procedure, the under-utilized Article 14 of the International Convention on the Elimination of All Forms of Racial Discrimination, both groups and individuals can file complaints.

The complaints procedure under the Economic and Social Council Resolution 1503 (XLVIII) is worth noting. It allows individuals and groups to submit petitions for demonstrating a consistent pattern of gross rights violations. The resolution is universally applicable, requiring no ratification or acceptance of instruments. Complaints received under the confidential '1503 procedure' are reviewed by the UN Sub-Commission on Prevention of Discrimination and Protection of Minorities, the Commission on Human Rights and their working groups.

Other treaties and resolutions adopted under UN auspices offer complaints procedures which are available and may be relevant to minorities. In addition, petitioners can ask ILO, UNESCO, the World Bank and regional organisations to look into State compliance under their respective human rights instruments.

Special Rapporteurs and Representatives of the UN Commission on Human Rights often address minority concerns in their country-specific and thematic reports. The country reports include those on Guatemala, Iran, Iraq, Romania, Rwanda and the former Yugoslavia, and the thematic reports include religious intolerance, racism, racial discrimination, xenophobia and related intolerance around the world. Groups have easy access to the Rapporteurs, and some of the reports have included excellent suggestions.

Expert committees under international human rights treaties routinely question government representatives about minority rights when they present State reports. This is true for the Human Rights Committee, the Committee on the Elimination of Racial Discrimination, the Committee on Economic, Social and Cultural Rights, and the Committee on the Rights of the Child. The committees scrutinize the reports and the replies of governments and make recommendations if discrepancies are found between the performance and obligations of the State concerned. Minorities can supply relevant information to the treaty bodies or to their individual members in anticipation of the examination of relevant State reports.

The UN Secretary-General, the UN High Commissioner for Human Rights and director-generals of specialized agencies and regional organizations have undertaken good offices or quiet diplomacy for the sake of groups in distress. Actions of this kind can be requested by both governments and groups, but their use is unlikely unless the monitoring procedures are deemed to be inadequate or too slow in the face of urgent human rights problems or peace-threatening situations.

Apart from the more formal procedures, public debates in intergovernmental fora about human rights standards and violations can attract attention and improve compliance. Governments do not welcome institutional pressure and criticism and would rather avoid it. Discussions about minority rights in the UN Commission on Human Rights and its Sub-Commission often embarrass governments whose records are under examination. The debates, under various agenda items, thus put political, diplomatic and public pressure on governments to mend their ways.

The observation has been made in the Sub-Commission that rights violations affecting minorities account for about two-thirds of the total number of human rights problems considered. NGOs are instrumental in bringing attention to the minority situations. Governments are clearly concerned about critical debates in the public forums of international organizations and will therefore take steps to avoid such embarrassment.

Documents adopted at OSCE gatherings contain far-reaching minority rights provisions which build upon the principles of non-discrimination and affirmative action. The texts also demonstrate a new approach which centres on dialogue, confidence-building and prevention. The High Commissioner on National Minorities and other OSCE institutions are involved both in the fact-finding process and in facilitating dialogue between the parties. The High Commissioner is a promising institution with a substantive mandate to involve both groups and governments in dialogue in order to prevent violent conflicts.[11] Much of the success is thanks to Max van der Stoel of the Netherlands, the first High Commissioner.

The new thinking is increasingly influential at the United Nations. The 1992 Declaration on the Rights of Persons belonging to National or Ethnic, Religious and Linguistic Minorities, the first UN human rights instrument devoted solely to minority rights, states clearly in the preamble and in Article 9 that organizations of the UN system have a role to play in 'the full realization of the rights and principles' set forth in the Declaration, and it expressly ties minority rights together with the 'development of society as a whole and within a democratic framework based on the rule of law'.

---

[11] See: Katherine Birmingham, *The OSCE and Minority Issues*, The Foundation for Inter-Ethnic Relations, The Hague (1995).

In a report to the Sub-Commission on the Prevention of Discrimination and Protection of Minorities, Special Rapporteur Asbjörn Eide of Norway dealt with constructive national arrangements for minorities based on human rights.[12] Such arrangements are intended to improve the relations between a majority and a minority and to inspire legislators, judges and other national leaders to achieve equal rights, particularly equal political representation, and to avoid ethnic conflicts.

In 1995, as a result of Eide's report, the United Nations established a new Working Group on Minorities (WGM). It reviews compliance with the 1992 Declaration, considers solutions to problems, promotes mutual understanding between groups and governments, and recommends measures for the protection of minority rights. At its sessions, the WGM has considered ideas, such as the facilitation of national conciliation machineries, the establishment of dialogue between the parties involved, early warning, and prevention of conflicts. Minorities and their representatives have free access to the WGM and can freely speak and submit documents at its meetings.[13]

Minority rights are increasingly included in international and bilateral technical cooperation programmes in the field of human rights. Assistance is now available for minority rights training and teaching, for the drafting of bills of rights and other laws which conform to international standards, and for the creation of national infrastructures which safeguard minority rights. Technical assistance should be made available not only to States, as is now the rule, but also to the groups working with national governments. In this way, technical assistance could be used to prevent and resolve conflicts.

International and regional standards with accompanying monitoring procedures are helpful only if people know about them. States are obligated to educate the public about human rights. Article 26 of the Universal Declaration, Article 13 of the Covenant on Economic, Social and Cultural Rights and many other instruments[14] stipulate that education, particularly human rights education, shall promote understanding, tolerance and friendship among nations and racial, ethnic and religious groups and further UN activities for the maintenance of peace. In 1995, the United Nations proclaimed a Decade of Human Rights Education for promotional purposes. More concrete work is essential because a lack of knowledge and understanding often leads to inter-communal distrust, prejudices and tensions.

Finally, NGOs are of crucial importance for the promotion and protection of minority rights. The NGOs perform a wide variety of relevant functions, includ-

---

12 His study on constructive national arrangements for minorities is contained in UN Docs. E/CN.4/Sub.2/1993/34 and Add. 1-4.

13 For the WGM mandate, see resolution 1995/24 of the Commission on Human Rights. WGM meets annually in Geneva and reports to the Sub-Commission. The reports of WGM are available on the home page of the High Commissioner for Human Rights at http://www.unhchr.ch.

ing research and fact-finding activities, informing and educating the public and otherwise generating public support, contributing to policy-making and legislative debates at all levels, pressuring governments to live up to their obligations, speaking up and speaking out on violations and abuses when governments and international organizations are ineffective or even silent, and bringing such issues to the attention of international and regional monitoring bodies, in particular complaints and investigative procedures.

Well-known international NGOs are actively involved in minority rights. They include Amnesty International, Article 19, Human Rights Watch, the International Helsinki Federation for Human Rights, and the Minority Rights Group. While requiring independent verification, the accumulation of NGO information on minority situations, together with views expressed by inter-governmental fact-finders and observers, strongly indicates that States in all parts of the world are experiencing difficulties which raise human rights concerns.

7. INDIVIDUAL AND GROUP RIGHTS

Most international human rights instruments emphasize the rights of individuals, or persons belonging to the group. Some texts declare that individuals enjoy rights in community with other members of their group, thus acknowledging the group element.

As pointed out above, group rights and group access are included in a number of instruments to ensure equality and effectiveness. Some instruments are straightforward in their establishment of rights for groups, including the International Convention on the Elimination of All Forms of Racial Discrimination. Article 14 of the Convention also empowers groups to submit complaints to the treaty monitoring body. The UNESCO Declaration on Race and Racial Prejudice contains a well-known phrase: 'All individuals and groups have the right to be different, to consider themselves as different and to be regarded as such'. In their monitoring work and/or dialogue functions, the WGM and the OSCE High Commissioner work with group representatives as well as individual group members.[15]

[14] For a survey of international and regional texts calling for human rights education and dissemination of human rights information, see: Gudmundur Alfredsson, 'The Right to Human Rights Education', in Asbjörn Eide, Katarina Krause and Allan Rosas (Eds.), *Economic, Social and Cultural Rights. A Textbook*, Dordrecht: Nijhoff, Finnish & Norwegian Institutes of Human Rights (1995), pp 213-227.

[15] For a survey of instruments containing group rights and for an elaboration of the reasons behind them, see Gudmundur Alfredsson, 'Group Rights, Preferential Treatment and the Rule of Law', Discussion Paper for Consultation on Group Rights at the University of Cambridge, Colombo: Law & Society Trust, (1995).

Group rights for minorities are necessary to guarantee a number of rights (including those to identity, culture and education), to otherwise approximate circumstances enjoyed by the majority, to allow individuals to draw on the strength of their groups, and to facilitate interaction of groups with the States in which they live and with international organizations. If group rights are rejected and preferential treatment denied, discriminatory patterns will persist and the equal enjoyment of human rights by minorities will never be realized.

8. A FEW CONCLUDING REMARKS

With thousands of distinct minority groups, the idea of one State for every group is far from the political reality. Groups without States which they feel like calling their own are vulnerable in a community of nation-States. These groups resent and resist integration through nation-building and are a frequent source of friction within and between States. The consequences of discriminatory practices are evidenced by the large number of ethnic conflicts of a violent nature, or the threat of the same, and by continued secession movements with ethnic, linguistic or religious undertones in many countries.

Interestingly, the sum total of international standard-setting, monitoring and conciliatory efforts surpasses that of many national legal systems. Many States are indeed reluctant partners in this line of work. Despite commitments to minority rights in international and regional instruments, government policies and practices are still heavily influenced by ideas of sovereignty, territorial integrity and national unity. Outdated 'nation-State' concepts reduce minorities to second class members of society.

Minority rights aim to achieve equal enjoyment of all human rights and non-discrimination in that enjoyment, with the support of special measures. The rights have been further developed by national legislation, reports by governments to international organizations, studies by Special Rapporteurs, views of other monitoring organs, the work of NGOs, and academic literature. Special measures and various methods of conflict resolution may need better elaborated standards, but much could be accomplished under current instruments if they were applied, as intended, on the basis of the rule of law, objectivity, impartiality and judicial or quasi-judicial review.

Much work remains to be done. Objectivity requires equal attention to countries of Eastern and Western Europe. Governments concerned only with the preservation of national unity and territorial integrity must learn to recognize the benefits of tolerance and pluralism. The will of the people is not only the will of the majority; for governments to be representative, they must also respect the rights of minorities. This is in the interest of all parties in order to keep the peace and to further prosperity. Loyalty is a two-way street; States must be loyal to all persons within their jurisdictions, including persons belonging to minorities, who in turn should be loyal to the State in which they live. The initiative should rest with the State as the stronger party.

The realization of minority rights is indeed intended to benefit all parties. States gain political and social stability and economic prosperity; the groups preserve their identities and improve the quality of life for individual members; and the international organizations maintain peace and stability which, after all, is the major reason for their existence.

Part One – Minorities in Croatia

POLITICAL AND SECURITY ASPECTS OF MINORITIES IN CROATIA

by Snežana Trifunovska

1. INTRODUCTION

Each minority group is characterised by its social, economic, political and security aspects. Which dimension(s) will prevail with respect to a concrete minority depends on various factors present on the part of the group itself and on the part of the State in which the members of that group reside. The numerical size of the group, its economic strength, its homogeneity, territorial location and density, as well as its claims based mostly on its historical past and sometimes on the changed contemporary conditions, are all important factors in determining a particular minority situation. At the same time, a given situation is to a large degree determined and directed by the State policy towards the minority, and the creation of the political, legal and economic conditions relevant for the maintenance of minority identity and its development. Of course, in some situations the role of the 'mother-' or kin-State has a significant if not decisive influence on the minority group which has a part of its population living within the borders of another State. Speaking in general and theoretical terms, this influence should have a positive impact on the position of the minority, its development, the relationship with the State in which it lives and the cooperation with its own kin-State. However, States with minority groups on their territories often face a situation of having to deal with a 'too protective' kin-State which they sometimes experience as interference in internal affairs and a violation of their sovereignty as one of the basic principles of international law.

This article intends to briefly discuss the present political and security aspects of minorities in the Republic of Croatia which is a multi-ethnic and multi-religious State with a number of minority groups differing in size and their characteristics.[1] Because of the size and the significance of the Serbs for the political stability of the country, further on in the text most of the attention will be paid to

[1] According to the last census held in 1991, out of a total of 4,780,000 inhabitants 84% constituted Croats, 12% Serbs, 0.9% Muslims, 0.5% Slovenes, 0.5% Hungarians, 0.4% Italians, 0.3% Czechs, 0.2% Albanians, 0.2% Montenegrins, and the rest represent some smaller groups like the Roma, Macedonians, Slovaks, Ruthenians, etc.

S. Trifunovska (Ed.), Minorities in Europe – Croatia, Estonia and Slovakia

the Serbian minority. Of course, in this discussion it will not be possible to avoid touching upon the recent past when developments took a dramatic course at the moment of the declaration of Croatian independence and sovereignty in 1991, when the issue of the Serbian population and its disagreement with the change of its constitutional position from a constitutive people to a minority directly brought about the war. It will also be necessary to look at the existing legal framework which provides for protection of minorities in order to establish whether it meets the internationally accepted criteria and requirements. Finally, an attempt will be made to assess the current situation and the actual position of minorities. Although any speculation as regards the future developments might be superfluous, it is a special challenge, indeed, to put the situation of the minorities in Croatia in the broader geopolitical and strategic context of the region of the former Yugoslavia.

2. THE IMPACT OF THE 1990 CONSTITUTION ON THE POSITION OF THE CROATIAN SERBS AND ON THE SECURITY SITUATION

The 1990 Croatian Constitution, which actually allowed for secession from Yugoslavia,[2] established a new political and legal system for the Republic. It introduced significant internal changes and facilitated the change of the international legal position of Croatia into a sovereign and independent State with full international legal capacity. It also introduced a change with respect to the constitutional position of the Croatian Serbs which proved to be of fatal significance for further developments. The Serbs 'became a minority, instead of a constitutive nation, political insignia were changed, while Serbs were removed from top positions in police and territorial defence, as they were overrepresented'.[3] This provoked a great deal of dissatisfaction among the Serbian population and hostilities commenced almost immediately after Croatia's declaration of independence in the regions populated by majority Serbs: Krajina along the Croatian-Bosnian border and in Slavonia in Eastern Croatia.

As M. Cherif Bassiouni, Chairman of the UN Commission of Experts established by Security Council Resolution 780 (1992), pointed out in his Report

---

[2] Though widely used in publications on Croatia, the term 'secession' is a matter of disagreement: the official Croatia as well as most of the Croats insist on the term 'dissolution' of Yugoslavia, which provides for no continuation of any legal personality in international law (on which Yugoslavia insists), meaning that all States which were created on the territory of the former Yugoslavia were to be treated equally as successor States. It should be pointed out that Basic Principle I of the 1974 Constitution of the SFR Yugoslavia departed from the right of self-determination including the right to secession for all the peoples of Yugoslavia, though it did not provide for a further procedure which would facilitate the exercise of this right to secession.

[3] Radovan Vukadinović, *The Break-up of Yugoslavia: Threats and Challenges*, Netherlands Institute of International Relations 'Clingendael' (1992) p. 13.

dated March 1994, the 'Constitutional nationalism, the doctrine that the constitution of a nation-State may acknowledge the domination of one ethnic group instead of treating all ethnic groups as equals – so long as it protects the rights of minorities – was reflected in the Croatian constitution adopted by the Croatian Parliament in December 1990. Its preamble referred to a " . . . thousand year national independence and State continuity of the Croatian nation . . ." and to the ". . . historical right of the Croatian nation to full State sovereignty"'.[4]

Some would certainly argue that the provision contained in the 1990 Croatian Constitution did not really change the position of the Serbs in Croatia as in the part entitled 'Historical Foundations' it defined Croatia as 'the national State of the Croatian nation and a *State of members of other nations and minorities who are its citizens: Serbs*, Muslims, Slovenes, Czechs, Slovaks, Italians, Hungarians, Jews and others . . .' (emphasis added). However, in the view of the Serbs this was exactly what had happened, taking into consideration that the previous 1974 Constitution of the Republic of Croatia explicitly only emphasised the Serbs as having the status of a people in Croatia.[5] '[T]he international recognition of Croatia, as well as documents adopted by the Croatian Administration prior to the recognition, stripped the Serbs in Croatia from their status of constituent nation and active subject in decisions concerning the Constitution of the Croatian State and especially the status of the Serbs in it. What does this mean? It means primarily that the Serbs in Croatia have been down-graded from nation to national minority, or to use a new European euphemism – an ethnic community'.[6]

According to the Association of Serbs from Croatia[7] this unilateral and sudden decision of the Croatian Parliament had the following consequences: Firstly, it had a decisive psychological effect on the Serbs in Croatia and inevitably provoked a number of associations linked to the Constitutional framework of the Independent State of Croatia (NDH). Secondly, the loss of political subjectivity made it impossible to establish political and national organisations representing the Serbs because of the following: such an organization would be futile if the Serbs – as they persisted in asserting – were denied the right to take part in the decision-making process; safety preconditions which would provide for an organization representing the interests of the Serbs were missing; and, there was a lack of readiness on the part of the Croatian Government to accept as a collocutor a pluralism-oriented and democratic organization of Serbs, which would embody

---

[4] M. Cherif Bassiouni, *Report on the Historical Background of the Civil War in the Former Yugoslavia*, UN Office in Geneva (March 1994).

[5] See the 1974 Constitution of the Socialist Republic of Croatia, Basic Principle I ('The Croatian people, together with the Serbian people and nationalities [*narodnostima*] in Croatia . . .' and Article 1 para. 2: 'Socialist Republic of Croatia is the national State of the Croat people, the State of the Serbian people in Croatia and the State of nationalities which live in it'.

[6] Association of Serbs from Croatia, *Serbs in Croatia – Types of Problems and Solutions for the Serbian Question in Croatia* (April 1993) (unofficial publication).

[7] Idem.

the interests of all Serbs in Croatia.[8] Although there are some views which hold that at that time the Serbs were not interested in cultural autonomy, proportional representation in legislative assemblies, and a guarantee of the rights of minorities offered by the Croatian Government,[9] initially there were, indeed, demands on the part of the Serbs for cultural autonomy which were treated with a striking lack of sensitivity.[10] Notwithstanding this, it was the position of the Serbs that as Croatia had the right to self-determination and separation from Yugoslavia, they had the right of (external) self-determination too, applying to the Krajina and Srijem regions in Croatia and the right to join their kin-State, Serbia: 'just as when Virginia joined the Confederacy during the War between the States and the US, what is now West Virginia seceded from Virginia and joined the Union'.[11]

2.1 The role of historic sentiments

Although it is not the intention of this article to commence on a detailed historic analysis, it should nevertheless be mentioned that from the very beginning of the joint Yugoslav State established in December 1918, throughout the period from 1918 up to the dissolution of what was known as 'the second' – the Socialist Federal Republic of – Yugoslavia in 1992,[12] there were some obvious differences in views and sentiments between the leading Croatian and Serbian politicians. These differences are presented and analysed in detail in the recently published book entitled *Croatia – A Nation Forged in War*, which provides an account of the rise, fall and rebirth of Croatia from its medieval origins to recent times. The author, Marcus Tanner, reveals, *inter alia*, the Croat dissatisfaction with what was perceived as the Serbian domination and cultural difference. He quotes a statement of a Peasants Party official Josip Predavec, dating back as far as 1934, who pointed out that right up to 1918 the Croats lived under the guidance of native Croatian officials and were responsible for four main internal departments of Government. 'Even under the Habsburgs, the Croat people were their own masters. Now, if you want to find those government departments, you must search for them at Belgrade . . . Every post is reserved for the predominant race, despite the fact that the Croatian people are by common consent a century ahead of the

---

[8] Idem.

[9] Vukadinović, op. cit. n. 3, p. 13.

[10] Robert F. Miller, 'Tudjman's Victory: Croatia, the UN, NATO and the US', in Aleksandar Pavković (Ed.), *The Disintegration of Yugoslavia: Inevitable or Avoidable?*, 25 Nationalities Papers (1997) No. 3, p. 503.

[11] Bassiouni, op. cit. n. 4, p. 35.

[12] As pointed out elsewhere in this book, it is considered that SFRY formally ceased to exist when the Arbitration Commission of the Peace Conference on Yugoslavia in its Opinion No. 8, dated 4 July 1992, declared that the process of dissolution of SFRY had been completed and that Yugoslavia ceased to exist.

Serbs in civilisation'.[13] The differences which were obvious at the early beginnings of the joint State and the dissatisfaction which resulted therefrom, were already at that time an indication of the limited prospects for a lasting joint State. The then Yugoslav Foreign Minister, Ante Trumbić, stated in 1935: 'The unity of Yugoslavia! There has never been such a thing . . . That unification, sir, is unification downwards. It is the illiterates who command the educated; imbeciles who command the intelligentsia . . . Between us and the pan-Serb *camarilla* which directs Yugoslavia today, it is not a question of force, for they are by far the strongest, but it is a question of time, a question of patience, until the day arrives when accounts will be settled'.[14]

Probably these sentiments, however harsh they were, remained deep-rooted throughout the whole period of joint life up to recent years, and the final separation in 1991. For, even if the pre-Second World War period had been forgotten, the Serb-Croat relations were never freed of the Serb emotions caused by the policy of the Ustasha regime during the Second World War when the NDH (Independent State of Croatia) 'made no secret of its intention to get rid of the Serbs'[15] and when in 1941 one of the new Ministers, Milovan Žanić, declared that Croatia 'must be the land of the Croats and no one else, and there are no methods that we Ustashe will not use to make this land truly Croatian, and cleanse it of the Serbs who have endangered us for centuries . . .'[16]

The sentiments relating to the past accompanied by the fear on the part of the Serbs of the idea of living together with the Croats in a Croatian State were invoked as arguments in their claims following the Croatian declaration of independence in 1991. Indeed, a number of authors in recent publications make reference to the fear of the local Serbs arising from the revival of Croatian nationalism.[17] Of course, one should be careful in assessing the historic or recent past as it is dangerous to point only at one reason or another attributed to one party or another which could be considered as a cause triggering certain developments. As somebody once said, history is too complex to summarise it in a few lines. And here again life proves that nothing can be described as being only black or white, as the situation is always more complex than it seems to be, and as there are

---

[13] See Marcus Tanner, *Croatia, A Nation Forged in War*, Yale University Press (1997) p. 127.

[14] Tanner, op. cit. n. 13, pp. 127-128 (quoting from Henri Pozzi, *Black Hand over Europe*, Zagreb (1994), reprint of 1935, pp. 15-20).

[15] Tanner, op. cit. n. 13, p. 150.

[16] This resulted in a large number of deportations and mass killings. According to the information provided by the Communist authorities to the UN Repatriation Committee the number of dead in Jasenovac, the NDH camp, was about 600,000, although a leading Croat historian, Ivo Banac, is of the opinion that there were about 120,000 victims, thus including the Serbs, among others, in all the NDH-run camps. Tanner, op. cit. n. 13, pp. 150-151.

[17] See for example: Peter W. Galbraith, 'Washington, Erdut and Dayton: Negotiating and Implementing Peace in Croatia and Bosnia-Herzegovina', 30 *Cornell International Law Journal*, No. 3 (1997) pp. 643-649, at p. 643.

many of what could be considered one's own truths. Therefore the above-mentioned is intended only to assist in our understanding of why, when in 1991 Croatia declared independence, the Serbs reacted so radically, and excludes any intention to justify in any manner whatsoever any use of force which followed in the period after 1990.

2.2 The role of the Federal Republic of Yugoslavia, i.e., Serbia

There is a widespread view, though strongly denied by Serbia, that its role as the kin-State was probably decisive in the development of the situation and events which took place in Croatia after its declaration of independence, by both instigating the separatism of the Croatian Serbs and by providing military support for the realisation of the Serbian secession from Croatia. It is the Serbian President, Slobodan Milošević, who is to blame for capitalising on the fears of the majority of the Serbs and for setting up a campaign for the unification of all Serbs, as well as for strengthening the belief of the Serbs that should Croatia secede from Yugoslavia, all the Serbs would still live in one country, a 'Great Serbia'. Moreover, he is seen as the main protagonist of the crisis on the whole territory of the former SFRY.[18] According to Ivo Banac the 'post-communist' nationalism of Slobodan Milošević, which has been taking shape since 1987, represents a new form of Serbian integral nationalism, with strains of fascist and communist influences and which aimed to create a nationally homogenous Great Serbia even on the most outlying territories of the Serb settlement.[19]

The Croatian Government understood the full range of the Serbian claim to live in one State on the basis of the right of self-determination, when the Serbs in Croatia initiated rebellion in response to Croatian independence, which in the summer of 1991 turned into a real war. The Serbian population occupied 30% of the Croatian territory and declared the Republic of Serbian Krajina (which was retaken by the Croats in May 1995). In the autumn of 1991 the Yugoslav People's Army (JNA) started shelling the towns of Vukovar and Osijek in Slavonia (which led to Vukovar's surrender to Serb forces in November 1991). Some sources indicate that the uprisings in the Serb-populated areas of Croatia 'were abetted and sometimes led by the armed paramilitary bands from Serbia proper, tacitly encouraged by Milošević'.[20] In that sense, and assuming that the JNA units and the Serbian territorial, paramilitary, irregular and volunteer units have from the very beginning of the hostilities militarily supported the Serbs in Croatia, the

---

[18] Vukadinović, op. cit. n. 3, pp. 13-14.

[19] Ivo Banac, 'Ancient Ethnic Hatreds and Recent Balkan Conflicts: the Role of Nationalism in Southeastern Europe', in Erasmus Ascension Symposium, *The Limits of Pluralism* (11-15 May 1994) pp. 139-153, at pp. 149-150.

[20] Miller, loc. cit. n. 10, p. 503.

international bodies requested their relocation outside and withdrawal from the territory of the Republic of Croatia.[21]

According to Vukadinović the Serbs in Croatia were used as puppets in a big political game and the undeclared war and suffering of the population intensified the hatred between the Serbs and the Croats.[22] For, one of the disastrous consequences of the Serbian claim to the right to self-determination and their declaration of autonomy was a large flow of refugees, initially of ethnic Croats, from the territories inhabited by the Serbian majority population, and later on – during the Croat military operations entitled 'Flash' (in Sector West) and 'Storm' (in Sectors North and South) in 1995 – of ethnic Serbs who fled from Krajina (mostly to the Federal Republic of Yugoslavia), both of these population movements being qualified as 'ethnic cleansing'.

3. THE LEGAL FRAMEWORK DETERMINING THE POLITICAL POSITION OF MINORITIES IN CROATIA

Of course, once there is a higher claim for secession raised by a group, as a rule it will be difficult for the State to provide a legal framework which would be satisfactory and acceptable to the group in question. Probably partly as a result of international pressure, Croatia, however, succeeded in establishing a sound legal framework for the protection of minority rights by taking into account the existing minority situation and by including a wide range of minority rights and freedoms. In this sense, the basic legal document relevant not only for the Serbs but for all minority groups in the Republic of Croatia is the Constitutional Law on Human Rights and Freedoms and on the Rights of National and Ethnic Communities and Minorities of 4 December 1991 (hereafter referred to as 'the Constitutional Law'), as amended and supplemented on 8 May 1992. In fact, the Law was drawn up in accordance with an agreement proposed at the Peace Conference on Yugoslavia, held in The Hague at the end of October 1991. It follows up on the basic guarantees of the rights of minorities including the right to cultural autonomy, contained in the 1990 Croatian Constitution. Besides the protection of human rights and freedoms which include all basic civil and political rights as contained in the major international documents and applicable to all citizens, the Constitutional Law provides for special collective rights of ethnic or national minorities, like cultural autonomy as well as proportional participation in representative and other bodies and local self-government in the areas populated with the Serb majority.

---

[21] See the so-called 'Vance Plan' which provided for the establishment of the United Nations Protected Areas in the regions of Eastern Slavonia, Western Slavonia and Krajina (UN Doc. S/23280, Annex III).

[22] Vukadinović, op. cit. n. 3, p. 14.

Chapter III of the Constitutional Law contains provisions for, *inter alia*, the full observance of the principles of non-discrimination, the right to identity, culture, religion, public and private use of minority languages and alphabets in education. It also guarantees equality in participation in public affairs, the right to political and economic freedoms in the social sphere, access to the media and in education and cultural matters in general.

In accordance with Article 18, paragraph 1 of the Constitutional Law, those minority groups which constitute more than 8% of the population of Croatia shall be entitled to proportional representation in the Croatian Parliament and Government, as well as in the supreme judicial bodies. For those minorities with less than 8% of the Croatian population the Law provides a possibility to elect a total of 5 representatives to the House of Deputies of the Croatian Parliament, which shall be obliged to protect the minority interests (Articles 18-20).

Moreover, districts (regions) in which ethnic or minority groups make up over 50% of the population according to the 1981 census, shall have a special status within the system of local self-government of the Republic of Croatia, so-called 'special status districts' (Articles 13; 21-57). The Law establishes and defines in Article 22 two autonomous districts with special status (Knin and Glina) with a number of municipalities (Dvor, Glina, Hrvatska Kostajnica, Vojnić, Vrginmost, Benkovac, Dojni Lapac, Graćac, Knin, Obrovac and Titova Korenica). It further establishes that the election or appointment of members of District and Municipal Assemblies of the special status districts and their Executive Councils shall be based on the principle of proportional representation of citizens with regard to their national and ethnic minority affiliation. With respect to competences, the Law lists all the fields which are relevant for the existence and economic and cultural development of the ethnic or minority group,[23] and determines the main bodies of the districts with special status (district assembly; district assembly executive council; President of the district assembly and district court).

Being such a comprehensive document, the Constitutional Law is one of the few examples of national legislation of European States providing for (a) a broad protection of human rights, (b) protection of all minority groups regardless of their size by ensuring cultural autonomy, and (c) providing for special forms of

---

[23] Pursuant to Art. 26 of the Constitutional Law, the districts with special status have competence in: (1) coordination and planning of urban development; (2) promotion of economic activities; (3) construction and maintenance of communication networks and other services and activities important for the district; (4) advancing environmental protection on its territory; (5) providing for satisfying conditions in the sphere of culture, in particular the preservation and protection of cultural heritage or interest to national and ethnic communities or minorities, the promotion of cultural and scientific activities, founding and maintaining museums, scientific and other libraries, etc., aimed at fostering minority traditions; (6) health protection and social welfare; (7) providing the conditions for the realisation of common interests in secondary education, science and the use of modern technology; (8) securing of public peace and order and traffic safety on its territory; and (9) ensuring special care for the human, civil and ethnic rights of all inhabitants.

protection for numerically more significant minority groups. In fact, the Law reflects an effort to satisfy the needs of all minority groups living on the territory of Croatia which, as pointed out above, substantially differ in their size, location, ethnic, religious and linguistic characteristics, as well as in political claims and aspirations. As an illustration of this, we only have to look at the provisions on proportional participation in representative and other bodies and the provisions on the special statute districts. They were introduced primarily to meet the needs of the largest, Serbian, minority as according to the 1991 census there are no other groups which constitute more than 8% of the total population of Croatia. At the same time, the Law does provide conditions for the smaller groups to participate in political life. So, one could argue that from the legal point of view the Law builds a sound framework for various minority situations ranging from those which require only maintenance of minority identity through cultural rights and religious freedoms, up to those which should satisfy the claims of larger minority groups to self-government and adequate participation in the political life and decision-making of the country.

In addition to the Constitution and the Constitutional Law there are some relevant provisions contained in other legal documents relating to the prohibition of discrimination on the basis of differences in race, colour or skin, nationality or ethnic origin, to the freedom of the use of minority languages, freedom of the media, elections, local self-government and administration, political parties, etc. The legal framework also includes a significant number of international human rights instruments to which Croatia has acceded since its independence, including the 1992 European Charter on Regional and Minority Languages and the 1995 Framework Convention for the Protection of National Minorities. Pursuant to Article 134 of the Croatian Constitution, international human rights agreements ratified and published in the Official Gazette become part of the internal legal order and have direct application and legal force over and above other legal provisions.

4. FACTORS HAVING AN IMPACT ON POLITICAL STABILITY IN THE POST-WAR PERIOD

At this moment in time it seems that the ethnic Serbs have renounced their secessionist claims. This is a result of: (1) the military defeat they suffered in 1995, which ended up, after the termination of the mandate of the United Nations Transitional Administration for Eastern Slavonia in January 1998, in the reintegration of the whole territory of Croatia; and (2) the normalisation of relations between Croatia and the Federal Republic of Yugoslavia provided for by the Agreement concluded between the two Governments on 23 August 1996. It also seems that the increasing Croatian integration in all major international and European institutions contributes positively to the internal political/security situation. However, a number of factors continue to play a role with respect to the political stability.

Among them, the following deserve attention: the creation of a legal framework and actual possibilities for effective participation of minorities in public life, which includes the building up of a network of governmental and non-governmental institutions aimed at fostering dialogue; confidence-building and the monitoring of the implementation of human and minority rights; compliance with the rules and the promotion of human rights protection; and the creation of sound living conditions and conditions for economic development.

4.1 **Participation of minorities in public life**

In general, the effective participation of minorities in public life and in decision-making in the issues affecting them is essential in channelling the minority needs and aspirations. This includes, and is dependent upon, the degree of representation in legislative, administrative and advisory bodies, the minority participation in decision-making, electoral rights and the issue of citizenship.

The inter-ethnic hostilities during the period 1991-1995 and the changes to the demographic composition in the areas populated by the Serbian majority, had a direct impact on the implementation of some aspects of minority legislation. This refers primarily to the provisions on political participation and the districts with special status, which were rendered inoperative as a consequence of the mass departure of the Serbs from their homes caused by the Croatian military operations 'Flash' and 'Storm' in 1995, aimed at the restoration of sovereignty of the Croatian State on the whole territory. Because of the changed demographic composition of the population,[24] the Croatian Parliament decided during its session from 19-21 September 1995, to suspend the implementation of Article 13 together with Articles 21-57 (on special status districts) and 18 (the right to proportional representation in the Croatian Parliament), until the next census which should take place sometime in the future. With respect to Article 18, one of the consequences of such a decision was a significant reduction of the participation of the Serbs in the Croatian Parliament. At present, in the House of Counties there are in total 7 representatives of minorities: 3 belonging to the Serbian minority (reduced from 13) and the rest representing Italian, Hungarian, Czech, Slovak, Ruthenian, Ukrainian, German and Austrian minorities.[25]

---

[24] According to some sources nearly one-third of the pre-war total of some 581,000 Serbs fled from Croatia to neighbouring countries (Special Report on Minorities, by Elisabeth Rehn, UN Doc. E/CN.4/1997/8, para. 101).

[25] In fact, pursuant to Art. 18 (2) of the Constitutional Law, members of ethnic and national minorities which comprise less than 8% of the whole population of Croatia, are entitled to elect a total of 5 representatives to the House of Representatives to the Croatian Parliament. According to the Law on the Election of Representatives to the Croatian Parliament, 7 seats are reserved for the elected members of minorities, as follows: 3 for the representatives of the Serbian minority; 1 for Hungarian; 1 for Italian; 1 for both the Czech and Slovak minority; and 1 representative for Ruthenians, Ukrainians, Germans and Austrians.

Apart from the fact that the suspension of Article 18 seems to have taken place in contravention of the provision referring to the demographic composition as established by the 1981 census,[26] the suspension of the key provisions relevant for the position and the autonomy of the Serbian minority was detrimental to the process of inter-ethnic reconciliation. In this sense the Council of Europe's Venice Commission for Democracy through Law emphasised that 'the suspension of the Law was not indispensable . . . the provisions could validly have continued in force, although in that case they would not for the moment have any practical application because of the demographic changes which have occurred'.[27]

Currently there are in Croatia 12 registered political parties representing specific minorities. It is interesting to note that Albanians, which according to the 1991 census presented 0.25% of the total population (12,032 people), have 3 registered political parties (Albanian Christian Democratic Party; Albanian Islamic Democratic Union; and Democratic Albanian Union), which is the same number as the largest, Serb minority has (Independent Democratic Serbian Party; Serbian People's Party; and Party of Danubian Serbs).[28] Only parties representing specific minorities also represent minority interests. At the 1992 general election no seats were gained by political parties representing minorities, though two persons belonging to minorities (both of Serb origin) have been elected to the House of Deputies from the list of parties other than those specifically representing minorities.

As in the House of Counties there are no reserved seats for the members of minorities, by using the powers given by Article 71 (4) of the Constitution,[29] the President of the Republic of Croatia, Franjo Tudjman, has nominated two representatives of the Serb minority in this body. This is a symbolic gesture which probably does not provide for a more significant influence of the Serbs in the decision-making; however, it does contribute to the development of inter-ethnic cooperation, making it possible for the voice of the Serbs to be heard and it thereby contributes to confidence-building.

---

[26] See Art. 10 of the Law on the Elections of Representatives in the Parliament (*Sabor*) of the Republic of Croatia of 17 April 1992 (*Narodne Novine* [Official Gazette of the Republic of Croatia] No. 22 of 1992) which requires that the share of the minority group exceeds 8% *as per the population census of 1981* (emphasis added), which has not been changed in the subsequent amendments in 1993, 1994 and 1995.

[27] The Council of Europe's Commission for Democracy through Law, *Report on the Implementation of the Constitutional Law on Human Rights and Freedoms and on the Rights of Ethnic Communities and Minorities in the Republic of Croatia*, Strasbourg (24 May 1996).

[28] There are also the following: Bosnian Democratic Party; Democratic Muslim Community; Croatian Muslim Democratic Party; Party of Democratic Action; Hungarian People's Party; and Party of Croatian Roma.

[29] It is the right of the President of the Republic to nominate up to 5 representatives to the House of Counties from among especially eminent citizens of the Republic of Croatia.

4.2 Building up a network of institutions of and for minorities

During the last few years a network of governmental and non-governmental institutions dealing with the issues of minorities has been established. The creation of various organisations, associations and institutions are aimed at confidence-building and their major tasks are to monitor the implementation of laws and regulations and to foster dialogue between minority and majority groups, aimed at the development of inter-ethnic tolerance and cooperation. Among them, worthy of mention is the Governmental Office for Ethnic and National Communities or Minorities,[30] the Croatian State Parliamentary Committee on Human Rights and Rights of Ethnic and National Communities or Minorities,[31] and the Council of Ethnic and National Communities or Minorities.[32] The Ombudsperson for Minority/Human Rights which is in fact a commissioner of the Croatian State Parliament, created in 1992, also has an important role to play.

There are 22 registered minority associations in the Republic of Croatia and 7 national NGOs dealing with minority issues. With respect to cultural activities it is worth noting that for the Italian minority there are 3 cultural societies currently active, whereas in the central association, the Italian Union, 40 Italian communities are active; the Czech national minority, for example, has 22 cultural societies located in various places throughout Croatia; the Slovaks 4; the Hungarian minority has 3 organisations and 9 amateur cultural societies; Ruthenians and Ukrainians have 8 cultural societies. Within the sub-committee of the Serb Cultural Society *'Prosvijeta'* the Serbian minority organises various activities, like exhibitions, panel discussions, workshops, etc.[33]

As part of their cultural autonomy each of the minority groups has its own newspapers, periodicals and other publications in their mother tongue. Only for

---

[30] The Office was established in 1991 as the main body responsible for the cultural autonomy of minorities in Croatia. Its tasks are to propose measures for the realisation of ethnic rights; to monitor the implementation of international instruments relating to the protection of national, religious, cultural and linguistic rights of minorities; to collect data and information concerning the realisation of ethnic rights in Croatia and in the world generally; and to propose the application of certain models for the enjoyment of such rights which have to date proven successful in practice.

[31] Established by the House of Representatives, the Committee consists of 15 representatives with the task of participating in the process of elaboration of minority legislation and to follow the implementation of the policy of Parliament concerning minorities. It has two Sub-Committees (a 7-member Sub-Committee on the Implementation of the Rights of Ethnic and National Communities or Minorities and an 8-member Sub-Committee on Croatian Minorities in European Countries).

[32] A non-governmental body, with coordinating and advisory functions established in 1997 to provide a setting for continued dialogue between the national minorities and the Government and bodies of state administration; to monitor the implementation of policies towards the preservation and promotion of national minorities; to examine issues and provide recommendations to draft legislation regulating the protection of national minorities.

[33] Government of the Republic of Croatia, *Implementation of Cultural Autonomy in the Republic of Croatia*, Prepared by Mila Šimic (1998).

the Serbian minority are there several journals and a number of other publications issued by the Serbian Cultural Society *'Prosvjeta'*, the Community of Serbs in Croatia, the Serbian Democratic Forum, the Initiative for the Serbian National Congress, and the association *'Tolerancija'*. There are also regular/periodical publications for the members of the German and Austrian national minorities, as well as for the Jews, Slovenians, Albanians, Bosniacs, Roma, Montenegrins and Macedonians. The Croatian radio and TV stations broadcast on a daily basis programmes on and for ethnic minorities in Croatia. For the Serbian national minority there is a 12-hour daily programme in the Serbian language which was launched on a number of radio stations at the end of 1997.[34]

The programmes of activities of minority associations and institutions are financially assisted from the State budget and the budgets of the units of local self-government.[35]

4.3 **Protection of human rights and enjoyment of freedoms**

Today the international community recognises that any disturbance to the political stability and security of a country by internal or external factors automatically affects various aspects of human rights and freedoms, and vice versa, a violation and disrespect for human rights, especially ethnically-based, will have a corresponding impact on the political stability and security of the country. Whereas there was massive suffering by all the people in Croatia during the period of the war and inter-ethnic hostilities, there were human rights violations and instances of harassment and discrimination (refusal of citizenship, job dismissals) against Serbs, Muslims and other non-ethnic Croats, which substantially affected their social and economic position. The human rights situation of the primarily Serb minority in Croatia continues to be affected in the post-war period in two major respects: the issue of citizenship and the return of refugees to their homes.

4.3.1 *Citizenship*

One of the problems of major significance which appeared following the dissolution of the former SFRY, especially in the republics like Croatia and Bosnia and Herzegovina which were faced with a large flow of refugees and displaced persons, is the issue of citizenship. The possibility to acquire Croatian citizenship was not only an important factor which played a role in the consideration of displaced persons whether to return to their homes, but also contained a political and economic dimension. The practical effect of not having a Citizenship Certificate, or *'Domovnica'*, was the restriction of the right to vote and to be elected in the

---

[34] A detailed list of the activities of each of the minority groups in Croatia is given in the Third Periodic Report submitted by Croatia to the Committee on the Elimination of Racial Discrimination under Art. 9 of the Convention (CERD/C/290/Add.1, paras. 78-86).

representative bodies on the national level, in the bodies of local self-government and administration units; restriction of access to free public schools; restriction in purchasing property; restriction of access to employment and to all subsequent rights; restricted travel (a passport could only be issued on the basis of the Certificate); etc. Whereas the Croatian Law on Citizenship adopted in June 1991 provided for the usual and mostly used forms of acquisition (descent, birth, naturalisation and in accordance with international treaties), it was still considered restrictive. This is true in particular for Articles 8 and 16 of the Citizenship Law.

In fact, Article 8, paragraph 1 provides for 5 preconditions for acquisition of citizenship by naturalisation: (1) that a person is 18 years of age and has not been denied the ability to work; (2) that a person has been dismissed from foreign citizenship or has submitted proof that it will be dismissed if Croatian citizenship is granted; (3) that before submitting the application the person has been resident for at least five years uninterruptedly in the territory of Croatia; (4) that a person has knowledge of the Croatian language and Latin letters; and (5) that the person's behaviour shows that he/she respects the judicial system and customs in the Republic of Croatia and accepts Croatian culture. Pursuant to Article 16 a member of the Croatian nation who does not have domicile in Croatia, can obtain Croatian citizenship if he/she fulfils the preconditions in Article 8 paragraph 1, items 4 and 5 of the Citizenship Law and if he/she submits a written statement that he/she considers himself/herself a Croatian citizen. In addition, Article 26 of the Law provides the Ministry of Interior with broad discretion to deny a petition from an applicant, although the prerequisites have been met, on the grounds of State interest. As noted by the Special Rapporteur, Elizabeth Rehn, the use of the provision contained in Article 8 is a pretext to deny citizenship to Croatian Serbs, many of whom have been long-time residents in Croatia.[36]

Whereas, according to not very recent statistics, in the period 1994-1996, out of 767,481 received applications citizenship was granted to 726,403 persons and 38,566 were denied,[37] some sources indicate that both Serbs and Muslims are reported to suffer from denial of citizenship.[38]

There are some remarks also with respect to the practical implementation of the Law and with respect to the pace in processing applications for citizenship where excessive delays are noticed, resulting in applicants losing social and educational benefits.

---

[35] For 1996 an amount of 15,867,464 Croatian kunas was allocated which is equivalent to US $ 2,864,370 (CERD/C/290/Add.1, para. 17). By the Ruling on Distribution of Funds Allocated for 1998 an amount of 6,143,250 Croatian kunas was given to non-governmental – primarily Serbian – associations and institutions (Government of the Republic of Croatia, op. cit. n. 33).

[36] Report on the Situation of Human Rights in the Republic of Croatia submitted by Elisabeth Rehn (E/CN.4/1998/14, para. 71).

[37] Third Periodic Report, *supra* n. 34, para. 73.

[38] Report on the Situation of Human Rights, *supra* n. 36, paras. 72-73, 100-102.

4.3.2 *Return of refugees*

For the time being this remains one of the most serious problems.[39] Security Council Resolutions 1009 (1995) of 10 August 1995 and 1019 (1995) of 9 November 1995 demanded that the Government of Croatia fully respects the rights of the local Serb population including the right to return in safety. However, the process of return has been taking place very slowly and until now only a relatively small percentage of the Serbs have returned or submitted requests to return. In the past the OSCE High Commissioner on National Minorities, Max van der Stoel, had been actively involved in the solution of the problem. He emphasised a number of legal and practical difficulties faced by those who want to return, as follows:[40]

Firstly, the returnees face difficulties in obtaining documents, accommodation, property and security, and for those who do not invoke family reunification it is virtually impossible to overcome these difficulties.

Secondly, if even formally it would be possible to obtain accommodation, practically many difficulties are encountered as many houses have been burned, mostly after the actual hostilities ended, and a great number of houses which remained have become uninhabitable as a consequence of 'extensive looting which continued for many weeks after the Croatian Army had re-conquered the area'. With respect to this, the High Commissioner referred to the UN Secretary-General's report (S/1995/1051 of 21 December 1995) which states that virtually every abandoned Serb property in the former Sector North and East has been looted.

Thirdly, a difficulty encountered by the Serbs wanting to return can be assumed in reclaiming their property. The Law on Temporary Take-Over and Administration of Specified Property had been amended so as to exclude any time-limits for an appeal against decisions of the Commission for the temporary take-over and usage of property abandoned by refugees, however the return of prop-

---

[39] According to the Croatian Government, by the end of 1992 there were 700,000 displaced persons and refugees in the Republic of Croatia, about 500,000 refugees were from Bosnia and Herzegovina. The return of Croatian displaced persons started after the military operations 'Storm' and 'Flash', while a large number of Serbs left the territories liberated by the Croatian Army. As of 1 November 1996, 13,173 Serbs returned to their homes. The Croatian Government emphasised that great difficulties in the process of the return of both Croatian displaced persons and Serbs are due to a lack of financial resources for the reconstruction of housing, infrastructure and especially the economy, as well as for the reconstruction of the formerly occupied territory which was totally devastated during the occupation. The situation as of February 1997 reveals that 366,135 displaced persons, returnees and refugees were still being accommodated in Croatia: 75.54% of whom were refugees from Bosnia and Herzegovina of Croatian descent, 27.73% were Muslims, 0.81% were Serbs and 0.91% were members of other national minorities. There were also 6,688 refugees from the territory of the Federal Republic of Yugoslavia, 94% of whom were ethnic Croats (CERD/C/290/Add. 1, paras. 65-69).

[40] Letter of the OSCE High Commissioner on National Minorities, Max van der Stoel, addressed to the Croatian Minister for Foreign Affairs, Mate Granic, on 22 February 1996.

erty was made the subject of regulation in the bilateral agreement between the Republic of Croatia and the Federal Republic of Yugoslavia on normalisation of relations. After the normalisation of relations has taken place the owner can retake his property only after appropriate property has been given to the person to whom the property had originally been allocated by the Commission. In the view of the High Commissioner, imposing the condition of normalisation of relations with the other State for exercising the right to property presents a violation of the right to property as recognized in the accepted international documents.

Finally, there is the question of security which could increase with the strengthening of confidence as well as with the increase of the police and its willingness to provide protection to ethnic Serbs willing to return to their homes.

5. CONCLUSION

It is true that since the cessation of hostilities in 1995 the situation in Croatia with respect to minorities has been improving. The restoration of peace as the most important precondition for the development of any human and minority rights has been realised and at this moment there is no reason to believe that in the near future the Serbian minority will present any security threat to Croatian integrity. The same goes with respect to other smaller minorities whose numerical size only adds to the ethnic richness and colourfulness of the country without being able to endanger its political stability. The situation with respect to inter-ethnic conflict in neighbouring Bosnia and Herzegovina is – in the presence of the NATO-led Stabilisation Force (SFOR) – relatively calm which has a positive impact on the situation of the primarily Serbian minority in Croatia. At this moment it also seems that there will not be any negative impact or disturbing effects emanating from the situation within the Federal Republic of Yugoslavia with respect to the Kosovo Albanians on the awakening of the claims of the Croatian Serbs.

However, as indicated by various national and international supervisory and monitoring bodies, in the wake of the inter-ethnic conflict there are still a number of problems which need to be addressed and overcome. As pointed out above, the issue of citizenship, return of displaced persons to their homes and the return of property continue to play a role. There are also economic and social difficulties which are present for some social groups without regard to belonging to an ethnic group, but they are probably more emphasised in the case of ethnic Serbs and some other minorities due to the restrictive citizenship legislation which generates further problems and difficulties. In fact, the existing problems could be divided into three major groups: (a) problems referring to the return of displaced persons; (b) the citizenship problem which is related, *inter alia*, to the return of refugees; and (c) the issue of ethnically-based discrimination and human rights protection.

The instances of discrimination and harassment are continuing to take place mostly in the regions inhabited by an ethnic Serb majority. In her Final Report of 14 January 1998 submitted to the Commission on Human Rights,[41] Elisabeth Rehn pointed out that though there were good reasons for optimism for the future, after more than two years of observing human rights trends in Croatia she was of the opinion that more still needed to be accomplished. As during the period since the military operations incidents of violence against remaining Serbs in the former sectors gradually decreased, some forms of abuse like ethnically-based harassment and intimidation, continued to be present.[42] The Reports of the Human Rights Field Operation note that there is even an increase in the level of harassment of Serbs in the Eastern Slavonian region.[43] In 1998 it was still possible to register 160 serious cases of harassment and violent attacks ranging from placing bombs or other explosives to threats and intimidation, including eight murders and 25 missing persons, most of which occurred in the Krajina region.

Croatia's failure to meet the comprehensive set of human rights criteria of the European Union, contained in the EU 'Regional Approach to Countries of South-East Europe', caused the EU to limit aid to Croatia to 6.65 million ECU for humanitarian assistance and 2.7 million ECU in support of an independent media. Croatia also remained ineligible for PHARE reconstruction aid.[44]

Contrary to expectations, the process of departure of Croatian Serbs from the Danube region continues. One of the major reasons is the fact that ethnic Serbs are still the victims of discriminatory treatment and intolerance which often occur also on their workplaces. The Croatian Helsinki Committee has indicated 61 ethnically motivated dismissals which took place during 1997. According to the High Commissioner for Human Rights the efforts undertaken by the Croatian Government to ensure equality of treatment have been insufficient, which has resulted in discrimination in important areas which include tenancy rights and reconstruction of war-damaged housing. Therefore the High Commissioner asked the Croatian President to ensure that displaced Croatian Serbs are given the same status and benefits as other Croatian citizens.[45]

The Committee on the Elimination of Racial Discrimination has identified the following principal subjects of concern: a lack of clarity as to the various definitions used in domestic legislation to describe ethnic and national minorities; the reduction of the proportionate representation of the Serbian ethnic community in the Croatian Parliament following the suspension of certain provisions of the Constitutional Law; the absence of legislative measures declaring illegal and pro-

---

[41] UN Doc. E/CN.4/1998/63.

[42] UN Doc. E/CN.4/1998/63, Sect. II B (1-3).

[43] These Reports mention, for example, that during a village carnival in Baranjsko Petrovo Selo, about 100 Croats gave fascist salutes, set Serb symbols on fire, and disturbed traffic (http://www.hri.ca/fortherecord1998/vol5/croatiafo.htm).

[44] http://www.hrw.org/hrw/worldreport99/europe/croatia3.html.

[45] Press Release HR/98/14 of 12 March 1998.

hibiting organisations which promote and incite racial discrimination; incidents of hate-speech directed at the Serb minority in the Croat media and the failure of the Government to take appropriate measures to investigate and prosecute those responsible for promoting hatred and ethnic tension through the print and audio-visual media. The Committee has also indicated the serious difficulties and violence encountered by displaced persons and others, in particular ethnic Serbs, when claiming their right to property; the difficulties of the return of Serbs and others in the region of Eastern Slavonia, Baranja and West Srijem; and that citizenship remains a problem as Articles 8 and 16 of the Croatian Law on Citizenship include excessive delays in the processing of applications for citizenship, etc. Departing from the points of concern the Committee recommended to the Croatian Government a number of corresponding measures.[46]

Croatia is one of the examples which proves that the change of State borders even if it means independence and sovereignty, can be a more painful than joyful process. Unlike in other countries which dismembered in the post-Cold War period (USSR and Czechoslovakia), in Croatia the process of becoming a sovereign State was followed by an inter-ethnic armed conflict which not only devastated the economy, but created and in some instances increased inter-ethnic hatred especially between the ethnic Serbs and Croats. As Marcus Tanner points out 'the price of a thousand-year-old dream [of independence] had been enormous. Apart from Bosnia, no State in Eastern Europe had suffered such material destruction and loss of life to win its independence'.[47] In such circumstances, by definition the normalisation and recovery cannot be an easy, quick and simple process. With all the necessary assistance from the international community it will probably take years for the country to recover economically from the material damage and devastation. At the same time, the inter-ethnic reconciliation will definitely be a longer process which will include a high degree of democratisation on all levels and in all segments of society. In the case of Croat-Serb ethnic relationships, of crucial importance will be confidence-building based on human rights protection and the elimination of all occurrences of human rights violations and/ or harassment. With an effort to intensively follow-up on the suggestions provided by various inter(national) human rights bodies, and to tackle on the grass-roots basis of the existing violations, Croatia will be able to definitely overcome problems in the implementation of and compliance with norms and regulations, so as to eliminate any possibility of a reverse process, and to continue the path towards democracy and the building of a European-model multi-ethnic State.

---

[46] Concluding observations of the Committee on the Elimination of Racial Discrimination of 10 February 1999 (CERD/C/304/Add. 55).

[47] Tanner, op. cit. n. 13, p. 301.

THE LEGAL STATUS OF MINORITIES IN CROATIA

by Budislav Vukas

1. INTRODUCTION

Throughout the centuries Croatia was a member of various State unions together with Hungary, Austria and neighbouring Slavic countries. Croatia's long history of forming part of multinational States was one of the reasons for the existence of ethnic (religious) minorities within its borders.

In this brief paper it is impossible to try to shed some light to the historic development of minorities in Croatia or to analyse their status in the distant past. However what will be necessary to point out for the purpose of this paper is the situation in this respect in the predecessor State of the independent Republic of Croatia – the Socialist Federal Republic of Yugoslavia (SFRY). Although formally a federal State according to its Constitutions (1946, 1963, 1974), this multi-ethnic State evolved from an actual unitary State to almost a confederation according to its last Constitution (1974). Under Article 1 of this Constitution, the SFRY was defined as 'a *federal State having the form of a State community of voluntarily united peoples and their Socialist Republics . . .*' (emphasis added).[1] The background to this norm was the fact that all the Republics, except for Bosnia-Herzegovina, were the historical results of the efforts of individual South Slavic peoples to establish their own national States. Therefore, a prominent commentator of the time, Kiro Hadživasilev, wrote in 1974:

> 'The exceptional character of this republic (Bosnia-Herzegovina – B.V.) does not negate, of course, the basic principle of the Yugoslav federal community that the national

[1] For the English translation of the Constitution see *The Constitution of the Socialist Federal Republic of Yugoslavia*, Cross-Cultural Communications, Merrick, New York (1976); *The Constitution of the Socialist Federal Republic of Yugoslavia*, Jugoslovenski pregled, Belgrade (1989). It has to be stressed that our reference to the existing translations either of the Yugoslav or Croatian Constitutions, or other municipal legal acts, does not mean that we literally quote parts of these translations. This cannot be done as all these publications do not contain accurate translations from the Croatian original. The major mistake is that the Croatian word '*narod*' (people), has regularly been incorrectly translated as 'nation'. If the drafters of the Constitutions had the notion/term 'nation' in mind, then they would have used the appropriate term for it in Croatian, which is '*nacija*'.

S. Trifunovska (Ed.), Minorities in Europe – Croatia, Estonia and Slovakia

> republics basically represent national states as the realization and guarantee of a nation's sovereignty and equality.'[2]

The SFRY consisted of six Republics which were defined as 'States based on the sovereignty of the people' with 'peoples and nationalities having equal rights' (Article 3 of the 1974 Constitution).[3] Although not expressly listed in the Constitution, Croats, Macedonians, Montenegrins, Moslems, Serbs and Slovenes were considered 'peoples' under the legal system of Yugoslavia. The term 'nationalities' was used instead of 'minorities' in order to convey the intention to provide minority groups with more rights than minorities are usually granted. In fact, the Yugoslav constitutional system pretended to be able to secure equality between the minorities (nationalities) and the majority (peoples).[4] However, this intention was not expressed with regard to all minorities. Namely, in the demographic statistics the minorities in Yugoslavia were divided into three groups: (a) nationalities of the SFRY; (b) other nationalities; and (c) ethnic groups. Although in principle the most numerous minorities belonged to group (a), the criteria for the mentioned division were never clearly stated. Thus, for example, although the Italian and the Vlach minorities in 1971 had almost the same number of members (22 000), the first belonged to category (a), and the second to category (b). Though the Slovak and Roma (Gypsy) minorities were of the same size (80 000), the Slovaks were considered a 'nationality of the SFRY', while the Roma were called an 'ethnic group'.[5]

Taking into account the historical, demographic and other features of each of the Republics of the SFRY, their Constitutions determined more precisely the 'peoples' and 'nationalities' (minorities) on their territories. Thus the Socialist Republic of Croatia was defined as the 'national State of the Croatian people, the State of the Serbian people in Croatia and the State of the nationalities living in it' (Article 1, para. 2).[6] The equality of 'all peoples and nationalities living in the Socialist Republic of Croatia: Croats, Serbs, Hungarians, Czechs, Italians, Slovaks, Ruthenians, Ukrainians and other peoples and nationalities' was proclaimed in Article 137, paragraph 1 of the 1974 Croatian Constitution.

The above quoted provisions show that in addition to the Croatian people, the only other 'people' of Yugoslavia expressly mentioned in the introductory Arti-

---

[2] K. Hadživasilev, 'National Equality and Social Self-Management', in D. Blagojević (Ed.), *Nations and Nationalities of Yugoslavia*, Međunarodna politika, Belgrade (1974) p. 84.

[3] '*Narodnost*' (nationality), used as a noun is a neologism in Croatian and some other South Slavic languages.

[4] Hadživasilev, loc. cit. n. 2, p. 85. The term 'nationality' was used for the first time in the 1963 Yugoslav Constitution. However, in Art. 43, para. 1 of this Constitution, the term 'national minority' was used alongside 'nationalities' in order to make clear that the two terms were synonyms.

[5] See D. Breznik and M. Sentić, 'Composition and Development of Yugoslavia's Population in Terms of Nationality', in Blagojević (Ed.), op. cit. n. 2, p. 20.

[6] *Ustav Socijalističke Federativne Republike Jugoslavije, Ustav Socijalističke Republike Hrvatske, Narodne novine*, Zagreb (1974), p. 199 et seq.

cle of the 1974 Constitution of Croatia was the Serbian people. This exceptional constitutional position of the Serbian minority in Croatia was due to its considerable size, but also to its influence on the history of Croatia and the dominant role of the Serbian people in Yugoslavia in general. According to the 1971 census the Serbian minority represented 14.2% of the population of Croatia, and all the other 'peoples and nationalities of SFRY' represented only 3.3%; 79.4% of the inhabitants were Croats.[7]

Yet, this special constitutional situation of the Serbs in Croatia had no legal consequences. While for all the minorities mentioned in the 1974 Croatian Constitution some form of education in the native language was provided, there was no special education in the Serbian language or indeed any teaching of that language. Namely, under Article 138, paragraph 1 of the same Constitution, Croatian was considered the language of both the Croats and the Serbs in Croatia, and therefore it was called 'the Croatian or Serbian language'.

It should be added that the Serbian Orthodox Church enjoyed all the rights granted in Croatia to the Roman Catholic Church and all other religious communities.[8]

2. THE 1990 CONSTITUTION OF THE REPUBLIC OF CROATIA

The unbearable situation in Yugoslavia in the late 1980s, caused by the authorities in Serbia wanting to replace the federal State by a unitary system, was the major incentive for the independent tendencies in all the other Republics. After the first free multiparty elections at the beginning of 1990, the six Republics engaged in negotiations on the future structure of Yugoslavia. Croatia, together with Slovenia, proposed the transformation of Yugoslavia into a confederation. Under the influence of the Belgrade Serbian regime, the Serbian minority in Croatia pretended to be frightened by the possible constitutional changes in the direction of the wishes and proposals of Croatia and Slovenia. The Croatian authorities were undertaking various initiatives in order to convince the Serbs in Croatia that any outcome of Croatia exercising its right to self-determination would not endanger the existence and development of this segment of the population of Croatia. Thus, in August 1990 the Croatian Parliament adopted the Resolution on the Protection of the Constitutional Democratic Order and the Rights of Minorities.[9] Yet, notwithstanding all these efforts, the Croatian authorities were

[7] Breznik and Sentić, loc. cit. n. 5, p. 26.

[8] The freedom of religion was regulated by Art. 173 of the Federal Constitution and Art. 258 of the Constitution of Croatia. The content of the two Articles was identical. No specific religions were mentioned in these provisions.

[9] *Narodne novine* [Official Gazette of the Republic of Croatia] (1990), No. 34.

losing control over the parts of Croatia inhabited mostly by the Serbian minority. Such resistance was not only aided by the authorities of the Republic of Serbia and paramilitary troops from that Republic, but it was also supported by the Yugoslav Army.

Taking into account the changes already undertaken in the economic and political systems, in the field of human rights and fundamental freedoms, and the desired transformation into a democratic State where government shall be organised by the principle of the separation of powers into the legislative, executive and judicial branches, Croatia had to adopt a new Constitution. This was done on 22 December 1990.

Still being a federal unit of the SFRY, Croatia had to formulate provisions on the status of peoples and minorities accordingly. Thus, in the Preamble to the Constitution ('Historical Foundations') Croatia is qualified not only 'as the national State of the Croatian people', but also as 'the State of the members of other peoples and minorities who are its citizens: Serbs, Moslems, Slovenes, Czechs, Slovaks, Italians, Hungarians, Jews and others, who are guaranteed equality with the citizens of Croatian nationality and the realisation of ethnic rights in accordance with the democratic norms of the United Nations Organisation and the free world countries'.[10]

In view of the negative reaction of Serbia and some of the Serbs in Croatia to this new Constitution, it has to be pointed out that *there are no substantial differences* between the 1974 Croatian Constitution and the new one in respect of the status of peoples and minorities in Croatia:

(a) In both Constitutions Croatia is defined as the 'national State of the Croatian people'.

(b) In the 1974 Constitution Croatia was also characterised as the 'State of the Serbian people living in Croatia'. In relation to this phrase, the 1990 Constitution contains two changes. First, Croatia is said to be a State not of the 'Serbian people living in Croatia', but of the 'members' of that people 'who are citizens of Croatia'. Second, Croatia is also considered to be the State of the members of other peoples who are its citizens. As at the time of the adoption of the Constitution Croatia was still included in the Yugoslav constitutional system, the term 'peoples' referred to the peoples of Yugoslavia. Thus, in addition to the Serbs in Croatia, Moslems and Slovenes were also expressly mentioned, as they are more numerous in Croatia than Macedonians and Montenegrins.

(c) Contrary to the 1974 Yugoslav and Croat Constitutions, but in accordance with international law terminology, the 1990 Constitution uses the term 'minorities', and not 'nationalities'. Czechs, Slovaks, Italians, Hungarians and Jews were

---

[10] Fourth preambular paragraph of the Constitution, *Narodne novine*, 1990, No. 56. Translation into English: Lj. Valković (Ed.), *The Constitution of the Republic of Croatia,* Sabor Republike Hrvatske, Zagreb (1991).

expressly mentioned, but it was indicated that there were also 'members of other minorities' who were citizens of Croatia.

The Serbian disappointment with the different way in which they were mentioned in the 1990 Constitution was somewhat artificial and/or exaggerated. Not only did the way in which they were referred to in 1974 not give them any special rights in Croatia, but this phraseology was rather a new invention in the constitutional texts of Croatia. Namely, the 1974 Constitution was the first to mention any specific people living in Croatia. Only a decade earlier the 1963 Croatian Constitution defined Croatia as 'the State socialist democratic community of the people of Croatia . . .' (Article 1, para. 1).[11]

In addition to the above-mentioned preambular provision, Article 15 of the 1990 Constitution also deals with 'peoples' and 'minorities'. Paragraph 1 proclaims 'equal rights' in the Republic of Croatia for members of all peoples and minorities. Paragraph 2 reads:

> 'Members of all peoples and minorities shall be guaranteed freedom to express their nationality, freedom to use their language and script, and cultural autonomy.'

As far as religious minorities are concerned, Articles 40 and 41 of the new Constitution should be mentioned. Article 40 provides that the 'freedom of conscience and religion and free public profession of religion and other convictions shall be guaranteed'. Article 41 reads:

> 'All religious communities shall be equal before the law and shall be separate from the State.
> Religious communities shall be free, in conformity with law, publicly to perform religious services, open schools, teaching establishments and other institutions, social and charitable institutions and to manage them, and shall in their activity enjoy the protection and assistance of the State.'

3. THE INDEPENDENCE OF THE REPUBLIC OF CROATIA

As there was no progress in the negotiations between the six Republics of Yugoslavia concerning the future of the Federal State, the Croatian Government organised a referendum concerning the future status of Croatia. On 19 May 1991 more than 93% of the inhabitants of Croatia opted for an independent Croatian State.

A month after the referendum, and on the basis of its results, the Croatian Parliament (Sabor) declared the Republic of Croatia to be a sovereign and independent State. In the Declaration on the Establishment of the Sovereign and Independ-

---

[11] *Ustav Socijalističke Federativne Republike Jugoslavije, Ustav Socijalističke Republike Hrvatske,* 3rd ed., *Narodne novine*, Zagreb (1964), p. 156.

ent Republic of Croatia (Part III), adopted on 25 June 1991, the Republic of Croatia guaranteed 'to Serbs in Croatia and to all national minorities living on its territory, respect for all human and civil rights, particularly freedom of speech and the cultivation of their own languages and promotion of their cultures, and freedom to form political organisations'.[12]

Together with the Declaration on Independence, the Croatian Parliament adopted another instrument specially dedicated to minorities – the Charter on the Rights of Serbs and Other Nationalities in the Republic of Croatia.[13] Its purpose was to appease the Serbs in Croatia, and to show to all the Yugoslav Republics and to the entire international community the good intentions of the Croatian Government. The purpose of the Declaration was already clear from the terminology used. Instead of using 'minorities', as in the 1990 Constitution, the Declaration reverted to 'nationalities', which was the term used under Yugoslav constitutional law.

The Croatian Parliament expressed its conviction in the Charter that 'a just solution of issues concerning Serbs and other nationalities in the Republic of Croatia is one of the essential factors of democracy, stability, peace and economic prosperity, and of co-operation with other democratic countries'. As the protection of the rights of minorities and their members is part of the international protection of human rights, it belongs 'to the sphere of international co-operation'. The rights of minorities to existence, self-preservation, cultural autonomy, economic and social development, are especially highlighted. Serbs and other minorities were promised proportional participation in local self-government and in 'government authorities'. They are also entitled to form organisations which would represent them both within the State and internationally. In order to protect their rights, minorities and their members are entitled to apply to competent international institutions. However, the rights of minorities and international co-operation do not permit 'any activities contrary to the principles of international law, and especially of the sovereignty, territorial integrity and political independence of the Republic of Croatia'.

Simultaneously with Croatia, the Republic of Slovenia also proclaimed its independence. The reaction of the Yugoslav Army to the proclamation of independence of the two Republics was brutal. It intervened in Slovenia and intensified its support for the rebellion in Croatia.

The European Community, which was closely observing the developments in Yugoslavia with great anxiety, undertook new initiatives to aid the interested actors to reach a peaceful solution. In order to contribute to these efforts, Croatia and Slovenia agreed to a three-month moratorium on the implementation of their decision on independence. As the aggression against Croatia by the Yugoslav

---

[12] *Narodne novine* (1991), No. 31; English translation in: *The Principal State Acts*, Parliament of the Republic of Croatia (Sabor), Zagreb (1993), p. 33.

[13] Ibid., p. 37.

Army and paramilitary troops from Serbia was unremitting, the Parliament of Croatia on 8 October 1991 adopted the Decision on the Sovereignty and Independence of the Republic of Croatia.[14] By that act Croatia dissolved all State relations with the other Republics and Autonomous Provinces of the SFR of Yugoslavia.

4. THE HAGUE CONFERENCE ON YUGOSLAVIA

In the meantime the European Community launched the idea of organising a conference in which the Yugoslav Federation and the Republics – assisted by the Community and its Member States – would try to find a peaceful solution for Yugoslavia.[15] As this initiative was accepted by all the Yugoslav parties, the Conference on Yugoslavia commenced in The Hague on 7 September 1991, under the chairmanship of the former British Foreign Minister, Lord Carrington. The Conference included the Arbitration Commission which was composed of five members of the highest courts of the European States, and it was chaired by Robert Badinter (France). Its task was to deliver opinions on legal issues submitted to it by the participants at the Conference.

The main issues to be negotiated were: institutional arrangements among the new entities emerging from the dissolution of Yugoslavia; protection of human rights in the area; and economic, political and legal co-operation. In accordance with the genesis of the war against Croatia, one of the major issues seemed to be the status of national minorities. That is why one of the first bodies established at the Conference was the Working Group of Experts on Minority Questions. It had to discuss the topic entitled 'The Rights of All in Yugoslavia'. The Group consisted of experts nominated by each of the six Republics and by the Federation, and it was chaired by Ambassador C.D. Barkman (the Netherlands). The Group met in The Hague on 16-18 September 1991. As it decided to adopt a list of rights and obligations pertaining to minorities, it invited an independent expert, Professor Giorgio Malinverni of the University of Geneva to help in this endeavour. Professor Malinverni was the best choice as only several months earlier the European Commission for Democracy through Law, on the basis of his draft, had adopted the Proposal for a European Convention for the Protection of Minorities.[16] Malinverni adapted the relevant parts of Chapter II of the European Draft Convention, which the Working Group adopted as 'sound guidelines for the protection of the rights of minorities in Yugoslavia'.[17]

---

[14] Ibid., p. 41.

[15] Declarations of 29 August and 3 September 1991.

[16] Council of Europe, European Commission for Democracy through Law, *Proposal for a European Convention for the Protection of Minorities*, Doc. CDL (91) 7, Strasbourg, 4 March 1991.

[17] Conference on Yugoslavia, Working Group of Experts on 'The Rights of All in Yugoslavia', *Chairman's Draft II*, The Hague, 18 September 1991.

This was only the beginning of the negotiations on a composite text on all the major issues relevant for a lasting peace on the territory of the former Yugoslavia. The negotiations continued on several levels (State presidencies, Ministers for foreign affairs, experts' groups), but they were often interrupted as none of the concluded cease-fires were observed.

The Draft Convention prepared by Lord Carrington and his experts, notwithstanding the changes which took into account the majority of the opinions and wishes of all the participants, was eventually rejected by Serbia.[18] Thus, the intended treaty between the new States established on the territory of former Yugoslavia was not concluded, and the Conference on Yugoslavia was reconvened only after a break. Yet, the provisions of the Draft Convention on 'Human Rights and Rights of National or Ethnic Groups' (Chapter II) retained their relevance as they influenced the subsequent Croatian internal legislation. The term 'national or ethnic groups' was used instead of 'minorities' because of the sensitivity about this term on the territory of former Yugoslavia.

In addition to a reference to the main international instruments dealing with the protection of minorities (para. 2), Chapter II of the Draft Convention listed the main minority rights included in these instruments (para. 3). Moreover, the Draft promised 'to persons belonging to a national or ethnic group forming a substantial percentage of the population in the Republic where they live but not forming a majority . . . a general right of participation of members of this group in public affairs, including participation in the government of the Republics concerning their affairs'.

All the above mentioned provisions of the Draft Convention would probably have been acceptable to all the Republics of former Yugoslavia. What was unacceptable to Serbia was paragraph 5 providing 'a special status of autonomy' for 'areas in which persons belonging to a national or ethnic group form a majority . . .' Although not expressly mentioned in the Draft Convention the status of autonomy was intended for areas in Serbia inhabited by Albanians, Hungarians and Muslims; areas in Macedonia where Albanians live; and areas in Croatia where Serbs represent a majority.

The sincerity of Croatia's acceptance of the entire text on minorities, including the 'special status of autonomy', was proved only a month after Serbia's rejection of the provisions proposed by the European Community. On 4 December 1991 Croatia adopted the Constitutional Law on Human Rights and Freedoms and the Rights of National and Ethnic Communities or Minorities in the Republic of Croatia, which was modelled on the Hague Draft Convention.[19]

---

[18] *Treaty Provisions for the Convention,* corrected version, 4 November 1991.

[19] Adopted by the Parliament of Croatia on 4 December 1991; *Narodne novine* (1991), No. 65.

5. THE CONSTITUTIONAL LAW ON HUMAN AND MINORITY RIGHTS

Although, in accordance with its title the Constitutional Law concerns human rights in general as well as specific rights of minorities, the first field is only marginally and summarily dealt with. Article 1 contains a list of international instruments on human rights which Croatia pledged to respect in its municipal legal system. Moreover, the Law restates part of the fundamental human rights and freedoms already proclaimed in the 1990 Croatian Constitution (Article 2). However, already in this Part of the Law (Part II), dedicated to 'Human Rights and Freedoms', Croatia promises to protect 'the equality of national and ethnic groups or minorities' and thus to encourage 'their universal development' (Article 3). Furthermore, Croatia engaged to assist the development of the relations between minorities and 'the people of their parent State in order to promote their national, cultural and linguistic development'. Minorities are also granted 'the right to self-organisation and association in order to realise their national or other interests in compliance with the Constitution and this Law' (Article 4).

As in the Constitutional Law itself or anywhere else in the Croatian legal system, there is no indication of a distinction between 'ethnic groups', 'national groups', 'ethnic minorities' or 'national minorities', we should stick to the term used in the 1990 Croatian Constitution – 'minorities' – which obviously covers all the above combinations. Three Parts of the Constitutional Law deal with 'ethnic or national communities or minorities', as follows:

– Part III of the Law elaborates the concept of 'cultural autonomy', generally granted to minorities in the 1990 Croatian Constitution (Article 15, para. 2), and it lists the other rights all national minorities and their members have in Croatia.
– Part IV deals with the proportional participation of minority representatives in central State bodies.
– Part V concerns communes (areas) with special self-governing (autonomous) status. Such a status was envisaged for communes (areas) in which members of a minority, according to the 1981 census, made up over 50% of the population.

As mentioned above, Part III mainly contains provisions which concern all the minorities in Croatia: the right to decide to which minority a person wishes to belong; non-discrimination of the members of minorities; protection of their survival; the right to identity, culture, religion, public and private use of their languages and script; the protection of equality in participating in public affairs; freedom of possession and the use of national and ethnic emblems and symbols of minorities along with the emblems and symbols of the Republic of Croatia; the right to organise information and publishing activities in their native language and script, and to receive financial aid for such purposes from public funds; freedom to found cultural and other societies (financed by public funds) aimed at preserving their national and cultural identity; the obligation of the State to protect historic monuments and the entire cultural heritage of minorities.

A special section is dedicated to the rights of minorities in the field of education. Minorities are entitled to kindergartens and schools in their own language and script, with programmes adequately presenting their history, culture and science. For these purposes, in addition to the funds of the communes, the Republic of Croatia itself has to provide adequate funding. Members of minorities may also found private kindergartens, schools and other educational institutions.

However, even in this Part of the Constitutional Law there are provisions which concern minorities in special circumstances:

(a) In those *communes* where *members of a minority represent the majority of the total population*, their script and language will be officially used together with the Croatian language and the Latin script (Article 7, para. 2). In addition to this obligation of the communes numerically dominated by minorities, there is an option for all local self-governing units (communes, districts, towns): they may decide to use two or more languages officially, taking into account the number of the members and the interests of minorities (Article 8).
(b) In *towns and other inhabited places* where *minorities represent a relative majority of the population, and the number of students allows for it*, separate schools or school departments will be established with classes held in the language and script of the particular minority, if such a wish is expressed. In cases where such schools or school departments cannot be established due to a small number of students, the instruction of the subjects which are related to the national affiliation of the students will be carried out within a separate school department by teachers of the same national affiliation, if such a wish is expressed by the students' parents (Article 15, paras. 1 and 2).
(c) In *towns and inhabited places* from which, during and after World War II, the autochthonous population belonging to some minorities *was expelled into parent countries or the policy of forced migration into parent countries was pursued,* the teaching of the language of these minorities can be introduced as an optional subject in elementary and secondary education, *regardless of the percentage of the total population* that those minorities represent in that region (Article 15, para. 3).

As already mentioned above, Part IV of the Constitutional Law deals with the proportional participation of minorities in State bodies.

Members of minorities who make up more than 8% of the population of Croatia are entitled to be proportionally represented in the Parliament and the Government of Croatia as well as in the supreme judicial bodies. Members of minorities whose share in the State population is below 8% are entitled to elect a total of five representatives to the House of Representatives of the Croatian Parliament.

Members of minorities are also entitled to be represented in the bodies of local self-government in proportion to their share of the total population of a particular local self-governing unit.

In order to apply the provisions of the Constitutional Law on minority rights in the field of culture, education, and access to the media, the Croatian Government has established its Office for Ethnic and National Communities or Minorities. For the territories of one or more communes where the number of the members of minorities and their interests so require, the Croatian Government will establish local offices for minorities (Article 20).

As well as the Convention planned by the Conference on Yugoslavia, the Croatian Constitutional Law contains provisions on self-governing areas. Part V of the Law contains elaborate rules on 'Communes (Areas) with Special Self-governing (Autonomous) Status'. Although this status was conceived primarily in order to meet the requirements of the Serbian minority in some parts of Croatia, the 'special status communes' were introduced as a general institution for all the communes 'in which members of an ethnic and national community or minority, according to the 1981 census, make up over 50% of the population' (Article 21, para. 1).

In the special status communes members of the commune assemblies and other commune bodies and services had to be elected or appointed taking into account 'the principle of proportional representation of citizens with regard to their national and ethnic or minority affiliation' (Article 23). Another general principle inserted in the introductory Articles of this Part of the Law is the protection of 'the national rights, status and interests of Croats as well as members of other national and ethnic communities or minorities' living in special status communes (Article 24).

Twenty lengthy Articles contain elaborate provisions on all the aspects of the legal order in the special status communes. Such communes were independent in deciding and administering affairs which, according to the Law, were 'within their *original competence*' (emphasis added), such as urban planning, communications, environmental protection, implementation of human rights, etc. (Article 26). On the other hand, bodies of such districts had to enforce laws and regulations of the central government authorities (*transferred competence*); in performing such activities they had to obey the instructions of the Croatian Government and other central bodies of the State administration (Article 28).

Besides the bodies of the special status communes (Assembly of the Commune, Commune agencies, Commune courts, Police administration), a commissioner had to be appointed by the Government of Croatia for every special status commune.

As the Constitutional Law was conceived, drafted and adopted in the course of the Conference on Yugoslavia, and before the international recognition of the independence of Croatia, it contains some provisions on the international monitoring of its implementation.

An international body for the supervision of the implementation of the provisions on the special status has to be established (Article 56). That body had to be created on the basis of a treaty concluded by Croatia; it is not stated who had to be the other parties to treaty. Although only reports and recommendations of that body were envisaged, Croatia was obliged to 'implement the recommendations'. In case of disputes concerning the implementation of such recommendations, a decision from the Court of Human Rights had to be requested. This Court was the one planned by the Conference on Yugoslavia (Article 58, para. 1), and provided for in its Draft Convention (Article 7(1) of the Draft). It had to consist of one member from each Republic of former Yugoslavia, and an equal number and one additional member being nationals of European States other than the Yugoslav Republics.

The Court of Human Rights was not only entrusted with disputes concerning the special status communes. It had the competence to deal with all the disputes concerning human and minority rights in respect of which all available internal legal remedies had been exhausted.

The Constitutional Law also contains a general provision promising the co-operation and consultation of Croatia with other States in order to promote the full realisation of human and minority rights (Article 57).

6. RECOGNITION OF THE REPUBLIC OF CROATIA

The status of minorities and the protection of their members were topics which were present not only in the negotiations by various bodies of the Conference on Yugoslavia and in the drafting of a Convention between the Republics of former Yugoslavia. It was also an important issue on which the Arbitration Commission had to express its opinion on several occasions.

Already in its Opinion No. 1 (7 December 1991), dealing with the disintegration of the SFR of Yugoslavia, the Commission expressed its view that '*peremptory norms of general international law* and, in particular, respect for the fundamental rights of the individual and *the rights of peoples and minorities*' (emphasis added) are binding on all the entities and parties to the succession of the SFRY.[20]

In Opinion No. 2, the Commission had to answer the following question put by the Republic of Serbia, and transmitted to it by Lord Carrington, the Chairman of the Conference:

> 'Does the Serbian population in Croatia and Bosnia-Herzegovina, as one of the constituent peoples of Yugoslavia, have the right to self-determination?'[21]

---

[20] 31 *International Legal Materials (ILM)* (1992) pp. 1496 and 1497.

Before interpreting self-determination in respect of minorities, the Arbitration Commission expressed some general views concerning minority protection. First, the Commission pointed out the right of minorities 'to recognition of their identity under international law'. Second, it reconfirmed its earlier opinion that 'peremptory norms of international law require States to ensure respect for the rights of minorities'. The Commission stressed that this requirement applied to all the Republics of former Yugoslavia *vis-à-vis* the minorities on their territory. As far as the Serbian population in Bosnia-Herzegovina and Croatia is concerned, the Arbitration Commission stated that it must be afforded every right accorded to minorities under international law as well as national guarantees consistent with the principles of international law and the provisions on minority protection proposed in the Draft Convention negotiated at the Conference on Yugoslavia.[22]

Paragraph 3 of Opinion No. 2 contains the Commission's interpretation of the application to minorities of the right to self-determination, inserted in Article 1 of the 1966 International Covenants on Human Rights. In its view, Article 1 'establishes that the principle of the right to self-determination serves to safeguard human rights'. The only mandatory consequence of that right for minorities is that 'by virtue of that right every individual may choose to belong to whatever ethnic, religious or language community he or she wishes'. However, the Commission saw another possible consequence of the principle of self-determination for the members of the Serbian population in Bosnia-Herzegovina and Croatia: *the two States could agree* that persons belonging to this population have the nationality of their choice.[23]

Simultaneously with the dissolution of Yugoslavia, the Republics of the Soviet Union also decided to establish their independence. Facing the request of the twenty new States for recognition, the Extraordinary European Political Co-operation Ministerial Meeting adopted rules for granting recognition. On 16 December 1991 it adopted the Declaration on the 'Guidelines on the Recognition of New States in Eastern Europe and in the Soviet Union'.[24] One of the conditions for recognition were 'guarantees for the rights of ethnic and national groups and minorities in accordance with the commitments subscribed to in the framework of the CSCE' (Conference on Security and Co-operation in Europe).

In addition to the requirements established for all the new States 'in Eastern Europe and in the Soviet Union', the mentioned European Ministerial Meeting adopted the Declaration on Yugoslavia, which contained additional requirements and the procedure for the recognition of the Yugoslav Republics.[25] The main additional requirement was a statement that they accept the provisions on human

---

[21] Ibid., p. 1498.
[22] Ibid., pp. 1498-1499.
[23] Ibid.
[24] Ibid., p. 1486.
[25] Ibid., p. 1485.

rights and rights of national or ethnic groups contained in the Draft Convention considered by the Conference on Yugoslavia. The Republics which wished to be recognised had to submit their applications through the Chair of the Conference to the Arbitration Commission for advice before 15 January 1992.

Croatia was one of the four former Yugoslav Republics (the others were Bosnia-Herzegovina, Macedonia, Slovenia) which requested recognition from the Member States of the European Community. According to the Declaration on Yugoslavia, all the applications for recognition were submitted to the Arbitration Commission before the implementation date of the Declaration (15 January 1992). The Commission considered all the applications on the basis of the Declaration on Yugoslavia, the 'Guidelines' and the materials submitted by the respective Republics. In addition to several other instruments, the Republic of Croatia supplied the Commission with the two main acts relevant to the treatment of minorities: the 1990 Croatian Constitution and the 1991 Constitutional Law on Human and Minority Rights.[26]

During the consideration of the Croatian application, on 10 January 1992 the Chairman of the Arbitration Commission, Mr Robert Badinter, sent a letter to the President of the Republic of Croatia, Dr Franjo Tudjman, requiring further information concerning the attitude of Croatia towards the Draft Convention produced by the Conference on Yugoslavia. The Croatian President answered the next day, reconfirming that 'all the provisions contained in the draft Treaty produced by the Conference on Yugoslavia on 4 November 1991 were accepted in principle by the Republic of Croatia at the meeting in The Hague chaired by Lord Carrington on 5 November 1991 . . . '[27] Moreover, President Tudjman stated that the Croatian Constitutional Law, adopted only a month earlier, was modelled on the Hague Draft Convention, and that Croatia was the only entity on the territory of the former Yugoslavia to adopt such an act.

The Arbitration Commission was of the opinion that the Constitutional Law does not fully incorporate the relevant provisions of the Draft Convention of 4 November 1991, notably those on the 'special status' areas. It therefore required that Croatia supplement the Constitutional Law in such a way as to satisfy those provisions. However, subject to these reservations, the Commission was of the opinion that Croatia had met the necessary conditions for its recognition by the Member States of the European Community.[28]

On the basis of the Opinion by the Arbitration Commission (Opinion No. 5), on 15 January 1992 almost all the Members of the Community recognised the Republic of Croatia.

---

[26] Arbitration Commission, Opinion No. 5 on the Recognition of the Republic of Croatia by the European Community and its Member States. Ibid., pp. 1503-1505 at p. 1504.

[27] Ibid., p. 1518.

[28] Ibid., p. 1505.

Notwithstanding the existing Croatian internal law and its already accepted international obligations in the field of human and minority rights, Italy expressed some concern about the treatment of the Italian minority in the two new neighbouring independent States. It therefore urged Croatia and Slovenia to accept a treaty on the protection of the Italian minority in these two States establishing their sovereignty on the respective parts of the peninsula of Istria, where the Italian minority has lived for centuries. Some of the provisions proposed by Italy and accepted by Croatia were so unusual and/or illogical, that it is difficult to blame Slovenia for not having accepted them. Eventually it was only Italy and Croatia that signed the Memorandum of Understanding on the Protection of the Italian Minority in Croatia and Slovenia (Rome, 15 January 1992). The most unrealistic provision was contained in paragraph 1 of the Memorandum which, notwithstanding the establishment of the independence of Croatia and Slovenia, held that the ethnic Italians in the two States should be treated as one minority. For this and some other unacceptable provisions (e.g. determination of only one organisation representing the Italians in Croatia), the Memorandum has never been submitted to the Croatian Parliament for ratification. On the other hand, Italy was obviously also aware of the peculiarity of the content of the Memorandum, and it accepted new negotiations with Croatia, this time on the protection of the Italian minority in Croatia and the Croatian minority in Italy (see Section 11, *infra*).

7. AMENDMENTS TO THE CONSTITUTIONAL LAW

Immediately after the adoption of the Constitutional Law Croatia started with the implementation of its provisions. The Office for Inter-ethnic Relations of the Croatian Government elaborated the Programme of Implementation of the Constitutional Law.[29] The Head of the Office was Mr Milan Đukić, a member of the Serbian minority. In accordance with Article 20 of the Constitutional Law, the Office was renamed in 1995: it was now called the Office for Ethnic and National Communities or Minorities.

Taking into account the Opinion of the Arbitration Commission concerning the necessity of amending the Croatian Constitutional Law, a memo annexed to a letter dated 22 February 1992 from the President of the Council of the European Communities to the President of Croatia indicated the suggested changes in the Constitutional Law.[30] On 8 May 1992 the Croatian Parliament adopted the

[29] See Vlada Republike Hrvatske, Ured za međunacionalne odnose [Government of the Republic of Croatia, Office for Inter-ethnic Relations], Doc. 012-02/91-01/03-50404-92-1 of 21 February 1992.

[30] Letter of João de Deus Pinheiro, President of the Council of the European Community to Dr. Franjo Tudjman, President of the Republic of Croatia, Lisbon, 22 February 1992.

amendments to the Constitutional Law on Human and Minority Rights.[31] These were the three main differences in comparison with the original version:

(a) 'Special status' was now granted to two districts (Knin and Glina) where the Serbian minority represented more than half of the population (Article 21). The 11 communes constituting these two districts were listed in Article 22. The reason for this change was the argument put forward by the European Community that a meaningful autonomy required a larger unified territorial area, and not autonomous communes divided between several counties. As a consequence of this change, all the provisions on the special status commune bodies were now to be applied to the bodies of the special status districts.
(b) The second major change was the introduction of a Provisional Court of Human Rights (Article 60, para. 3) for the period up to the establishment of the Permanent Court of Human Rights (see Section 5, *supra*). The Provisional Court had to be composed of five members. The President and two members had to be nominated by the Presidency of the European Community from among the ranks of citizens of its Members States, and two members had to be nominated by the Parliament of the Republic of Croatia from among Croatian citizens.
(c) Finally, the third change was the deletion of Article 62 of the original text of the Constitutional Law, which made its application subject to the establishment of a complete and lasting peace throughout the Croatian territory and the holding of free elections in areas with special status.

On 4 July 1992 the Arbitration Commission analysed the amended Croatian Constitutional Law.[32] It noted the changes to the 1991 original text, and pointed out some restrictions to which the autonomy accorded to the areas with special status were subjected. According to the Commission, the restrictions concerned the following: the fields in which the authorities of the areas concerned exercised sole jurisdiction; the procedure for the appointment of the political and judicial authorities in the areas concerned, which left the final choice to the central government; the judicial, political and budgetary control to which the authorities in the areas with special status were subject.

In addition to these remarks concerning the adopted 'special status', the Arbitration Commission noted that the Constitutional Law made no mention of the demilitarisation of such areas, provided for in the Hague Draft Convention.

However, the Arbitration Commission was in an awkward situation: it scrutinised the only legal act of one of the States established on the territory of the

---

[31] *Narodne novine* (1992) No. 27; the Constitutional Law as amended: ibid., (1992) No. 34; the translation of the amended Constitutional Law into English in: *The Principal State Acts*, op. cit. n. 12, p. 45 et seq.

[32] Conference for Peace in Yugoslavia, Arbitration Commission, Comments on the Republic of Croatia's Constitutional Law of 4 December 1991, as last amended on 8 May 1992, 31 *ILM* (1992) pp. 1505-1507.

former Yugoslavia which had been formulated on the basis of the proposals of the Hague Conference. The other States to whom the proposals were addressed were not even considering the adoption of such a comprehensive act on minority rights, and the Conference on Yugoslavia was no longer considering the Hague Draft Convention. That is why the Arbitration Commission had to admit that 'the draft Convention . . . does not define in detail the concept of autonomy and adjustments may be made by agreement between the republics'. It added that 'even if the Constitutional Law in question does sometimes fall short of the obligations assumed by Croatia *when it accepted the draft Convention of 4 November 1991, it nonetheless satisfies the requirements of general international law regarding the protection of minorities*' (emphasis added).[33]

Be that as it may, the non-accomplished Hague Convention and both versions of the Croatian Constitutional Law did not have any effect on the attitude of the insurgent Serbs, the remaining units of the Yugoslav Army, and the paramilitary forces from Serbia in the areas to which 'special status' had to be applied (Knin and Glina), and other areas beyond the control of the Croatian Government (Central and Eastern Slavonia, Baranja and Western Sirmium). Any status short of independence they did not even want to consider; the only solution they would have accepted was the independence of these micro-entities and their right to be associated with the 'New Yugoslavia', i.e. Serbia (see Section 8, *infra*).

8. THE LONDON CONFERENCE ON THE FORMER YUGOSLAVIA

After the recognition of the new States established on the territory of the former Yugoslavia (Bosnia-Herzegovina, Croatia, Macedonia, Slovenia), and the admission of some of them (Bosnia-Herzegovina, Croatia, Slovenia) to the United Nations (22 May 1992), a new international conference on the former Yugoslavia was organised. On 26-27 August 1992 the International Conference on the Former Yugoslavia was held in London.

One of the principles endorsed by the London Conference as the basis for a negotiated settlement of the problems of former Yugoslavia was the 'implementation of constitutional guarantees of the human rights and fundamental freedoms of persons belonging to ethnic and national communities and minorities . . . '[34]

As the Conference intended to 'remain in being until a final settlement of the problems of the former Yugoslavia has been reached', it established various organs for its further activities. One of the six Working Groups in continuous session at the Office of the United Nations in Geneva was the Ethnic and National Communities and Minorities Working Group. Its task was to recommend initia-

[33] Ibid., p. 1507.

[34] The London Conference, Statement of Principles, Doc. LC/C2 (FINAL), 26 August 1992. Ibid., p. 1524.

tives for resolving ethnic questions in the former Yugoslavia; it was chaired by a German diplomat, Ambassador Gaert Ahrens.[35]

At the first plenary meeting of the Working Group (15 September 1992) the delegations of Bosnia-Herzegovina, Croatia, Macedonia and Slovenia were present. According to the UN Secretary-General's Report, 'all those present reconfirmed their commitment to the Conference principles, particularly to the Treaty Provisions for the Convention adopted at The Hague'.[36] However, no efforts were undertaken to finalise the Hague Draft and formally to adopt it. On the other hand, as far as municipal law was concerned, the minority protection concept enshrined in the Hague Draft was reproduced only in the Croatian Constitutional Law.

In the course of the work of this Group, the international community gained a clear picture of the stance of the rebel Serbs concerning the possible solutions of 'ethnic problems' in Croatia. The UN Secretary-General reported:

> 'On the Serbs in Croatia, the Working Group had a talk with Mr. Goran Hadžic, "President of the Republic of Krajina", and several meetings with Croatian representatives. In Belgrade on 25 September, Mr. Hadžić said that he was quite prepared for talks on human rights, economic and communication issues, but *not on any form of Serbian autonomy inside Croatia. He further said that the Krajina would rather resort to renewed warfare than become a part of Croatia again. It was not possible so far to convince Mr. Hadžic or any other Knin representative that a solution has to be found on the basis of the London Principles*' (emphasis added).[37]

Notwithstanding various efforts to change this attitude of the Serbian leaders in 'Krajina', and the agreements they concluded with the Croatian authorities in 1993 on some economic and communication issues, this intransigent stance remained unchanged among people like Mr. Hadžić. That is why they also rejected the Draft Agreement on the Krajina, Slavonia, Southern Baranja and Western Sirmium proposed by the international community on 18 January 1995.[38] This Draft Agreement (called plan Z4) went even further than the previous proposals in granting a broad autonomy to the areas controlled by the rebel Serbs, and even offered them a limited international personality (the right to enter into some international agreements). Notwithstanding the strong resistance of many political factions in Croatia, the Croatian Government expressed its readiness to resolve the problem of the Serbian mutiny on the basis of this Draft Agreement.

---

35 Ibid., p. 1535.

36 UN Doc. S/24795, 11 November 1992, para. 83, reproduced in ibid., p. 1570.

37 Para. 89 of the Secretary-General's Report, ibid., p. 1571.

38 Draft Agreement on the Krajina, Slavonia, Southern Baranja and Western Sirmium, 18 January 1995, p. 43.

9. THE REINTEGRATION OF THE OCCUPIED AREAS

1995 was the decisive year for the reintegration of all parts of the Croatian territory under the control of the Government of Croatia. As any peaceful solution with the rebellious Serbian authorities in the Krajina proved to be impossible, the Croatian Government undertook two military operations in May and August 1995 in order to restore control over Western Slavonia and the areas which under the 1991 Constitutional Law had to enjoy the special status (the districts of Knin and Glina). The two actions, and particularly the second one ('Storm' in August 1995), resulted in an exodus of Serbs from Croatia, which was an expected result of the suicidal policy of the local Serbs which had been instigated by the Belgrade regime.

As a consequence of these events, the realities which were the reasons for many of the provisions of the Constitutional Law have been changed. The provisions on 'special status districts' had never been applied due to pressure from Belgrade and the unwillingness of the leaders of the population of the areas where this status had to be applied. Now, due to the exodus of the Serbian population there were no more areas where ethnic Serbs would represent the majority of the population. In this new situation, on 21 September 1995 the Croatian Parliament adopted a new Constitutional Law suspending some of the provisions of the 1991/1992 Constitutional Law on Human and Minority Rights.[39] Until the publication of the results of the next census in Croatia, suspended are:

(a) The provisions on the special rights and protection of the minorities who made up more than 8% of the population of Croatia under the previous census;
(b) Part V on districts with special self-governing status;
(c) The provisions on the conclusion of an international agreement for the supervision of the provisions on the special status;
(d) The provisions on the Court of Human Rights and the Provisional Court of Human Rights.

While the suspension of the provisions under (a) and (b) are the result of the changed ethnic composition of the population in the areas concerned, the provisions mentioned under (c) and (d) have been suspended due to the changed international status of Croatia. These provisions were inserted in the Constitutional Law at a period of time when the protection of human and minority rights in Croatia was discussed at the Conference on Yugoslavia. At the moment of suspension Croatia had already become party to all UN treaties on human and minority rights, it was bound by all the OSCE commitments and it was a candidate for joining the Council of Europe and acceding to its treaties on the protection of

[39] *Narodne novine* (1995) No. 68.

human and minority rights. On the other hand, there are no longer any reasons for the establishment of special human rights courts in Croatia as the Croatian judicial system, and particularly its Constitutional Court, provide for judicial control over the implementation of human and minority rights.

Another occupied area of Croatia was freed without the use of force. On 12 November 1995 a delegation of the Croatian Government signed with a 'Serb Negotiating Delegation' the 'Basic Agreement on the Region of Eastern Slavonia, Baranja and Western Sirmium' (Croatian Danubian Region). The Agreement was witnessed by the UN representatives, and its implementation in the next two years was monitored by the United Nations Transitional Administration for Eastern Slavonia (UNTAES).

The complex process of reintegration of this part of Croatia cannot be described here. As far as the minorities are concerned, it is noteworthy that not only Croats, but also several minorities (Hungarians, Slovaks, Czechs, Ruthenians, Ukrainians) were the victims of the aggression and a five-year long occupation of this area. The return of all the refugees and displaced persons, and the establishment of confidence and coexistence with the Serb population is the major, but difficult task of the Croatian authorities and the local populace. As far as the Serbian community is concerned, in addition to its representation in local government bodies, its interests and rights should be monitored and promoted by the Joint Council of Communes, provided for in paragraph 12 of the Basic Agreement. The Council was established on 23 May 1997.[40]

In the process of its admission to the Council of Europe, Croatia was required to reconsider the suspension of some of the provisions of its Constitutional Law. In October 1996 the Croatian Government established the Working Group for the Revision of the Constitutional Law. According to an *aide-mémoire* of the Croatian Government, before undertaking any amendments to the Constitutional Law it is crucial to carry out a census, which will be feasible only once the situation has stabilised and the refugees have returned to their homes. For the time being, a major step in this direction has been the reintegration of the Croatian Danubian region, completed on 15 January 1998.

One of the international bodies involved in the question of the implementation of the Croatian Constitutional Law has been the European Commission for Democracy through Law (Venice Commission). On the basis of its recommendations, Croatia undertook two measures. In January 1998 the Council of National Minorities was set up to act as an independent consultative body defining the interests of minorities and proposing actions in this respect to the Croatian Parliament and the Croatian Government. Secondly, the Croatian Constitutional Court has accepted the Venice Commission's proposal on the participation of international advisors in the work of the Court in cases dealing with minority issues.

---

[40] Ibid. (1998) No. 137.

10. THE 1997 AMENDMENTS TO THE CROATIAN CONSTITUTION

Notwithstanding the fact that Croatia had adopted the 1990 Constitution when still in the position of a Yugoslav Republic, and that its independence has been won in a lengthy and cruel war, few amendments to the Constitution were necessary in the new circumstances. These amendments were adopted on 12 December 1997.[41] Mention will only be made of those amendments which concern minorities.

The preambular provision on peoples and minorities in Croatia from the 1990 Constitution had to be changed as a consequence of the now independent Croatia. However, the changes have not been formulated in the most clear manner. The provision reads:

> '. . . the Republic of Croatia is hereby established as the national State of the Croatian people and as the State of the members of autochthonous national minorities: Serbs, Czechs, Slovaks, Italians, Hungarians, Jews, Germans, Austrians, Ukrainians, Ruthenians and others who are its citizens and who are guaranteed equality with the citizens of Croatian nationality and the realisation of ethnic rights in accordance with the democratic norms of the United Nations Organisation and the free world countries.'

Three changes have to be mentioned in comparison with the 1990 text:

(a) There is no longer any reference to other 'peoples' in addition to the Croatian people. This is the consequence of the fact that the population of Croatia consists of the Croat people (80%) and of minorities. No more a federal unit of Yugoslavia, Croatia is not bound to call its Serb, Slovene, Moslem, Macedonian and Montenegrin citizens 'peoples'. The term 'peoples' has also been omitted from the Article 15 of the Constitution, now granting equal rights, freedom of expression of their nationality, freedom of the use of their language and script, and the right to cultural autonomy only to the members of national minorities.
(b) The term 'minorities' in the 1990 Constitution has now been replaced by 'autochthonous national minorities'. While the adjective 'national' is in accordance with the European usage, the introduction of the adjective 'autochthonous' is surprising and gives rise to many questions.

Already in the 1991 Constitutional Law (Article 15, para. 3) the rights of the 'autochthonous population' belonging to some minorities that 'was expelled into parent countries', were specially dealt with (see Section 5, *supra*). At variance with the language of this provision, a new paragraph (Article 15, para. 4), added to the Law in 1992, dealt with 'autochthonous minorities'. This provisions insists on the necessity of protecting some collective rights of autochthonous minorities

[41] Ibid. (1997) No. 135.

regardless of their share in the total population. The adjective 'autochthonous' has not been specially defined or even discussed in international law, there is no definition of 'autochthonous minorities' in the Constitutional Law, and none of the minorities in Croatia is indicated in the Law as being an 'autochthonous minority'. And, indeed, it is very difficult to characterise specific minorities in Croatia as 'autochthonous'. Why should the Slovak and Czechs minorities be called 'autochthonous' as well as the Italian and Hungarian minorities, when thousands of years separate their arrival in the territory of the present Republic of Croatia? Why are the national minorities in the preamble of the Constitution called 'autochthonous national minorities', and in Article 15, dealing with minority rights, only 'national minorities'?

(c) What are the reasons for not including the Slovenes and Moslems (Bosniacs) among the 'autochthonous national minorities'? The fact that these two minorities have not expressly been listed in the amended Constitution has not been officially explained. They have lived in Croatia for centuries, and there are more members of the Bosniac and Slovene minorities than some others mentioned in the amended Constitution (Austrians, Germans, Ukrainians, etc.). Anyhow, it must be pointed out that the list of minorities in the Constitution is not exhaustive. After listing ten minorities, members of other minorities who are citizens of Croatia are equally mentioned. The fact is that not only Bosniacs and Slovenes, but four other minorities not mentioned in the Constitution (Roma, Macedonians, Montenegrins, Albanians) also enjoy the status of minorities in Croatia.[42]

11. INTERNATIONAL OBLIGATIONS OF CROATIA DEALING WITH MINORITY PROTECTION

Since the recognition of its independence, by way of succession the Republic of Croatia has become a party to all the UN treaties on the protection of human rights, including those containing specific provisions on minorities, such as the Convention on the Prevention and Punishment of the Crime of Genocide, the Convention against Discrimination in Education, the International Convention on the Elimination of All Forms of Racial Discrimination, the International Covenant on Civil and Political Rights, and the Convention on the Rights of the Child. At the time of the adoption of the Declaration on the Rights of Persons Belonging to National or Ethnic, Religious and Linguistic Minorities Croatia was already a Member of the United Nations.

Speaking about the Croatian international obligations in the field it is important to point out that according to the Croatian Constitution (Article 134), treaties to which Croatia is a party are part of the internal legal order of Croatia and in

---

[42] See M. Šimić (Ed.), *Implementation of Cultural Autonomy of National Minorities in the Republic of Croatia*, Government of the Republic of Croatia, Bibliotheca Documents, Zagreb (1998).

terms of legal effect they rank higher than Croatian laws.

After Croatia's entry into the Council of Europe, it signed and ratified the two treaties on minority issues adopted in the framework of this organisation: the European Charter on Regional and Minority Languages[43] and the Framework Convention for the Protection of National Minorities.[44]

Being a member of the Organisation on Security and Co-operation in Europe, all the substantive and procedural provisions on the protection of human rights and national minorities adopted within this organisation also apply to the Republic of Croatia. Croatia also participates in the Central European Initiative (CEI), a grouping of sixteen States which in 1994 adopted the CEI Instrument for the Protection of Minority Rights.[45]

In addition to its commitments assumed on a regional or global level, since its independence (8 October 1991) Croatia has been engaged in accepting minority provisions in various instruments concluded with its neighbours. Already on 15 December 1991 Croatia acceded to the Declaration on the Principles of Co-operation concerning the Granting of the Rights of National Minorities, concluded between Hungary and Ukraine on 15 May 1991. That same day (15 December 1991) Croatia and Hungary concluded the Protocol on the Principles of Co-operation in Preserving the Rights of National Minorities. On the basis of this Protocol, the two States established a joint, Mixed Commission entrusted with the implementation of the mentioned Declaration. In this Commission the representatives of Croatia and Hungary drafted the Agreement on the Protection of the Hungarian Minority in Croatia and the Croatian Minority in Hungary, which was signed in Osijek, on 5 April 1995.[46] An interesting feature of the Agreement is the composition of the Mixed Intergovernmental Committee established for the monitoring of the implementation of the Agreement. It is composed not only of government representatives: members of both minorities nominated by minority organisations are also members of the Committee. In its first three meetings the Committee discussed many relevant issues for the two minorities, and adopted various recommendations to the two Governments.

As already mentioned, Croatia had already concluded a treaty on minority protection with Italy on 15 January 1992. In order to replace this poorly drafted trilateral treaty, which Slovenia did not want to sign, Croatia and Italy engaged in new negotiations. After protracted negotiations, the Treaty between the Republic of Croatia and the Italian Republic concerning Minority Rights was signed in Zagreb on 5 November 1996.[47]

[43] Text in: *European Treaty Series (ETS)*, No. 148; ratification: Web site: http://www.coe.fr/tablconv/148t.htm, 30 November 1998.

[44] ETS, No. 157; ratification: *Human Rights Information Bulletin*, No. 41, doc. H/INF(98)1.

[45] CEI Instrument for the Protection of Minority Rights, CEI – Center for Information and Documentation, Trieste, 1996.

[46] *Narodne novine – međunarodni ugovori* [Official Gazette – Treaties] (1995) No. 8.

[47] Ibid., (1997) No. 15.

A new, realistic approach to the position of the Serbian minority was adopted by the FR of Yugoslavia in the Agreement on Normalisation of Relations between the Republic of Croatia and the Federal Republic of Yugoslavia, signed in Belgrade on 23 August 1996.[48] Instead of claiming the right of the Serbs in Croatia to independence, their union with Serbia, etc., the FR of Yugoslavia adopted the position that they, as well as the Montenegrins in Croatia and the Croats in Yugoslavia, should be treated in accordance with international law, which means that they enjoy the status of minorities in the Republic of Croatia:

> 'The Contracting Parties shall guarantee the Serbs and Montenegrins in the Republic of Croatia and the Croats in the Federal Republic of Yugoslavia *all the rights they entitled to under international law*' (emphasis added – Article 8).

The two States agreed that the protection of the respective minorities should be the subject of a special treaty. Croatia was entrusted with proposing the first draft, which it had already done in the autumn of 1996. The proposed draft generally followed the model of the Agreement which Croatia concluded with Hungary. For the time being, there is no progress in the drafting of the treaty.

Croatian authorities have mentioned the possibility of concluding bilateral treaties on the protection of minorities also with Slovenia and Slovakia, but there is no report of any concrete measures being undertaken in this respect.

12. FINAL REMARKS

This article has no intention to provide a complete picture of the legal situation of minorities in Croatia and to embark on the analysis of all legal rules applicable to the protection and promotion of minority rights in the field of education, culture, participation in public life, etc. Its goal is rather to indicate in a chronological order the developments of the Croatian constitutional rules concerning minorities, particularly the rules determining their relations with the Croatian people. It was these rules that influenced the attitude of the minorities, particularly of the Serbs in Croatia, towards the Republic of Croatia. As this analysis proves, it was not the content and implementation of those rules that determined the reaction of the Serbian minority towards the constitutional changes in Croatia. The constitutional rules have been misinterpreted in order to foment fear among the Serbian minority as regards an independent Croatian State. Resistance against the Croatian State emerged even before the adoption of any change of the constitutional rules. The irrelevance of the legal solutions proposed and adopted in Croatia is best demonstrated by the rejection on the part of the rebellious Serbs of the Constitu-

---

[48] Ibid., (1996) No. 10; English translation in the Annex to UN Doc. A/51/351-S/1996/744 of 12 September 1996.

tional Law on Human Rights and Freedoms and the Rights of National and Ethnic Communities of Minorities. The Law was based on the proposals of the international community as the highest standard for minority protection, offering autonomy in addition to regular, general minority rights. Totally negative reactions were also expressed in respect of other international proposals, such as the so-called Z4 plan in 1995.

This negative stance by a part of a minority towards its life in the independent Croatian State, and the terrible consequence of such an attitude, makes us neglect the other minorities too often. Their attitude has been realistic and constructive: they try to get the best legal position possible, they have always co-operated in the drafting and implementation of the Croatian legal rules affecting their situation, they co-operate directly with their kin in the neighbouring countries, and they participate in the international relations established by Croatia for the sake of promoting minority rights. It is to be hoped that in the future there will be no exceptions to such a positive stance from the side of the minorities, and that the Croatian Government will be able to implement all the minority rights provided for in its municipal legal rules and its international obligations.

THE ECONOMIC POSITION OF MINORITIES IN THE REPUBLIC OF CROATIA

by Mirjana Domini

1. INTRODUCTION

In determining the right to development to be one of the fundamental human rights, the General Assembly of the United Nations at its 34th session[1] confirmed that all human rights are unique, mutually linked, interdependent and conditioned towards each other and can only be considered in a comprehensive and integral way. In other words, it is not possible to divide human rights into civil and political categories, on the one hand, and into economic and cultural rights, on the other. At the same time, as established in a Report by the UN Secretary-General,[2] States, peoples and minorities are all subjects and beneficiaries of these rights.[3]

Since the right to development presents a dynamic category, being in constant development and continuously appearing in new forms, and at the same time dependent on general social movements and the degree of economic development of the area concerned, a multi-disciplinary approach and the use of various data sources is needed in order to follow its materialization, as well as the position of the recipient of this right. In States like Croatia, which in the recent past have experienced fundamental social and economic changes, the problem of how to present the economic position of minorities as bearers and recipients of the right to development presents an especially complex task.

2. MINORITIES IN THE REPUBLIC OF CROATIA IN THE PERIOD OF THE FORMER SFRY

In the former multinational Yugoslavia, of which Croatia was a component part, according to the federal[4] and republic[5] constitutional provisions, the integral

[1] UN GA Resolution 34/46 accepted on 23 November 1979; UN GA Resolution 32/130; Declaration on the Right to Development of 4 December 1986 (41/128).

[2] Report of the Secretary-General, UN, E/CN. 4/1334, 2 February 1979.

[3] In the former Yugoslavia these rights were also acknowledged to belong to peoples and minorities, but also to insufficiently developed territories through its self-managing system.

[4] E.g., Arts. 154 and 245 of the Constitution of the SFRY.

[5] E.g., Art. 229 of the Constitution of the Republic of Croatia.

S. Trifunovska (Ed.), Minorities in Europe – Croatia, Estonia and Slovakia

members of peoples and minorities were placed on the same level and – as self-managers – were included on an equal footing with the management of production, trade and other economic activities. This was especially the case in planning the development of the areas which they populated, by means of delegation in decision-making processes on the level of the commune, the region and the republic. In accordance with the legal system, they were able to establish business and other organisations of private ownership based on economic, and not ethnic interests.[6]

In other words, the need for the manifold development of minorities was built into local and regional plans for the socio-economic development of ethnically mixed areas as well as into documents regulating town-planning, utilisation and similar arrangements while economic equality was seen as the basis of every other equality.

The following could be considered to be major factors which implicitly affected the economic position of minorities in the Republic of Croatia in the period when it was a constitutive part of ex-Yugoslavia:

(a) Migration flows. Whether or not migrations were the result of spontaneous population movements from one area to another ('shift for oneself', marriage migration and the like) or of migrations imposed and implemented by the State official authorities (colonisation) whereby ethnic and economic components were combined, they nevertheless changed the demographic composition in territories in which these changes took place and thereby also the ethnic map. This had its functional and developmental dimension as well. In general, migration processes are especially important for multi-ethnic States, as the former Yugoslavia was, because they had an impact on the demographic homogeneity of the territory and on the already established internal relations among traditionally settled ethnic groups.

Changes in the demographic composition were reflected in the inhabitants' way of living, but they also manifested themselves in the outward appearance, function and development of the territory itself (particularly in the case of mass (im)migration), even to the extent of the so-called culture of living, changing socio-ethnic/cultural and socio-economic determinants. However, this mutual impact – of a person on the space and of the space on a person – was not given serious attention. On the contrary, aimed at the suppression and neutralisation of ethnic individualisation, it was thereby neglected.

---

[6] According to the general commitment that only work and the results of work with socially-owned means of production and performing activities in citizens' ownership schemes determine the economic and every other person's position and human rights, the Constitution of the Republic of Croatia makes equal and places on an equal footing all working people and citizens regardless of race, sex, national and ethnic affiliation, religion, language, education or social position.

(b) Forced industrialisation. In addition, favouring rapid and forced industrialisation and the 'working class' led to a rapid breakdown of the ethnic communities and ties between their members. This happened together with the mass population movements to urban centres; classic village communities which had the function of preserving cultural heritage and traditions were replaced by modern industrial, mobile communities acting on different social and cultural principles. In that sense any effort to establish an ethnic participation by means of economic parameters seems to have been rather difficult if not impossible.

The self-managing economic system, which was the economic concept of the Yugoslav socialist system, suppressed private companies and private ownership, and in this way it also completely neutralised ethnic traits. As a consequence, one can conclude that minority members as individuals, together with ethnic communities, shared the fate of the rest of the population of narrower areas (geographic units, territorial and administrative units, local self-government) and the whole community.

2.1 **Territorial settlements**

In the former multinational Yugoslavia[7] there were six national groups which had a minority status in the Republic of Croatia:[8] Czechs, Hungarians, Slovaks, Ruthenians, Italians and Ukrainians, whereas the Roma were considered as an ethnic group.[9] Italians and Czechs had the highest demographic settlement in Croatia whereas the numbers of other minorities were far larger in other parts of ex-Yugoslavia (e.g., over 93% of the Hungarian minority lived in Vojvodina, the autonomous province of Serbia), which had a corresponding impact on the concentration of minority resources important for the prosperity of an ethnic community and its economic development.

The above-mentioned ethnic groups numbered 68,388 members in total out of the 4,601,469 inhabitants of Croatia which represented 1.48% of the population.[10]

---

[7] Croatia and Slovenia were the first republics of the former SFRY which, on 15 January 1992, were recognized as independent and sovereign States. Otherwise, officially it seems to be accepted that the post WW II Yugoslavia existed until July 1992 when the Arbitration Commission of the Peace Conference on Yugoslavia in its Opinion No. 8 (of 4 July 1992) expressed the view that 'the process of dissolution of Yugoslavia referred to in Opinion No. 1 of 29 November 1991 is now complete and that the SFRY no longer exists'.

[8] The term 'nationalities' was, according to the 1974 Constitution, used for national minorities in order to formally actualise the principle of equality as the basic approach to the arrangement of a minority position in the constitutional and legal order, as well as to neutralise the 'majority-minority' relationship. It was used for 'the parts of the nation whose mother country borders with Yugoslavia and for the members of other nations permanently living in Yugoslavia'. (English translation of the SFRY Constitution and of the Explanation of the expressions used in the Constitution, p. 307).

[9] Sometimes the Roma were placed in the category of an ethnic group without distinction as regards nationality, but most often they remained on the margin as a 'civilisation-related problem'.

[10] 1981 census, Central Bureau of Statistics.

They were dispersed over the whole territory of Croatia, in 114 out of 115 then existing communes,[11] but only in 26 of them were minorities statistically significant. Reducing this to a more palpable numerical proportion, the existing statistical data show that more than 100 members of the Czech minority lived in 20 communes of the administrative-territorial constitution of Croatia at that time, Hungarians were to be found in 31 communes. The 18.6% of the Hungarians present in the city of Beli Manastir was the greatest concentration of minority members in one commune. The Italian minority had more than 100 members in 10 communes, Slovaks lived in 8 communes, Ruthenians in 4 and Ukrainians in 3. The Roma, as a rather specific population group, whose process of settlement in one place and the abandonment of the traditional nomadic way of life only appeared recently, counted more than 100 members in 7 communes, although it can be said with certainty that this number was at least twice as large, but they had no registered residence nor properly issued documents.[12]

According to the administrative-territorial system of that time, communes were organised in 10 associations of Communes,[13] and the aforementioned nationalities were most numerous in the association of Communes of Bjelovar, Osijek and Rijeka. Individually, Czechs were the most numerous in the association of Communes of Bjelovar, Zagreb and Osijek; Hungarians in the association of Communes of Osijek and Bjelovar and in the city association of Communes of Zagreb; the greatest concentration of Italians was located in the territory of the association of Communes of Rijeka and far less so in the territory of the association of Communes of Split and Zagreb; Slovaks were mostly concentrated in the territory of the association of Communes of Osijek and the association of Communes of Sisak; Ruthenians in the association of Communes of Osijek; Ukrainians in the association of Communes of Osijek, the association of Communes of Sisak and in the city association of Communes of Zagreb; and the Roma in the association of Communes of Varaždin and in the city association of Communes of Zagreb.

From the available data as well as from a more detailed analysis, it is obvious that on the level of communes and settlements the usual statement that minorities lived in underdeveloped or less developed areas which affected their economic and social positions, cannot be applied here. This assertion could, to some extent, also be applied to a part of the Roma population who, due to their way of living

---

[11] The commune was defined as 'the territory of a basic socio-political community, in which peoples and minorities exercise their rights, conditions for satisfying their material, social, cultural and other joint needs are realised . . . work and employment is ensured . . . direct execution of the Law is guaranteed, the protection of freedoms realised, the development of the economy and social activities directed and co-ordinated'.

[12] See M. Domini, 'Manjine u Hrvatskoj', in *Manjine u alpsko-jadranskom prostoru*, Zagreb (1991) p. 94.

[13] In the former administrative-territorial constitution the association of Communes was a 'social community and a unit of political authority for the area comprising several communes'.

and spontaneous settlement in 'free' – most often unattractive – areas remained on the margins of economic and social development. Though, it should be pointed out, that there are settlements like, for example, Pitomača, where, according to their standard of living and accommodation, the Roma can be placed far ahead of the rest of the population in this area.

2.2 **Employment**

For an assessment of the economic position of minorities in Croatia valuable data can be found in the proportion of active working minority members in relation to the rest of the population, their qualifications and their education level. The data from the period of the former Yugoslavia show that minorities had a 1.52% share of the active working population which was slightly higher than their share in the total population (1.48%). Accordingly, it can be concluded that there was no significant difference as regards the total active population of Croatia. However, there were considerable differences among the minorities themselves: the Czech minority had the greatest number of active working population (51%) which was almost 9% higher than the Croatian average while the Roma had the lowest percentage with only 20.8% of the total Roma population in Croatia being in employment. The representation of women belonging to minority groups in the active working population showed that only the Czechs had similar numbers to the Republic average (40.3%), while this rate was the lowest with respect to the Roma women (18.3%).

2.3 **Occupation**

With regard to occupation,[14] minority members were most often to be found in the category of 'Agricultural and similar workers' – 17% more than was the case with the other inhabitants of Croatia. On the other hand, the share of minority members in the second, most frequent, occupational category: 'Miners, industrial workers and the like', was 5% lower than the Republic's average. With regard to other occupations, minority presence was roughly equal or slightly less (0.5-3.2%). There were, however, some exceptions among certain minorities. For example, the Italian minority had the largest number of management staff, while the Roma had none; likewise, in relation to the total number of minority members the Italian minority counted the largest number of persons employed in the 'Managing, administrative and similar workers' category as well as among the 'Experts and artists' occupations. The Czechs had the greatest share of their active working population in the category 'Agricultural and similar workers' (above 50% of those employed), a category which counted the least number of Italians (slightly

[14] The nomenclature of occupations used herein is according to the *Statistical Yearbook of Croatia* (1987).

more than one-sixth of all working persons). Hungarians and Italians were mostly 'Miners and industrial workers and the like', occupations which had the least number of Slovaks. Among the 'Managing and administrative personnel' the most represented were the Italians and Ruthenians, and the least were the Roma whose number was the smallest also in the category of the 'Experts and artists' in which the Italians, Hungarians and Czechs were predominant.

2.4 **Education**

Since, in principle, one's integration into the economic system depends to a large extent on the degree of education and qualifications one possesses, the economic position of every individual, as well as of a group as a whole, depends on qualifications and the kind of work one performs. This had a special significance for the realisation of the actual equality of minorities with the majority nation. According to the available data it is unquestionable that the education and qualifications of minorities had been improving during last decades of the former Yugoslavia, although certain differences among minorities themselves as well as in relation to the rest of the population of Croatia still existed.

Some 70% of the members of the Hungarian minority either lived in the countryside or had their origins there. Their qualifications and education revealed a considerable qualitative shift: 90% of Hungarians, after ending primary school, continued and successfully completed their secondary education in Hungarian-language and majority Croatian-language national schools respectively. The number of students of Hungarian nationality in institutions of higher education corresponded to the average for the rest of the population of Croatia. A similar situation was to be found as regards the Czech minority whose elder generation was mostly agricultural, while young people were completing their education and trying to find employment in urban centres. Slovaks were still more distinctly involved in agriculture and similar occupations so that integration into the education system was directed to this end. The level of education of the Italians was, on the other hand, above-average, mostly due to the rather developed educational system in their mother tongue and to their significant presence in urban centres which produced a precious personnel functioning successfully in economic and social structures. This contributed to the preservation and increase of Italian self-conscienceness and the protection of the national interests of the Italian community.

With regard to the level of literacy and education, Ruthenians and Ukrainians were in a similar position to the Italians, since they had a small number of illiterate persons, while the number of secondary school pupils and university students greatly exceeded the Croatian average. However, the situation of the Roma was quite the contrary; in the majority of cases they were placed at the bottom of the social scale and social emancipation. The large number of illiterate and semi-literate Romas (even of younger generations), as well as particular and recognisable ways of earning their living, made the integration of the Roma difficult. Even though certain attempts had been made to accelerate the material and cultural development of the Roma in Croatia, the integration problems were still significant.

3. THE ECONOMIC POSITION OF MINORITIES IN THE INDEPENDENT REPUBLIC OF CROATIA

By the independence of the Republic of Croatia and its establishment as a sovereign State in international law and relations, in addition to the already existing minority groups, members of the former constituent nations were also afforded the status of minorities. This resulted in the enlargement of the list of already existing minority groups (of six nationalities, plus the Roma), with the following national communities/minorities: Montenegrins, Macedonians, Muslims, Slovenes and Serbs. Besides, the minority position of Austrians and Germans, who lost their minority status after WW II due to their 'historical sins', has now been restored; Albanians (although recognized as a minority in the former Yugoslavia, did not enjoy this status in Croatia) were also granted minority status; as were the Jews who were formerly not granted minority rights owing to their insufficiently clearly declared religious and national elements in the identification. Though the Russians, Greeks, Turks, Roumanians and others, have been represented as separate groups, due to their small numbers, dispersion and the lack of organisation (the members did not show any interest in organising themselves in order to preserve their national and cultural identity) they remained on the level of merely being present in the Croatian multicultural space.[15]

Some of the 16 minority communities today existing in the Republic of Croatia can be considered as autochthonous in the real sense (Italians, Hungarians), others are considered autochthonous with respect to their long-lasting residence (for several centuries) on the territory of Croatia (Czechs, Slovaks, Ukrainians, Ruthenians, Jews and others) while newcomers consist mainly of groups like Muslims, Albanians, Macedonians, and others. The Republic of Croatia makes no formal distinction between autochthonous and alochthonous minority groups,[16] but it depends rather on the actual situation it faces in moulding the

---

[15] According to the last census held in 1991 on the basis of the unique methodology of ex-Yugoslavia, Croatia had a total of 4,784,265 inhabitants. Croats constituted the majority population (4,496,429 inhabitants or 78.1%). The second largest group were the Serbs who made up 12.1% of the total population. A relatively high percentage (6%) of the population remained nationally undeclared or its national attainment was not established (although this percentage is considerably lower than that of 1981 which amounted to 10.2%). Members of twenty-two clearly stated national groups constituted 3.7% of the population and those whose nationality was not registered by name (the 'Others' category) amounted to 0.1%.

[16] However, not all the minorities are equally satisfied with their principally equalised position. The Serbian minority has not accepted the loss of the status of a 'nation' guaranteed by the 1974

joint existence of different ethnic groups within the State and its legal territory.[17]

In addition to other changes that have taken place (like the introduction of multi-party democracy, the establishment of State sovereignty, the change in the political and social system, etc.), the Croatian State has turned towards changing the economy into a market economy. This, in the first place, has meant the transformation of ownership, i.e., the transformation of the so-called social ownership and self-management system into private ownership and private business. In the economic sphere, ethnic or national affiliation has no special importance. Economic strength or the role of minority groups does not depend on their origin, but – just like for the Croatian population – their economic prosperity is rather dependent on how much they manage and succeed in adapting to the altered economic conditions. In this sense, in matters of the economy and development, minorities are not regarded as a specific subject which by means of culture, the manner of using resources and management over them, develop any forms and functions of development and structures specific to their ethnicity. Although, this would be possible to maintain in a negative sense, with respect to some of the Roma population who have maintained their traditional way of life.

From the genuine economic situation in which minorities are not differentiated from the majority population, one should point to the still existing consequences of the Serbian aggression against Croatia with the participation of part of the Serbian population in Croatia in anti-Croatian activities.[18] In addition to the problem of the Serbs, there also remains the problem of the Roma population. Their 'wild' settlements are often located on private property or on land expropriated under the former system, so that every attempt at cultivating their settlements and bringing them to the level of life-style acceptable to the community is met by the obstructions of establishing a proprietor's right and rights of use and thereby any legal change in debatable areas is difficult to attain.[19]

Constitution of the Republic of Croatia; others, living for centuries on the territory of the present Republic of Croatia, are not pleased be being rendered equal with so-called new minorities while some minority groups consider that they have the right to greater aid from the State due to their traditional underdevelopment or rights which had been formerly achieved.

[17] The Constitutional Law on Human Rights and Freedoms and Rights of Ethnic and National Communities or Minorities in the Republic of Croatia, adopted in December 1991, uses the terms national community, minority and ethnic community, thereby not making any difference in the scope of guaranteed rights and freedoms, but leaving it to each minority community to accept an appropriate term for itself in accordance with its own discretion.

[18] In the past when Croatia was a constituent part of Yugoslavia, the Serbian population present in certain socio-economic segments had a privileged and favoured position which had direct impact on their economic power.

[19] As an example of this the village of Strmec (Međimurska County) can be taken in which financial aid from international institutions for improvement of socialisation of the Roma children could not be made use of because of the fact that the facility for socialisation was placed in the settlement which had been illegally placed on private property, within two communes, and legal allowances for bringing in water and the arrangement of other communal sanitary connections were needed.

3.1 Entities with the status of minority communities

A statistical overview for the period 1948-1991 reveals the following:

Table I *Groups which after 1991 continued to have the same – minority – status in the Republic of Croatia:*

	1948	1953	1961	1971	1981	1991
Czechs	28,991	25,967	23,391	19,001	15,061	13,086
Hungarians	51,399	47,725	42,347	35,488	25,439	22,355
Slovaks	10,097	9,570	8,182	6,482	6,533	5,606
Ruthenians	6,397	5,980	6,290	3,728	3,321	3,253
Italians	76,093	37,565	21,103	17,433	11,661	21,303
Ukrainians	Included in Ruthenians			2,793	2,515	2,494
Roma (ethnic group)	405	1,261	313	1,257	3,858	6,695

Table II *Constitutive nations of the former SFRY which after its disintegration received minority status in the Republic of Croatia:*

	1948	1953	1961	1971	1981	1991
Montenegrins	2,871	5,175	7,465	9,706	9,818	9,724
Macedonians	1,387	2,414	4,381	5,625	5,362	6,280
Muslims	10,097	9,570	3,113	18,457	23,740	43,469
Slovenians	38,734	43,482	39,103	32,497	25,136	22,376
Serbs	543,795	588,756	624,991	626,789	531,502	581,663

Table III *Other ethnic and minority groups which, after the declaration of independence of the Republic of Croatia in 1991, were afforded minority status:*

	1948	1953	1961	1971	1981	1991
Germans	10,144	11,248	4,214	2,791	2,175	2,635
Austrians	1,387	749	510	352	267	214
Jews	10,097	413	406	2,845	316	600
Albanians	635	1,001	2,126	4,175	6,006	12,032

3.2 Legal guarantees for minorities in Croatia

Under the 1991 Constitutional Law on Human Rights and Freedoms and on the Rights of Ethnic and National Communities or Minorities, which is an act of the highest legal force after the Constitution, minority communities existing and functioning in the Republic of Croatia are guaranteed cultural autonomy throughout the whole State territory. Ten chapters and 62 articles of the Law establish the following:

– the protection of human rights and the prohibition of discrimination based on the Constitution of the Republic of Croatia and on existing international instruments;
– the protection of ethnic and national communities or minorities, the right to development and the right to exercise cultural autonomy and other rights for the benefit of this community;
– the right of the members of ethnic and national communities or minorities to proportional participation in representative and other organs of the Republic of Croatia;
– areas with a special self-governing (autonomous) status, the way of their functioning, as well as the manner and conditions under which the citizens of these areas can participate in moulding and decision-making for satisfying their particular needs with respect to their national affiliation; and
– judicial protection against violations by the Constitution by means of this and other laws as well as by human rights and the rights of ethnic and national communities or minorities guaranteed by international instruments and the establishment of the Court of Human Rights.

The Law also prohibits any activity which could hamper the realisation of human rights and the rights of ethnic communities as well as the continuity of rights acquired in the former system whose legal successor is the Republic of Croatia.

The realisation of some rights and the way they are exercised are built into and expounded by the statutes of local units. In areas in which a certain minority make up a simple population majority (according to the 1981 census), the Constitutional Law provides for the establishment of districts with a special status, i.e., territorial autonomy, whose constitutions should not be contrary to the constitutional system of the Republic of Croatia as a unitary and integral State. In such districts the Croats and other inhabitants not constituting the majority population enjoy all special rights defined under the Constitutional Law for the members of ethnic and national communities or minorities.

The protection of human rights and the rights of national and ethnic communities and minorities established in the legal system builds upon and succeeds the rights already achieved and acknowledged in these areas before Croatian independence; it restores those rights and freedoms which were repressed or invalidated and those respectively imposed by the concurrence of events as a result of the established statehood of Croatia. Accordingly, new possibilities have been developed for national communities, for the articulation of minority facets, the valuation of achievements in the cultural, scientific and artistic sphere, for new incentives and for the improvement of communication with compatriots, other national communities and the majority nation. At the same time and in conformity with the Constitution and the Croatian legal system, members of minorities are ensured participation in social and economic life on an equal footing with other citizens.

3.3 **Indicators of the economic position of minorities**

In order to be able to provide an evaluation of the current economic position of minorities in Croatia, some relevant indicators are needed which would, to a certain degree, reveal the level of the inclusion of minorities in the economic structures and their development in the areas in which they live. Unfortunately, such indicators are lacking. As the process of the dissolution of the former Yugoslavia did not take place in a peaceful and civilised way (although the 1974 Federal and the Republic Constitutions did guarantee the right to self-determination and even separation), Croatia was rather a victim of Serbian aggression with the participation of a part of the Serbian population living in Croatia. Besides, war damage and the destruction of material goods in the war-torn areas as a result of which some minorities especially suffered,[20] the forced abandonment of their own homes and their displacement all over the country[21] and in the neighbouring countries, as well as their permanent emigration to some European and overseas countries,[22] all present real obstacles to establishing the actual facts and, in gen-

[20] In the first place this refers to Hungarians, Ukrainians, Germans, Ruthenians, Slovaks and Czechs whose centres of gathering and activities were just inside the territories of Eastern and Western Slavonia where the greatest concentration of their members was to be found.

[21] In December 1992 Croatia may have been considered to be the greatest refugee camp in the world if the total number of inhabitants of Croatia is compared to the number of those given refuge by Croatia whether on the basis of their refugee status (those who had escaped from Bosnia and Herzegovina or other parts of ex-Yugoslavia) or the status of exiles (the inhabitants of Croatia who were forced to leave their homes owing to Serbian aggression and war destruction). They constituted 15% of the population. Among them, minority members were numerous, especially from Eastern and Western Slavonia (the territory with the greatest concentration of minorities). There were 663,493 officially registered persons, although a considerable number of persons who found shelter with their relatives and friends and were not being cared for by the State, should be added to this number. An illustration is the fact that out of 13,153 Hungarians settled in Eastern Slavonia before the war, 7,554 left this area; 4,530 of them had the status of exiles in Croatia and 2,548 were registered as refugees in Hungary. (Source: Teleki László Foundation Ms 2380).

[22] The greatest number of refugees from Croatia in European and overseas countries were registered by the end of 1991 (148,000). Their repatriation to liberated areas did not begin until mid-1995. At the same time, the number of persons having left the Republic of Croatia permanently showed a different trend, i.e., their numbers increased so that in May 1998 there were 283,000 regis-

eral, will certainly also have long-term negative consequences on the whole population as far as economic development is concerned. Many hundreds of thousands of refugees and exiles who, as a result of 'ethnic cleansing', had left their homes and everything they had merely to save their own lives will still have to return,[23] which poses the question whether the basic assumption for return in areas devastated by war can and will soon be realised.[24] Though, it should be pointed out that after the Croatian sovereignty and legal system were reinstated in the internationally recognised State boundaries as result of both the liberation action in certain areas and of the process of so-called 'peaceful reintegration' which commenced, some preconditions for their return have been fulfilled.

As already pointed out above, currently there are no relevant data specifically dealing with the economic position of minorities in Croatia. It is not possible to obtain some indicators regarding the inclusion of minorities in the economic development and structures even in the 'minority areas' on the basis of the last census results,[25] and neither are there any comparative analyses in relation to the situation concerning the existing political, social and economic changes. Taking this into consideration, it is only possible to indicate the determinants which may have an influence on the economic position of minorities in Croatia and their participation in the economic system.

The economic position of minorities can be equated with the majority nation with respect to both the economic structure and economic development.

The economic situation affects minority members and thereby all the minority groups indirectly, to the extent of their ability to adapt to or to use the opportunities offered by the new rules on ownership and property. The general problems appearing in certain branches of the economy (especially in respect to agriculture) and the current high unemployment rate[26] are roughly the same for all

---

tered persons who had decided to emigrate permanently. Among them, the most numerous were Serbs who had left Croatia on a massive scale after Croatia's liberation (from Krajina and Western Slavonia) and the peaceful reintegration of Eastern Slavonia into the state and legal system of Croatia.

[23] E.g., according to the data of the Office for Refugees and Displaced Persons of the Government of the Republic of Croatia by the end of 1998 there were 4,474 registered Hungarians waiting to return. A considerable number did not or were not able to register at the Office because they had no intention whatsoever of returning to the areas from which they had fled.

[24] The estimates of the number of exiled and displaced Serbs range from 283,000 (the Office for Refugees and Displaced Persons of the Government of the Republic of Croatia for the 1991 1998 period) whereby the number of returnees to 350,000 according to SRY sources, was not taken into account.

[25] The last census took place in 1991 (the Central Bureau of Statistics), and it is expected that the next census, according to the usual ten-year period, will be held in 2001. Only then will it be possible to evaluate the changes during not only the last 10 years but rather 20 years (since the 1981 census).

[26] According to official Croatian sources, the unemployment rate is currently estimated to be 11% and 19% respectively (dependent on the method of calculation), but unofficial sources, particularly for some counties (so-called minority areas are not in question) speak about a much higher rate.

Croatian citizens, regardless of their national belonging. In the same way the gravitational force of urban centres (especially the big cities) is independent of ethnic belonging.[27]

Certain advantages of belonging to a national community for the economic position of that community and its members respectively can be observed as regards the minorities living in areas which border their kin-State. The joint language, culture and ethnic affiliation as well as comparative advantages of one or the other border area give rise to transfrontier contacts that most often start in the field of culture and continue in the field of economic exchange and are shaped by coming in touch with the institutions on local and regional levels. This cross-border co-operation is especially significant for the Italian, Hungarian and Slovenian minorities in Croatia while, with the normalisation of relations between the Republic of Croatia and the Federal Republic of Yugoslavia, possibilities have been created for the development of cultural and economic relations between the Serbian minority and its kin-State within the framework of accepted international standards.[28] The normalisation of relations with the SR of Yugoslavia will, in the future, also have consequences for trans-border co-operation between the members of the Hungarian, Slovakian and Ruthenian minorities in Croatia as the majority of their compatriots have remained separated in the SR of Yugoslavia (in Vojvodina) by the State border, and whose traditional cultural, economic and family ties were broken during the period of hostilities. It can be assumed that increasing opening-up of frontiers and development of private business and the initiatives between ethnically-kindred participants will shape some new forms of 'ethnic economy' that will animate the economic interests of minorities.

The opposite situation, i.e., the one with a negative influence of ethnic belonging is to be found in the Roma population.[29] The greatest losers of the changing system (the transformation of the economy and privatisation) have been the qualified, semi-skilled and auxiliary Roma workers, employed in socially-owned/State firms, who have been redundant. With the increase in the unemployment rate and the problems of retraining, as well as a difficult adaptation to changed working conditions (especially by private contractors), more and more of the Roma have been thrown out of work and income. They consider their position to be completely hopeless, finding an explanation for such a situation in their Roma origin. The ones who live on social aid and those illiterate/unskilled Roma (who live on casual or seasonal work) are in a special situation besides everyday liv-

[27] For the majority of minority members this means hastened assimilation.

[28] The collaboration of Serbs from Croatia with their kin-State was very intense during the war (1991-1995) and before peaceful reintegration of Podunavlje into the State and legal space of Croatia (1997) as well, but this did not contribute to the cultural and economic prosperity of the Serbian minority in Croatia, but rather to the secessionist Serbian movement.

[29] A thin stratum of the Roma population are well versed in making use of the possibilities of a market economy. In this way the families dealing with intermediate trade and collecting secondary raw materials have become 'prominent'.

ing problems they have acceptance problems, even within their own Roma communities.[30]

3.4 Minority settlement areas

With respect to minority settlements, the current estimates are even more questionable than in the period of the former Yugoslavia, if the consequences of war destruction, a destroyed infrastructure, forced displacement, large-scale immigration, reconstruction difficulties and the expedited return of displaced persons are all taken into account.[31] This should be added to the already-mentioned fact that all minorities are dispersed all over Croatia[32] and that only within some counties do certain minorities have a more significant concentration, but not a proportional majority of the population. The exception to this in the past were only the districts in which Serbian inhabitants constituted the majority population[33] and to which a special self-governing (autonomous) position was ensured[34] on the basis of the Constitutional Law.[35] However, this self-government has never been implemented because of the fact that the Serbs inhabiting these areas from the very beginning obstructed the Croatian legal system wanting, by establishing the so-called Krajina, to separate from the Republic of Croatia. As a consequence of this (and maybe for the time being),[36] the formal requirement for the establishment of territorial autonomy, based on the ethnic principle, has disappeared.

---

[30] This is part of the Roma population who live in a manner unacceptable to their environment, often dealing in crime; acting violently or not being able to take care of themselves due to alcoholism or poor health.

[31] It is a question not only of the reconstruction of housing facilities and the clearing of mines, but also the renewal of the infrastructure since this will enable the inhabitants to find jobs and existential security as well as indispensable cultural, educational, religious and other institutions necessary for a normal life.

[32] According to the 1991 census results members of all 16 minorities live in all 20 counties and the City of Zagreb with the exception of Ličko-senjska County where no Roma were registered.

[33] These districts are Glina and Knin in which the Serbian population made up the absolute majority. In the district of Glina Serbs constituted over 71% of the population and in the district of Knin almost 76%.

[34] In the field of economic rights and development of the areas with a special status the Constitutional Law guaranteed: '. . . the protection of equal participation in public affairs as, for example, the enjoyment of political and economic freedoms in a social sphere . . .' (Art. 6); the Republic of Croatia and local self-government bodies financially support the implementation of minority rights in conformity with their possibilities (Arts. 10 and 16); the co-ordinating of rational use and arrangement of the area and regional development on the territory of a commune; the stimulation of the development of economic activities in agreement with a general economic policy of the Republic; the protection of nature and the environment; the construction and maintenance of infrastructure (Art. 25) etc.

[35] Chapters V and VI, Arts. 21-55 of the Constitutional Law.

[36] The return of Serbs who have fled is in progress, but according to estimates from the Croatian, Serbian and international sources, it will be much lower in percentage terms in relation to those having decided to permanently emigrate from Croatia.

The situation in the regions with the greatest concentration of minorities[37] reveals that, on the basis of economic and structural indicators, the Italian minority have the most favourable position and their members are mainly concentrated in Istarska County which was largely unaffected by the war and has therefore continued to develop without serious turbulence. In contrast to them, the Hungarians, Czechs, Slovaks, Ruthenians, Ukrainians and Germans had the largest numbers of their members (and their minority institutions as well) in the counties exposed to war (Osječko-baranjska, Vukovarsko-srijemska, Sisačko-moslavačka, Bjelovarsko-bilogorska and Brodsko-posavska), while in some of their territories (particularly in Osječko-baranjska and Brodsko-posavska County) ethnic cleansing was carried out so that many of them still have exile or refugee status and are waiting to return or to 'take root' in new environments.

3.5 Education as a factor of the economic situation

The education[38] and qualifications of minority members to a large degree determine their position in the economy and their possibilities to adapt to new, changed conditions. However, education only still remains relevant at the level of individuals who, although they sometimes bring the elements of traditional occupations into the economic life of an area or region, are not markers by means of which the minority economic position within the whole system could be estimated. Namely, in order to speak of this national aspect within the system it would be necessary for a minority group to have its own independent economic institutions organised on the national principle and governed by a separate minority economic institution. However, such institutions do not exist. Even those economic facilities (like production, services etc.) owned by minority members in which, perhaps, only minority members are employed, cannot be regarded as minority economic institutions since administrative minority authorities have not participated in their establishment.

---

[37] Here it is also necessary to emphasise that it is not a question of 'minority' regions because in the territory of the counties in which their concentration is the greatest, the percentage of their representation is actually low. Thus, e.g., the Italians constitute only 7.5% of the population of Istarska County, Hungarians 3.7% of Osječko-baranjska County, Czechs 5.8% of Bjelovarsko-bilogorska County, etc. (data based on the 1991 census results).

[38] The possibility (or impossibility) of education in the mother tongue as a part of the need to safeguard and develop the feeling of national belonging and the level to which such education is ensured as well as the existence of possibilities to make choices between occupations (for which education in the mother tongue is possible) gives a special significance to the educational component.

3.6 Additional aspects for the evaluation of the economic position of minorities

As regards the economic position of minorities, the additional 'inputs' of financial assistance to minorities coming from the Republic of Croatia, kin-States, and/or from the international institutions supporting various segments of minority communities or certain activities, should not to be forgotten.

For the realisation of cultural autonomy the Republic of Croatia assigns financial means to minorities (on the basis of their programmes) from the Central Government budget through the agency of the Office for National Minorities of the Government of the Republic of Croatia and through authorised institutions of the Republic which are responsible, professionally and administratively, for certain fields of the social life of all Croatian citizens. The special needs of minorities are financed along with the fulfilment of conditions for their achievement.[39] Although it is not a direct investment in stimulating the economic position of minorities, it does contribute to the preservation of their identity and the conscience of national belonging, thereby animating cohesive elements within the minority groups which might have an indirect/positive impact on their economic development.[40] The aforementioned funds are provided in addition to the means set aside at the level of local self-governments and counties, in conformity with their material possibilities and the concentration of minority groups.

Certain minorities receive significant financial aid and other forms of material support from their mother-countries and from international institutions as well, but its practical distribution and worth often becomes a stumbling block within the minority group itself,[41] while at the same time others may view such aid being clouded by 'a veil of secrecy'.

The denationalisation and restitution of goods removed or expropriated[42] and the compensation for the losses caused by the forceful seizure of property and ownership rights, will, in the future, provide a special dimension in the evaluation of the economic position of minorities in Croatia.

---

[39] The Central Government Budget for 1999 provides 24 million kunas (3.45% more than in 1998) for financial support to minorities.

[40] Thus, e.g., the Ministry of Education and Sport (besides ensuring financial means) organises, co-ordinates and exercises full control over the education of minorities in their mother tongue.

[41] Nowadays newspaper articles discuss the question of where the leaders of the Italian minority have spent the 90 thousand million liras they received the from Italian State (*La Voce del Popolo*, *Novi list*, *Delo* and others).

[42] Some minority groups like Jews, Germans and Italians were especially affected by such deprivation of property and expropriation in the former regime.

4. Instead of a conclusion

In most areas inhabited by minority groups (and marked, in a way, by their ethnic belonging, for example with respect to certain occupations, the means of using resources, construction, etc.) the changing of the social structure from an agrarian to a non-agrarian one, and a relatively high degree of urbanisation and industrialisation, have been taking place during the last few decades. There have also been significant socio-economic changes within the minority groups (and within the majority nation as well), while spatial mobility has intensified by the dynamic attraction of urban centres, and ethno-identification codes have been modified. The demand for new communication channels and co-operation that will not always make the ethnic dimension visible and operative, especially not at the group level, has been more important than the minorities and the majority population. This is present in the field of economic relations and evaluations of the economic position of a minority group within a broader environment in particular.

Part Two – Minorities in Estonia

POLITICAL ASPECTS OF THE RUSSIAN MINORITY IN ESTONIA

by Marina Martynova

1. INTRODUCTION

The proclamation of independence by the Baltic States has provoked an unprecedented ethnic crisis. Developments which were assumed to be primarily political gave rise to ethnic detestation, which shook the Estonian society. The strong bond of the political positions with respect to the ethnic question was the reason why inter-ethnic relations in Estonia were disturbed, as also happened in Latvia. Of course, the actual impact on the minority groups in question, as well as for the whole of society, was much wider than that in the political sphere.

The radical political and economic transformations, which took place in Eastern and Central Europe, caused the ethnic factor to become one of the decisive aspects of modern life. The awakening of national self-consciousness and the creation of the nation-State, on the one hand, and the cultural revival of ethnic groups, on the other, became central to the process of transformation. As long as this 'national' idea united only part of the community, it was opposed by other ethnic groups. In brief, the growth of ethnic self-consciousness, and the movement towards sovereignty, directly contributed to the creation of problems in inter-ethnic relations.

At the beginning of the 1990s the ethnic Russians who had remained outside the Russian Federation experienced similar problems in all the republics of the former Soviet Union: as parts of what used to be the dominant (Russian) nation, in the new States they became national minorities or migrants. Now those so-called 'title' ethnic groups of the federal republics, who used to be minority groups in the former USSR, gained leading positions in the bodies of power and authority in all spheres of life. The Russians had lost their privileged positions. In addition, that was inundated with serious legal, economic, practical difficulties – not the least important being psychological ones – such as their new identity, the choice of citizenship, the learning of State languages, and retaining contact with relatives abroad, etc. If there was a difference in the position and actual and legal situation between the Russians in various newly created States, it was determined mostly by the general State policy towards minorities which ranged from respect

S. Trifunovska (Ed.), Minorities in Europe – Croatia, Estonia and Slovakia

for cultural pluralism to the policy of assimilation, as well as by the level of inter-ethnic pressure or conflict interactions within the region.

As regards the issue of independence the Russians were divided among themselves in their attitude towards the desire of the Baltic people to regain sovereignty in their countries: in 1990 only about 26% of the Russians living in Estonia were in favour of a fully independent Estonia, whereas a large part of the Russian community preferred a partially independent Estonian Republic.[1] However, at that time the number of the Russians who supported the idea of Estonian independence was increasing.

On the other hand, the position of the ethnic Estonians was based and had its roots and its history in the Soviet period, when the concept and idea of ethnocentrism prevailed in Estonia. At the time when the liberation movement started at the beginning of the 1990s two clearly distinctive positions clashed: one part of the ethnic Estonians supported the integration of the society, but another, radical, view of ethnic exclusion prevailed. At the same time the Russians did not wish to be assimilated (which is proved by the fact that in the USSR period only 15% of the Russians in Estonia were able to communicate in the Estonian language), and neither were they willing to allow themselves to become second class citizens. As a consequence, a confrontation between the ethnic Estonians and other minority groups of the population followed, which divided society in Estonia along ethnic lines.

However, shortly after Estonia's independence developments took a positive turn. The gradual building of a civic society within Estonia caused a change in its conception of inter-ethnic relations. Its position and view towards minority groups and migrants were increasingly determined by the situation within the country and by its international position. The fact that Estonians no longer feared the possibility of the restoration of Soviet rule also contributed to these developments. At the same time, the danger for society of the existence of non-integrated groups was realised in Estonia. It became evident that large numbers of non-citizens living in Estonia were detrimental to several spheres of life in the country such as, *inter alia*, social, cultural, economic and security aspects. Estonia admitted the incontestability of the coexistence of various ethnic groups in its territory and embarked on the process of integrating the non-Estonians into Estonian society.

Notwithstanding this integration, during the past few years non-ethnic Estonians have faced various problems such as economic problems (the restructuring of the State-run system, where the majority of the Russians happened to work), social problems (the integration of Slavs), political problems (replacing the political elite with the necessary demotion of the old ones – who happened to be mostly Slavs, and the search for the legitimacy of the new ones, who made use of ethnic-

[1] Aksel Kirh, 'Karta politicheskih sil v Estonii', 12 *Sociologicheskie iisledovanija* (1990) p. 55.

based discourse to gain popular support), legal problems (the lack of a legal framework), military problems, and so on. All these problems were linked to the political one. However, in the existing human rights situation in Estonia one of the most serious problems, closely connected with the political situation, remains the status of ethnic Russians, some of which speak no other language but Russian, and the issue of the preservation and development of their culture and language.

2. A BRIEF COMMENT ON THEORETICAL ASPECTS OF ETHNIC PROBLEMS

The position and rights of the non-indigenous population in Estonia are linked with the theoretical view on the essence of what is a nation. In reality the subject of discussion is the choice between the ethnic and the civic principle in State-building, though it has not been formulated in these terms. As is broadly known, in Eastern and Central Europe a significant provocative factor for ethnic revival was the principle of State-building.

An explanation for the 'Estonian case' lies in the theories of the Soviet past. The Marxist-Leninist view on the concept of a nation was based on the ethnic principle. It defined members of a nation as an ethnic community and not as citizens of a State. In accordance with this, the former USSR had an ethno-federal structure according to which territorial administrative units were identified with a particular nation. Each titular group attained a privileged standing within its home republic and was afforded special powers in socio-cultural, economic and political life. Sovereignty thus resided with each particular ethnic group, the members of which were the only ones who could decide on the fundamental questions of State form and identity. Robert Hiyden has defined it as constitutional nationalism,[2] though it could also be called territorial nationalism. In Estonia, as well as in other Soviet Republics, the situation was complicated by the migration movements within the borders of the former USSR, and especially by the 'Russification', which is a term used to reflect a process of permanently populating these areas with a large number of ethnic Russians.

3. POPULATION STATISTICS

3.1 **Background**

Any analysis of the current minority situation should start from the ethnic composition of the population in Estonia. The 1922 census reveals the following

---

[2] 51 *Slavic Review* (1992) No. 4, pp. 655-656.

population composition in the early 1920s: Estonians – 969,976; Russians – 91,109; Germans – 18,319; Swedes – 7,850; Jews – 4,566; other nationalities – 14,505. Thus, the total non-Estonian population amounted to 12.4%.

The 1934 census shows the following demographic structure: Estonians – 88%; Russians – 8%; other nationalities (Germans, Finns, Jews, Swedes, etc.) – 4%.[3]

During the years 1945-1989 the total number of Estonians increased by 22%, but the number of non-Estonians in the same period grew 26-fold, meaning that during the Soviet period the population of the Estonian Republic became very heterogeneous. The largest group of non-Estonians were the Russians – they grew from 20,000 (in 1945) to 474,800 (in 1989), whereas the total number of Slavic-language peoples (consisting of Russians, Ukrainians and Belarusians) was 551,000, or 35% of the population of Estonia. The Russians constituted 91.4% of all non-ethnic Estonians.

3.2 **The latest data**

Data released by Estonia in January 1999 sheds some long-awaited light both on the country's ethnic composition in the post-Soviet era and on the legal status of the non-indigenous population. Compiled by the Citizenship and Migration Board, the data show the population to be composed of 65.1% of ethnic Estonians; 28.2% of ethnic Russians; 2.6% of Ukrainians; 1.5% of Belarusians; and 2.6% of several other ethnic groups.

Out of the total registered population of 1.454 million, 1.075 million have Estonian citizenship, whereas 323,000 are documented resident aliens and the remainder are undocumented resident aliens. The 'alien', which is a legal and not an ethnic category, indicates the Soviet-era population influx. According to the situation in July 1998, 311,000 individuals belonging to the group of aliens or non-citizens, had fixed-term residence permits and almost 12,000 had permanent residency permits. At the same time, there were 8,849 retired Soviet military personnel with 7,400 dependants residing in Estonia by special permission. During 1997, 101,000 resident aliens were granted citizenship through naturalisation.[4]

The data show, firstly, that a small nation which had seemed destined to be turned into a minority in its own country has gained an irreversible lease of life through post-Soviet demographic changes. Secondly, the figures indicate that Estonia is making progress towards becoming an inclusive society through naturalisation, which is based on clearly defined residency and language qualifications. Third, the figures suggest that the enfranchisement of the non-indigenous population can be managed without throwing the political system off balance, provided

---

[3] Katus Kalev, 'Easti demograafiline areng labi sajandite', *Eesti edasivastes*, Metroo kolinas raamat, Tallin (1990) p. 22.

[4] Bureau of National Statistics (23 November 1998).

that the enfranchisement process remains gradual and is thereby implicitly pegged to the alien population's generational change.

4. THE SITUATION OF THE RUSSIAN POPULATION IN ESTONIA

The Russians in Estonia are in many ways not homogeneous, and differ amongst themselves with respect to their political perceptions, the length of time they have resided in Estonia, the level of integration in Estonian society, their plans for the future, etc.

According to the territorial location of ethnic Russians, three groups can be distinguished: the first is composed of ethnic (indigenous) Russians of the regions Prichudje, Narva and Setumaa, who have been residing in these areas for several generations and for that reason stand a good chance of having integrated into Estonian society. The other two groups, that is about 70% of the Estonian Russians, are migrants from the Soviet period who live in different regions of Estonia. Theoretically speaking, they also have a chance of integration. However, if one looks at the map of Estonia and at their geographic location it becomes immediately clear that this chance is very slim due to the fact that they are demographically concentrated in the North-Eastern part of Estonia and in Tallinn, which means that there is no practical need to study the State language, which is a precondition for genuine integration with the other population. In these areas there is no practical use of the Estonian language in everyday life as the prevailing population is non-Estonian. For example, 97% of the total population (of 80,000) of Narva is non-Estonian. So, in this area as well as in some more distant places in the country with a similar ethnic composition, integration is not stimulated by the needs of everyday life.

The Russians in Estonia used to be mostly workers, the administrative staff of the industrial enterprises and the officers of the Soviet army.

It deserves to be mentioned that the assimilation processes in Estonia had been quite specific. Among the non-Estonians it mostly involved assimilation by the Russians, due to the fact that the majority of non-Estonians are Slavs. The assimilation of Ukrainians, Belarusians and other Slavs was made possible through education which was carried out mostly in the Russian language.[5] This brought them closer to their Russian cultural surroundings, but at the same time it endangered their national identity. Thus, the position of the Russians used to be very strong

[5] Due to their concentration in industrial areas, other groups of non-Estonians were living in a special, Russian-speaking social and cultural environment. There were some offices (for example, railway and militia offices) and even localities (mainly in the North-East region) where it was impossible to communicate in Estonian, although it was possible to communicate in Russian almost anywhere in Estonia.

since it was the only national minority in Estonia with the possibility for schooling their children in their mother tongue.

5. CITIZENS AND NON-CITIZENS IN ESTONIA

The period leading to Estonia's independence started with the Declaration of the (then) Supreme Soviet of the Estonian Soviet Socialist Republic on the Sovereignty of the Estonian SSR from 16 November 1988.[6] This was followed by what is considered to be the first blow to the Russian-speaking people, the adoption of the new Language Law on 18 January 1989.[7] The Law declared Estonian to be the official language of the Estonian Republic and, *inter alia*, created an obligation for certain job holders, especially within State administration, to know the Estonian language. It could be assumed that political decisions and administrative consequences with regard to the Law were aimed at the restoration of the use of the Estonian language in public functions and at forcing out the Russian language from the government, administration, industry, science, etc. According to the Law the opportunity to be employed depended on the knowledge of the Estonian language. As the Law contained a paragraph which required a knowledge of the State language for certain professions, for the Russians, especially in the regions where they numerically prevailed, it created a significant problem.

The Law on National Rights of Citizens of 15 December 1989, which introduced differences between citizens and residents of Estonia, has to be mentioned.[8] The Law should be considered as a legal basis for the implementation of the rights of ethnic Estonian as indigenous people of Estonia to its ethnic territory and self-determination. Besides, it affords the right of Estonian citizens in accordance with the ethnic origin of their parents, to establish their national origin.

That the legal and political position of the ethnic Russians was radically changed became clear in 1992, after the adoption of the new Constitution (on 3 July 1992), the Law on Citizenship adopted by the Decree of 26 February 1992[9] and after the Parliamentary elections had been held. In fact, the most critical situation in relations between the Estonians and ethnic Russians was the position of the new State concerning the issue of citizenship. After the collapse of Soviet power (in 1991) Estonia restored its independence in accordance with the principle of legal continuity. As it was admitted, the Estonian State had continued to exist from 1918 to 1990. Estonia did not therefore consider itself to be a new State, but rather a restored State. Citizenship was determined by the application of both the principle of historical and legal continuity. It meant that all individu-

---

[6] *Estonija. Konturi etnopoliiticheskoii evolucii*. Sbornik dokumentov, p. 122.

[7] Idem., p. 140.

[8] Vedomosti. ESSR 1989/40/6181.

[9] Vedomosti Estonskoi Republiki, 1992/7/109.

als who had Estonian citizenship before 1940 and their direct descendants, were considered to be automatically citizens of the Estonian Republic. At the same time those who had settled in Estonia under Soviet rule and whose citizenship did not date from before 1940, were classified as aliens. They had to apply for citizenship in accordance with the new Law. In the larger geo-political context which includes the countries of the Commonwealth of Independent States and the Baltic Republics, the issue of naturalisation had certain consequences if one takes into consideration the fact that the Russian Diaspora consists of the natives who once all lived in one State. As pointed out above, the migration flows during the last fifty years led to a substantial shift in the ethnic composition within all the republics of the former Soviet Union. As a result, large non-indigenous communities currently live in the new States. The individuals belonging to these communities are legally prevented from automatically acquiring citizenship, notwithstanding the length of the period they have lived in these territories.

As in 1991 Estonia's demographic situation and political polarisation in the ethnic sphere was rather complicated, the political parties refused to apply 'the zero option' which would have implied that all persons being permanent residents in the territory of the State on the date of the entry into force of the Citizenship Law were included *ipso facto* in the initial body of citizens. Consequently, the Estonian Government decided to reinforce the Estonian Law on Citizenship from 1938. The version valid on 16 June 1940 was once again put into force as from 30 March 1990, and was approved by a Decree on 26 February 1992.

The procedure for the acquisition of Estonian citizenship by naturalisation was regulated by the Decree of the Government from 1992. All those wishing to apply for citizenship had to know the Estonian language, to be older than 18 years of age, to have lived in Estonia for a minimum of 2 years and they had to wait for one more year after they had filled in the necessary forms.

These relatively strict conditions resulted in 30% of the Estonian population becoming non-citizens. However, as regards the Russians, the majority had been born in Estonia or had settled there a long time ago and resided there permanently. They considered Estonia to be their homeland, a country which, paradoxically enough, had now made them stateless persons.

With the entry into force of the new Estonian Constitution and the Law on Citizenship the Russian-speaking population became divided into 3 categories: (a) citizens of the Estonian Republic; (b) citizens of the Russian Federation and other former Soviet Republics; and (c) persons with an indefinite status.

5.1 **The difference between citizens and non-citizens in Estonian laws**

Obviously the most decisive step for the future relations between indigenous Estonians and the ethnic Russians living in Estonia was finally undertaken with the approval of the new Estonian Constitution, which entered into force on 3 July 1992. The Constitution combined Estonian legal traditions from the time of its first phase of independence with the developments of the later period.

Like most constitutions in the world containing a part on constitutional rights and freedoms, the Estonian Constitution differentiated between rights guaranteed only to citizens and rights guaranteed to any person. According to the Estonian Constitution, the rights, freedoms and duties are equal for citizens and people migrating to Estonia. But this important guarantee of human rights in reality has some limitations. It only covers persons 'migrating' to Estonia, but not residing there.

The favouring of Estonian citizens is obvious from Article 6 (Estonian as the State language), and Articles 8 and 9 (constitutional rules for the acquisition of Estonian citizenship, constitutional rights of citizens), Article 30 (state officials preferably Estonian citizens), Article 36 (prohibition of extradition, right to settlement in Estonia), Article 37 (language in administration and before the courts), and Articles 57-59, 61, 81 (right to vote, right to be elected President). Only citizens of Estonia have the right to be elected to Parliament, to work in the state and local administration, to buy land and to join the armed forces. Non-citizens do not have a right to own real property, they can only rent land.

Citizens of other countries residing in Estonia can vote and be elected in their home countries. Since the early 1990s they have only had the right to take part in local elections, but not to be elected themselves (The Law on Elections into Local Soviets of 8 August 1989). The new Law on the Local Elections of May 1993 determined that residents without Estonian citizenship had no right to vote in Estonia, even in the districts where they are in a majority.[10]

Besides, it deserves to be mentioned that the Language Law established a barrier for the professional careers of the Russians. According to the data from September 1993, about 30,000 Russian highly-educated specialists had lost their jobs.[11]

The 1993 Law on Aliens introduced conditions which contributed to the increase in the number of citizens from other States.[12] Estonian law does not allow dual citizenship. For this reason 300,000 non-Estonian citizens, i.e., residents without–citizenship, were obliged to choose their citizenship. They had until the deadline of 12 July 1995 to apply for Estonian, Russian or any other citizenship. At the same time, all residents who did not have Estonian citizenship became foreigners. Every 5 years they have to undergo a formal procedure to extend their residence permit.[13] The Law denies officers of the former Soviet armed forces and members of their families from acquiring citizenship in the foreseeable future or even to be granted resident permits. As the Law on Aliens replaced the 1990 Estonian Immigration Law, it likewise lays down an annual immigration quota.

---

10 Sergei Savoskul, *Latvija. Estonija*, p. 107.

11 Idem., p. 107.

12 See the English translation in Legal Acts of Estonia 1993/3/637.

13 The process of issuing residence permits commenced in 1994.

At the end of 1998, from the 420,000 Russians living in Estonia only 120,000 had acquired Estonian citizenship. More than 40,000 ethnic Russians were unable to obtain citizenship because of the provisions of the Law.

The Law on Citizenship, especially the language requirements for gaining Estonian citizenship, and the Law on Aliens led to a wave of protests by the Russian public, the mass media, and finally to official protests by the Russian Government within the OSCE and the Council of Europe. Conclusions were sent to the Estonian Government by the OSCE High Commissioner on National Minorities, by the Council of Europe, as well as by the United Nations.

5.2 **The modification of the Laws**

The Prime Minister of Estonia in his speech on the political situation in the country in May 1995 noticed that the large number of foreigners who had not been integrated into society presented a factor of instability. In his view it would be a strategic mistake of the national demographic policy if the access of Russians to Estonian society would remain restricted.[14]

Under the special decree of the Estonian Government of 16 June 1992[15] Soviet passports ceased to be valid from 1995 onwards, and so the Estonian Government insisted on a prompt solution to the citizenship problem. The Law on Aliens (1993) imposed an obligation on all residents to choose and apply for citizenship before 12 July 1995. Non-citizens received resident permits for a period of 5 years after which they were allowed to request permanent resident permission. Thus, the problem of citizenship remained actual.

With the new 1995 Citizenship Law, the conditions for the acquisition of citizenship by naturalisation became even more harsh. The required period of residence within the territory become longer and demands for the knowledge of the Estonian language stricter. The applicant had to fulfil the requirements of the Constitution and the Citizenship Law, as well as to communicate and fill in all the documents in the Estonian language. As provided by the Law, temporary resident permits were prolonged until the year 2005. However, the Law still did not allow dual citizenship.

In addition, in 1995 the new Language Law was also enacted. Whereas under the 1989 Law the Estonian language received the status of the state language, under the new Law it became the only language to be used in official life. All employees and workers, who in their jobs communicated with other people, were obliged to declare that they had knowledge of this legal provision. Non-Estonians had to pass an examination, which would demonstrate the level of their knowledge of the Estonian language.

---

[14] Sankt-Petersburgskie vedomosti, 1 June 1995.

[15] Vedomosti Estonskoi Respubliki 1992/27/364.

The Amendments to the Law on Aliens, of June 1995, provided some kind of political compromise in this very difficult period for the ethnic Russian population.[16] By the Governmental Decree of January 1996, which introduced a new passport for aliens, a further step was taken in finding a solution to the citizenship problems of non-Estonians. At the same time, residence permission for servicemen of the former Soviet armed forces and members of their families was prolonged. (In March 1996 residence permissions were granted to 100 of them).

In 1997 the new Amendments to the Law on Aliens were adopted.[17] For the next three years the time-fixed residence permits became equivalent to the permanent permits. In October 1996 about 80,000 'foreigners' voted in the local elections.

Despite the fact that the Russians in Estonia had faced a great deal of political and social problems, 80% of them wanted to acquire Estonian citizenship. Sociological research, which took place in 1996, showed that young Russians did not hurry to apply for Russian citizenship and were loyal to the Estonian State. 10 % of them in the 20 to 29 age group already had Russian citizenship, however two-thirds of the Russian residents in the 18 to 29 age group preferred to have Estonian citizenship.[18]

In the 5-year period from 1989 to 1994, 63,000 Russians left Estonia. Their share in the population of the Republic decreased from 30.3% to 29%. Out of 110,000 persons with Russian citizenship residing in Estonia, 28% obtained Russian citizenship in 1995 and 36% in 1996. In 60% of these cases the reason for obtaining Russian citizenship was the desire not to be stateless because of the impossibility of acquiring Estonian citizenship; 31% of the Russians thought that with Russian passports it would be easier to go to Russia in the future; 21% noted their ethnic identity as a reason; and 16% explained their choice by the conviction that Russia would protect its citizens.[19]

The years 1995-1996 formed the period when the non-Estonian population were actively choosing their citizenship. Up to February 1996 Estonian citizenship had been granted to about 70,000 persons, split up as follows:[20]

- 25,000 ethnic Estonians from other States;
- 23,000 residents of Estonia who had passed the examination in the State language;
- 21,000 so-called 'supporters of Estonian independence';
- 600 persons considered to be 'especially deserving'.

---

16 *Molodez Estonii* (28 June 1995).

17 *Molodez Estonii* (25 September 1997).

18 *Estonija* (4 January 1997).

19 *Russkaja gazeta*, Tartu (1994) 2 J.07. P. 7.

20 *Molodez Estonii* (1 February 1996).

In June 1996, of the 450,000 Russians in Estonia, 190,000 had acquired citizenship. The numbers of persons with Russian citizenship was also increasing at that time, as follows:

- in January 1996, of the 382,000 legal non-citizens, 82,000 were citizens of Russia;
- by April they had increased to 94,000;
- by February 1997 they had increased to 121,000.

In 1996 the Government had decided to issue aliens' passports to everybody who still had not chosen their citizenship. One year later there were 100,000 persons with this kind of passport. But one further category of non-Estonians existed – those who did not have any kind of legal documents (Soviet passports were no longer in use). In July 1997 it was decided to start registering illegal aliens.

So the circumstances had divided the Russians in Estonia into 3 categories: Estonian citizens, Russian citizens, persons without citizenship. In 1997 their number was about equal, but interests were different and in some cases even opposite. It seemed that these groups had only one feature in common – the Russian language.

6. POLITICAL CONSOLIDATION OF THE RUSSIANS

As in a politically divided society the desire to form different political units comes as natural, the first political units of the Russians in Estonia had already been organised in 1989, immediately after the adoption of the Language Law. Until that time the Russians had not revealed any kind of opposition views. They even supported the Estonian national movement. The Russians started to consolidate when they felt their positions in Estonia to be threatened.

During that period the so-called 'Inter-movement' was organised. But it was not supported by the majority of the Russians because of its orientation to the central power. Of more substantial influence was the United Council of the Working Collectives,[21] which in the spring of 1989 united with the Inter-movement. But the events which took place during 1991 left the non-Estonian population without any political institutions, mainly due to the fact that the Russian deputies in the Estonian Supreme Soviet did not support the proclamation of independence. The prohibition of the Russian organisations was formally based on

[21] It had arisen like the ecological organization of the enterprises subordinated to Moscow. They had a very weak dependence on the local administration. So the opportunity for Estonian independence, which seamed to become more and more real, made their status unprofitable.

the Constitutional provision which allowed the establishment of political organisations only by Estonian citizens.[22]

The first multi-party elections to the Estonian Supreme Soviet in 1990 ensured for the Russians 21 deputy mandates from 104, or 20% of the total. But the first Parliament of the independent Estonia, according to the elections which took place in October 1992, was monoethnic. One third of the population of Estonia was not democratically represented in Parliament.

Evidence of the positive developments in the Russian-Estonian dialogue were the elections to Parliament which took place in March 1995. The block of Russian parties called 'Our home is Estonia' won 6 seats which provided representatives in the most important Parliamentary Commissions: Economic, Social, Legal, Constitutional, for Foreign Affairs, Culture and Education.[23]

The latest results reveal that in 1998 there were about 30 organisations which united the Russian-speaking population of Estonia.[24] Some of them were proclaimed as the successors and followers of the Russian organisations which existed in Estonia before 1940. The Union of the Slav Enlightenment and Charitable Societies, and the Russian Community of Estonia sought all-Russian unification in Estonia. However, there was no consensus amongst the leaders on the basic issues of the development of Russian culture in Estonia: some of them favoured integration into Estonian society, and others wanted to preserve their identity.

All the Russian parties have been established somewhat recently. None of them have had enough members and funds to solve the problems mentioned in their programmes. As a result of this, the Russian organisations did not succeed in establishing an 'umbrella system'. Their role and place within Estonia has been modest, though as emphasised by some experts they tried to gain the support of the Russian deputies, who could provide the 'Russian voices' to be heard in Parliament.

(a) In February 1993 'the Representative Assembly of the Russian-speaking Population in Estonia' was established, aiming to facilitate a dialogue with the Estonian political forces and the Estonian Government, as well as to secure the human rights protection of the ethnic Russians. The leaders of the Representative Assembly commenced on the establishment of relations with the Russian Federation and, even more importantly, the Estonian Government was ready to commu-

---

[22] It is worth mentioning that at the end of August 1991 an attempt was made to establish a democratically orientated organization – the Russian Democratic Movement. The idea was supported by the Prime Minister of Estonia, E. Savisaar. As the organization was not widely supported by the Russians it formed no real opposition.

[23] *Molodezii Estonii* (15 January 1996).

[24] Tatjana Poloskova, *Diasporii v sisteme mezdunarodnih svjazei*, Mezdunarodnaja kniga (1998) p. 56.

nicate with the Assembly. But the existence of this organization was not long-lasting.
(b) The Coordinate Council of the Assembly for National Minorities was only formal as it did not function actively and did not have any political power.
(c) More considerable were the Russian Party of Estonia which was officially established in 1994 proclaiming itself as the successor of the Russian National Union which had existed since 1920, and the Russian People's Party of Estonia which was also set up in 1994 with a different orientation and political programme from the former. In 1996 these two parties merged together under the name Russian Party of Estonia. Its members numbered 403.

The basic notion in the programme of the Russian Party of Estonia is to unite all political forces of the non-Estonian population in the Republic. As proclaimed by the leaders, the main aim of their activities has been the achievement of equal rights for all Estonian residents. For that purpose they were prepared to cooperate with other organisations combating discrimination against non-Estonians. Their plan of action was based on the conviction that the Estonian Government had a well-thought plan to displace the non-Estonians from the country.

The opposition character of the Russian Party of Estonia attracted persons with a low social status, who had not found their place in the new Estonian society and in the world of the market economy.

The third party, the United People's Party of Estonia, was also organised in 1994, gathering among its membership representatives of the Russian intelligentsia. The platform of the United People's Party of Estonia is more realistic and flexible than that of the Russian Party. It supports the integration of the Russians into Estonian society and declined a compromise with the Government. This party is well attuned to the current situation in Estonia and has potential in the future of becoming some kind of legal opposition. In the Russian mass media the United People's Party of Estonia is treated as the initiator of the split in the Russian movement and is condemned for flirting with the Estonians.

During the Parliamentary elections in 1995, the three above-mentioned parties: the United People's Party of Estonia, the Russian Party of Estonia, the Russian People's Party of Estonia, had united in the 'Our home is Estonia' block. However, the plurality of interests prevented the fortification of the Russian fraction in Parliament and in 1997 it was practically disintegrated. As emphasised by the mass media, the main reason why the fraction became isolated from other political forces in Estonia was the fact that it was more oriented to solving the problems of the Russian citizens in Estonia than of the ethnic Russians with Estonian citizenship. However this was in a way understandable because of the hardship being suffered by non-citizens in Estonia.

The Estonian Republic Union of the Citizens of Russia is the political party of the residents of Estonia with Russian citizenship. The political orientations of the Estonian Russians are also different. According to the political rating in 1997 only 10-20% of the non-Estonians supported the Russian Party of Estonia.

At the same time the United People's Party of Estonia became more and more popular, as did new organisations – the Russian Party of Unity and the Russian Christian Union. On 15 December 1997 these three parties signed an agreement on the new Russian electoral union with the same name as the previous Russian 'Our home is Estonia' block.[25] This indicates to an unification of Russian forces which will create genuine opportunities in the next Parliamentary elections.

Though it seems that there is not much sense in stimulating the unification of the Russian Diaspora in the Baltic States, the organization capable of uniting the Russians of the whole region already exists. It is the Association of the Russian Population of the Baltic States. It has the potential to play a positive role in the lives of the Russians.

7. THE NOTION OF RUSSIAN CULTURAL AUTONOMY

It is important to explore the issue of how realistic the creation of cultural autonomy for the districts where the Russian-speaking population predominates would actually be. As already pointed out, in the industrial centres of Silomaje and Narva the problem of integrating Russians into Estonian society is linked to the social, cultural and language problems.

On 26 October 1993 the Estonian State Assembly passed the Law on Cultural Autonomy for National Minorities which seems to be of the utmost importance for the Russian population. However, as the Law only considers Estonian citizens to qualify as national minorities, a large part of the Russians without Estonian citizenship are excluded from having this status. Nonetheless, in the present situation cultural autonomy should be one of the variants of the opportunity to preserve and develop Russian culture in Estonia. What hinders this opportunity from being realised?

During 1996 the Russian scholar Tatjana Poloskova carried out sociological research into the issue of the realisation of the cultural autonomy of the Russian population in Estonia.[26] For this purpose she interviewed representatives of the Russian cultural and political units of Tallinn, Tartu, Narva, members of the Russian fraction in the Estonian Parliament, scientists, directors of the Russian schools and journalists about their opinion concerning this problem. The research showed that among the representatives of the Russian organisations there was not much divergence in their views concerning the Law on Cultural Autonomy. Most of them considered it as discriminative for the following reasons:

---

[25] *Estonia* (5 January 1998).

[26] Poloskova, op. cit. n. 24, p. 36.

– it is not applicable to the large group of Russians without Estonian citizenship;
– it does not include the principle of financing cultural activities on a proportional basis, the funding is not dependent on the numerical size of national minorities; and
– according to the Estonian Law on the School System cultural autonomy has no influence on the educational system in any legal way. The State guarantees the possibility for education in the Russian language only at secondary-school level. The State has postulated that by the year 2007 (previously it was to be by 2000) education at high-school level will be encouraged only to use the Estonian language.

The Russian leaders in Estonia still do not have a joint view concerning the possible amendments aimed at the liberalisation of the Law. According to the members of the United People's Party of Estonia and the Russian Cultural Centre in Narva, it would be more efficient to struggle for a revision of the existing laws on citizenship (Estonian citizenship should be granted to all residents), language (two State languages should be recognized), and on aliens (a special status for the citizens of Russia permanently residing in Estonia should be recognized). Initiating the process of amending the Law on Cultural Autonomy should, in their view, be the second step of the legislative liberalisation.

Some experts note that any initiative to amend the Law on Cultural Autonomy by the Russian deputies would not be supported by the Estonian Parliament. In their view attention should first be paid to exploring the possibilities already granted by Estonian legislation.

At the same time some representatives of the Russian organisations in Estonia insist on the necessity of amending the Law on Cultural Autonomy in the following sense:

(a) the status of the Russian language should be determined in the Law. Russian should be used as an official language in the districts where the Russians and Russian-speaking population are predominant;
(b) the Russian-speaking population should be informed of the possibilities of education in the Russian language. The Russian schools and high schools, as well as the Russian departments at the universities, should be retained. At the same time, in providing for the implementation of the right of parents to choose the language in which their children will be educated, the Russian schools and university departments should be financed by the State and municipal funds proportional to the numbers of students;
(c) the aspirations for the preservation and the development of Russian culture in Estonia should depend on the numbers of Russians in any given area; and
(d) the existing ethnic situation in Estonia makes it necessary for the Law on Cultural Autonomy to recognize its application to all Russians without regard to citizenship.

For the time being and in the absence of a concept providing for Russian autonomy, the Russian leaders in Estonia do not know in which way the autonomy could be realised. Besides, there is no consensus between the leaders on several points regarding Russian cultural autonomy in Estonia:

Firstly, the Russian leaders are aware of the negative attitude of the Estonian administration towards any attempt aimed at liberalising the Law on Cultural Autonomy, and towards the efforts of the Russian leaders in this direction. The attitude of the Estonian authorities is closely connected with the intention of the Estonian Republic to build a mono-ethnic society. In this sense, the Russian leaders notice that their wish to establish Russian autonomy is considered as disloyal.

Secondly, it is evident that some parts of the Russian-speaking population will remain outside any cultural autonomy because of the lack of Estonian citizenship. This could make the existing split between the Russians even deeper. Moreover, the creation of autonomy would bring about extra/supplementary taxes, which some Russians would not be ready to pay. Of importance is also the fact that a group of well-adopted Russians in Estonia prefer to be assimilated and do not have any need for cultural autonomy.

In addition, the fact that Russian autonomy would include some non-Russian groups also has a negative side. The idea of Russian autonomy was criticised, for example, by the Koreans and Ukrainians who seem to be afraid of the reinforcement of Russian hegemony.[27] This all goes to show that there is no unified position among the Estonian and non-Estonian population concerning the issue of Russian cultural autonomy.

8. INTEGRATION OF THE NON-ESTONIANS AS A TASK

During the last few years much attention has been paid by the Estonian Government to the integration of society. It was often stressed that integration should be one of the highest priority tasks of the State organs and other non-governmental organisations. A specific Advisory Council for Integration Processes working at the office of the Minister without Portfolio dealing with the issues of national affairs was established in the spring of 1998. Special integration-supporting programmes and projects have been launched. Initiated in 1997 the Estonian Language Strategy document and the Estonian Integration Strategy document were adopted in 1998.

Discussions on the two political documents have not yet finished. But it is absolutely clear that both of them are aimed at facilitating the future integration of children and young people into society. As it is mentioned in the Estonian Integration Strategy document, Estonia supports the ideology of a united Europe.

[27] *Estonia* (7 April 1996).

As the main and important strategic tasks of the integration policy the document mentions a necessary decrease in the number of stateless persons, the critical need for a change in the teaching of the State language, the need for real participation on the part of non-Estonians in the life of Estonian society. The concrete steps to be taken in order to solve these problems should be the following:

– he attitude towards the non-indigenous population needs to be changed. The perception of non-Estonians that they are the problem, should be changed in a way that their residing in Estonia is considered as a complementary potential for the development of the new Estonian society;
– the task of decreasing the number of aliens requires adequate changes to the Estonian citizenship policy. As Estonian citizenship should prevail in the country, the rules for acquiring citizenship by naturalisation should become more liberal. It also includes the need all children born in Estonia, regardless of the nationality of their parents, to become Estonian citizens;
– education is seen as one of the most influential tools in the process of integration. The teaching of the State language in the non-Estonian schools should be on a level which would allow the acquisition of Estonian citizenship without the need for any examinations. Knowledge of the Estonian language should remove any cultural barrier to subsequent education and employment. A special document entitled the Development Plan for Russian Education in Estonia, recently prepared by the Ministry of Education, presents the first official and written document containing the position of the Estonian Government on this matter, which should serve as a starting point for commencing dialogue within society;
– the State is supposed to ensure teaching in a non-Estonian language and to provide education on the history and development of the country of origin. This requires urgent measures to provide a higher level of knowledge of the State language among the non-Estonian groups;
– regional differences in the population structure should be overcome by encouraging Estonians to relocate, so as to be among the non-Estonians. This could reduce the number of areas where the Russians live as compact groups; and
– the non-ethnic Estonians with Estonian citizenship should be integrated into the political life (governmental structures) of the State.

During the last few years a great deal of effort has been made in order to harmonise the existing national laws with the international standards and principles of human tights. In that sense, during the period 1997-1998 some concrete legal steps were taken which were aimed at establishing a sound basis for the integration process, though it seems not to be a quick and simple task. Unfortunately, in January the Estonian Government refused to support the initiative of the Russian politicians' project for the liberalisation of the Law on Citizenship, which basically contained a suggestion to simplify the process of naturalisation and to grant citizenship without language examinations to all the under-age residents, invalids, pensioners and the spouses of Estonian citizens. The instigators of the project have also suggested granting citizenship without examinations to all the residents with residence permission who came to Estonia before 1 July 1990.[28]

On 19 November 1997 the amendments to the Law on Language were enacted. Forty-five deputies from the existing 101 had voted in favour, but none of the six Russian deputies had done so. Knowledge of the State language was admitted to be obligatory for all employees and businessmen who had to communicate with other persons during working hours. In order to discover the level of knowledge of the Estonian language, the Ministry of Education has established a special examination. This examination is compulsory for everybody who has not been educated in the State language.

According to the Russian Party of Estonia this document limits the rights of the non-Estonian population and creates conditions for the removal of competitors in policy, business, etc. This Law, as is emphasised by the ethnic Russians, will safeguard ethnic Estonians' own interests and will hinder normal relations among the Estonian and non-indigenous populations.[29]

Some indication of the improvement in bilateral Russian-Estonian relations is the fact that the Estonian President was not prepared to agree to the Amendments according to which the deputies in Parliament and those wishing to ascend to the position of the President of the Republic had to pass the language examination. In his view, this would give the Government too much authority considering that it has to establish electoral commissions.[30]

On 10 September 1997 the Parliament adopted the amendments to the Law on Education. Until 2007, when education in Russian at the basic and secondary level will be supported by State funds, the non-Estonian schools will have to provide a sufficient knowledge of the Estonian language which will enable the pupils to continue their education in the State language.[31]

9. THE INTERNATIONAL STANDARDS AND POLICY ACTIVITIES OF RUSSIA

In view of the OSCE High Commissioner on National Minorities, Max van der Stoel, who visited Tallin in 1997, the position of nationality in Estonia had changed for the best during the previous three years. However, as he advised, Estonia should provide a policy which will assist in reducing the number of non-citizens, as well as integrating non-Estonians into Estonian society. All children

---

[28] *Estonia* (1 July 1998).
[29] *Molodez Estonii* (24 November 1997).
[30] *Molodez Estonii* (6 December 1997).
[31] *Molodez Estonii* (12 September 1997).

born in Estonia should automatically become Estonian citizens. Experts have recommended a liberation of the status of non-citizens.

On the United Nations level various efforts have also been undertaken to catalyse Russian-Estonian dialogue and to find complementary approaches with the main priorities being to facilitate the integration of the non-indigenous population into Estonian society, an initiative which was launched by the UN some time ago.

The Russian Federation for its part is trying to ensure the protection of the rights and interests of Russians living outside Russia. The Russian Law on Citizenship gives the Russians an opportunity to acquire Russian citizenship. The strategic tasks of Russia in this sphere are contained in the Presidential Decree No. 1681 of 11 August 1994, on the Guidelines for the Russian Federation State Policy concerning Compatriots Living Abroad, and these tasks are confirmed by the Russian Government to be a field of priority.

The starting point of the Government of the Russian Federation has been that the States in which ethnic Russians live should be responsible for the implementation of social, political, economic, social and cultural rights of their non-indigenous population. One of the main tasks of Russian foreign policy is to find an answer to the isolation of ethnic Russians in the Diaspora from their homeland, as well as to discourage compulsory assimilation and discrimination. At the same time, Russia's strategic approach towards its compatriots abroad is to assist in their voluntary integration into the society of the new States, their adaptation to local cultures with possibilities to preserve their own cultural identities.

10. CONCLUSION

The status of the Russian Diaspora is a common problem for all new States established on the territory of the former Soviet Union. But in none of these countries has the indigenous population so strongly supported the State policy of displacing ethnic Russians from the country as happened in Estonia and Latvia. There were some historical reasons for this. The emphasised negative attitude towards the Russians was created in the Baltic States during the period of the former USSR. The decrease in the numerical size of the indigenous population in these countries, followed by a fear among ethnic Estonians that they could have been assimilated during the period of the domination of Russian culture, resulted in the Estonian State establishing its society on ethnic principles after it had regained independence.

Without doubt the size of the non-indigenous population in the Baltic States is a factor which plays a role in stability inside and outside borders in international relations. The problems which the non-indigenous population is faced with should not be ignored and need to be adequately solved. It seems that the interaction between the position of minorities and internal stability has been recognized by the Estonian leaders. As a result, the political strategy has been reconsidered and the integration of the non-indigenous population into Estonian society is seen as the main task of State policy. That has also contributed to positive changes in the normative field. All these factors provide a sound basis for an optimistic view as regards the future.

ESTONIA'S MINORITIES AND ALIENS: TIME FOR A 'YES-CAMPAIGN'

by Peter van Krieken

1. INTRODUCTION

At Marc Chagall's autumn 1998 exhibition in Liege, one of the first paintings to catch the eye was a depiction of the artist's atelier at Narva (1910). During the period when this famous French painter of Russian origin lived and worked at Narva, the city belonged to the Russian Empire as, indeed, did the whole of Estonia. For Narva this was just a chapter in its long history which also saw it under Swedish rule (until 1721), and during which time Dutch builders were co-shaping the town. Estonia had throughout its history been the object of conquest and war by several powerful neighbouring States. Estonia's 5 krooni banknote symbolises this reality: it depicts the Narva river with fairly pleasant weather on the Western bank, and rather stormy weather on the Eastern bank.

Following the First World War, Estonia gained independence.[1] For its admittance to League of Nations membership Estonia was required to undergo tests on the treatment of minorities, which on the one hand was a specific feature of that time, and on the other, proves that the issue of minorities has for a long time been present in the Estonian political and legal life.

Following its loss of independence in 1939, its suffering during the Second World War, as well as its plight during the time when it was part of the USSR, Estonia happily regained independence in late 1991. But virtually immediately, the minority issue came once again to the fore. The first reactions were to look back to the 1920s and to treat minorities in accordance with the requirements of those days. Another reaction was to focus on humanitarian law, and to emphasise that the deportation of the civilian population was strictly forbidden under that particular brand of international law. It could indeed be easily argued that both the deportation of Estonians to far away places – including the Gulag – was strictly illegal, as well as the 'im-portation' of tens of thousands of Russians into

[1] The word 'gain' might be incorrect as it can be established that the beginning of Estonian sovereignty took place around the year 997. A period of initial statehood, or rather the existence of a geopolitical entity, lasted until 1227. Teutonic knights and the Danes moved in. In fact the name Tallinn means 'town of the Danes'.

S. Trifunovska (Ed.), Minorities in Europe – Croatia, Estonia and Slovakia

Estonia. Such an approach might indeed have survived in court, but it was politically suicidal. Estonians, with their pragmatic, practical, Lutheran minds, understood that law, justice and reality are often three different aspects of the complex life of an independent State. Estonia, therefore, came to the conclusion that a pragmatic approach should involve the voluntariness of the population involved.

This article briefly deals with legal rather than practical aspects of minorities in Estonia, or, more precisely, with 'newcomers'[2] and with those individuals belonging to minority groups who, after the independence of Estonia in 1991, remained without Estonian citizenship. What follows is to some extent an inventory of Estonia's present state of legislation, its accession to relevant international human rights instruments, institution-building and implementation.

As far as the existing legal framework is concerned, it is herein submitted that, in general, Estonia has made significant progress since it regained independence. As the legislative parameters relevant for minority groups and protection of the rights of persons belonging to minorities seem to be in place, it seems that problems are once again to be found in the field of their practical implementation, both with respect to the setting of the tone and to the interpretation of the existing legislation.

It should thus be underlined that due attention needs to be paid to an effective implementation of the existing legislation which is aimed, on the one hand, at stimulating those individuals allowed to stay on the territory of the Republic to integrate, and, on the other, at encouraging those who for legal/formal reasons or of their own free will are not able to continue to live in Estonia, to leave.

In addition, it is suggested that the focus should shift from the formally established legislative and administrative frameworks and the presumed 'wrongdoers', to the potential beneficiaries, be they relative newcomers, like asylum seekers and refugees, or persons born 40 years ago into a Russian family. One should expect that besides the respect for the established and accepted international legal norms and standards and internal legal and political frameworks and realities which often pose limitations to the existing wishes, there are also responsibilities on the part of the beneficiaries or barriers corresponding to their rights.

Since Estonia's ratification of the 1950 European Convention on Human Rights, non-nationals are fully entitled to address the Strasbourg institutions (as per 1 November 1998: institution, singular) in view of their *locus standi* under that Convention. The proof of the pudding is in the eating; the ball is now in the court of the potential beneficiaries. It is time for a 'yes-campaign', along the lines of the Northern Irish campaign to endorse the 1998 Irish Good Friday Agreement: a campaign to convince the non-nationals to actively strive for citizenship, to strive for co-habitation, integration, mutual understanding and *mutua fides*.

---

[2] 'Newcomers' are herein considered to be all non-Estonians who settled in the territory of Estonia in the period 1945-1989.

2. DEMOGRAPHIC SITUATION

Currently Estonia counts 1.6 million people,[3] which reveals a certain increase in comparison with the demographic situation in the late 1930s when the total population amounted to 1 million. At that time some 10% of the population belonged to minority groups (the five biggest groups being Germans, Russians, Jews, Swedes and Latvians; smaller groups consisted of Ingrians, Tatars and Roma). In fact, throughout the 50 years preceding the Molotov-Ribbentrop Pact (of 1939), the Estonians themselves formed 88%-91% of the population. This number increased to 95% at the end of the Second World War, in view of the departure of Germans and Swedes, the horrible plight of the Jewish population, and the transfer of some territory to the Russian Federation (like the villages east of Narva). This meant that out of the total population of 900,000, there were 850,000 ethnic Estonians.

As the official statistics showed, by 1989 out of the total population only 62% turned out to be ethnic Estonians (930,000), whereas 38% were non-Estonians (meaning that in the 44 years of the post-Second World War period the number of non-Estonian population had increased significantly, i.e., from 50,000 to 570,000). A comparison of the numerical situation of non-ethnic Estonians with the pre-Second World War figures (9% to 38%) indicates an almost four-fold increase. Of relevance for this discussion is also the number of foreign-born persons. The 1989 Soviet census revealed that more than 25% of the total Estonian population had been born outside Estonia: 'such was the legacy of Soviet rule, which Estonia bore as it regained its statehood'.[4] It reflects the enormous immigration of Russians into Estonia. It could be submitted that in 1998, with due reference to a 1.7% fertility rate, the number of foreign-born persons in Estonia is still above 20%, which, according to European standards, is an extremely high percentage.

3. SOME GENERAL OBSERVATIONS ON THE LEGAL AND INSTITUTIONAL FRAMEWORK

3.1 An inventory of the relevant international human rights instruments

Since its admission to United Nations membership, on 17 September 1991,[5] Estonia has acceded to a large number of international instruments in the field of hu-

[3] Minority Rights Group, *World Directory of Minorities* (1997).

[4] This quote, as well as some of the figures mentioned herein can be found in Aksel Kirch (Ed.), *The Integration of Non-Estonians into Estonian Society*, Tallinn (1997) pp. 12-15.

[5] The Declaration recognising the compulsory jurisdiction of the International Court of Justice was issued on 21 October 1991.

man rights and humanitarian law, such as: the 1948 Convention on the Prevention and Punishment of the Crime of Genocide (21 October 1991, accession); the 1966 Covenants on Human Rights cum Optional Protocol (21 January 1992); the 1984 Convention Against Torture (21 October 1991); the 1989 Convention on the Rights of the Child (21 October 1991); the 1949 Red Cross Geneva Conventions with the 1977 Protocols on international and non-international armed conflicts (18 January 1993, accession); the 1950 European Convention on Human Rights with all Protocols (with exception to Protocol No. 6 on the abolition of the death penalty which was adopted only in March 1998) including Protocol 11 (May 1993 up to May 1994), instruments of ratification deposited on 16 April 1996; the 1957 European Convention on Extradition (July 1997); the 1977 European Convention on the Suppression of Terrorism (June 1997); the 1987 European Convention for the Prevention of Torture and Inhuman or Degrading Treatment or Punishment (ratified by Estonia in 1996) and the 1993 Protocol Nos. 1 and 2 (ratified by Estonia in 1996); and the 1951 Refugee Convention with 1967 Protocol (February 1997).

In addition, in the period from 1995-1998, Estonia signed readmission agreements with Latvia, Lithuania, Finland, Norway, Sweden, Iceland, Slovenia, Italy and Switzerland.

Though the list of legally and politically binding human rights documents to which Estonia has adhered in the last few years is impressive, there are some more important documents for the Estonian situation missing from the list, like the 1954 Convention Relating to the Status of Stateless Persons and the 1961 Convention on the Reduction of Statelessness. The accession to these Conventions would benefit both Estonia and the stateless persons concerned, particularly as Estonia already appears to live up to the standards set in these Conventions.

3.2 **Institutional framework**

Apart from the normative framework, there are a number of bodies falling under the responsibility of the Ministry of the Interior dealing with migration in general, like: the National Board of Border Guards, the Estonian Police Board, the Estonian Security Police Board, and the Citizenship and Immigration Board. Besides these, in the field of migration certain tasks and responsibilities belong to: the Border Guards; the Ministry of Social Affairs and the Judiciary.[6] The Citizenship and Migration Board has tasks to carry out the population policy set by the Government of Estonia on citizenship and migration; to implement the documentation/ID-card policy; to deal with matters of citizenship; to issue, extend and revocate residence and work permits; to issue visas; to collect information con-

---

[6] For more details on this issue see in particular my paper entitled 'Disintegration and Statelessness', in 1 *Netherlands Quarterly on Human Rights* (1994) pp. 23-33, as well as 'Nieuwe Medelanders', in *Ars Aequi* (1993).

cerning migration; to prevent illegal migration; to receive applications on asylum and prepare the necessary decisions thereon; and, to manage the relevant databases. It could be noted that during the last decade the Citizenship and Migration Board has undergone a substantial transition. The move from the charming, yet very medieval office in the old town to the functional renewed office building at Endla symbolises the change. The new Statute of the Board was approved in April 1998 and the new structure of the organization has been in place as from 1 July 1998.[7]

The activities of these bodies leave an impression that until now they have been rather cooperative in dealing with the issues within the frameworks of their tasks. It is of importance, however, to underline the need for effective communication and transparency. The Ministry will have to ensure that the conditions therefor are fully met.

4. LEGAL FRAMEWORK AND A PRAGMATIC APPROACH TO THE ISSUE OF CITIZENSHIP

4.1 Pragmatism

Upon the (re-)gaining of independence, various aspects of international and internal law started playing a role, like the issue of State succession including the difference between gaining and regaining independence, citizenship law, property law, war damages, expropriation, reinstating nationalised property, the return of the exiled and deported, the presence of those who migrated during 'occupation' or colonial times, etc. These issues, of course, became topics of discussion within and on Estonia, as they also became issues of mutual concern. Mutual, because

---

[7] Without the intention to enter into a deeper analysis, a few remarks should be made with respect to the Citizenship and Migration Board:

(a) It is in charge of carrying out a great number of politically sensitive tasks; the balance between efficient implementation and political awareness needs to be kept at all times.

(b) Although a centralized institution, its main tasks are carried out in the field (it has 20 regional offices and a special Narva branch). This is the logical result of the Board's main activities: registration and deciding upon the applications for citizenship which shall be basically dealt with at or near the place of residence of the applicant.

In virtually all the organizations the staff appear to be highly motivated and well trained. It should not be denied that over the last seven years many donors have invested heavily in providing individual scholarships, training, etc. The investments seem to be paying off, but due attention needs to be paid to training at university level and below, to prepare society and its individuals for dealing with non-Estonians, asylum seekers, refugees, migrants as well as rejectees. On the university level, for example, it should be ensured that the various faculties introduce into their curricula elements such as the following:

- refugee law, human rights, minority rights, migration law
- integration v. non-integration; counseling towards return.

not only the Estonians themselves were interested in the outcome, but also the Russians residing in Estonia, as well as the Russian authorities in Moscow. In that sense the interest revealed by the Council of Europe, the OSCE, the European Union and various UN organs, indicates the complexity of the issues playing a role in Estonia. Faced with all the legal and practical issues to be solved, as pointed out above, the Estonians themselves showed a remarkable level of pragmatism, which enabled them to overcome emotions and to stick to rational approaches.

4.2 Citizenship

This is especially true with respect to the issue of nationality or citizenship. Though vehemently discussed in academic circles, in Estonia it has been and remains for the time being the most salient one. In addition, it should be noted that the nationality issue as such has hardly been touched upon in international law. Some more important instruments date back to the early 1930s,[8] notwithstanding the fact that the issue of migration and nationality has always been present within the State boundaries.

The 1948 Universal Declaration on Human Rights explicitly confirms that everyone has the right to a nationality and that no one shall be arbitrarily deprived of nor denied the right (Article 15 paras. (a) and (b)). This provision, however, was not taken over in the 1966 International Covenant on Civil and Political Rights that followed and in which it is only stated that children are entitled to acquire a nationality (Article 24).[9] Within the frameworks of the CSCE/OSCE documents, of importance is the 1992 Helsinki summit, which on the one hand reaffirmed the right to nationality, and at the same time emphasised that regulations concerning citizenship are, above all, a matter of national law. It posed a duty on States 'not to increase statelessness' and not a duty to take measures for its decrease. It reads:

> 'The Participating States
>
> 55. Recognize that everyone has the right to a nationality and that no one should be deprived of his/her nationality arbitrarily;
> 56. Underline that all aspects of nationality will be governed by the process of law; they will, as appropriate, take measures, consistent with their national framework *not to increase* statelessness;' (emphasis added) [10]

---

[8] For example, the Convention on Certain Questions Relating to the Conflict of Nationality Law, The Hague, 1930.

[9] The situation has not been changed by the adoption of the 1989 Convention on the Rights of the Child, which in its Art. 7 confirms the right of the child, *inter alia*, to acquire a nationality.

[10] Helsinki II Decisions (1992), Chapter VI – The Human Dimension.

Apart from the weak framework established by international documents, of significance is the famous *Nottebohm case (Liechtenstein* v. *Guatemala)*[11] which describes nationality as:

> '. . . a legal bond having as its basis a social fact of attachment, a genuine connection of existence, interests and sentiments, together with the existence of reciprocal rights and duties.'

This indeed indicates that the nationality issue does not concern a calculated relationship. Aspects like sentiments, and one may thus say, loyalty, are part of the bond.

What seemed to be the Estonian dilemma concerning the issue of nationality, initially involved the issue of whether to embark on a policy stimulating departures of those considered as the 'newcomers'. Some efforts (like building apartment blocks in Russia for those who would return) proved that this was an unrealistic idea and an impossible task. There was also an option to follow the Lithuanian example on the so-called 'zero option', which meant granting citizenship to everyone legally residing on the territory of the country at the time of (re-)gaining independence.[12] However, the Lithuanian situation was not comparable to the Estonian one: only 15% of the Lithuanian population belong to minority groups (Russian, Polish, Belarusian, Jewish, Ukrainian, Tatar, etc.), which means that the integration and consequently the acceptance of Lithuanian as the official and day-to-day language would be accepted almost automatically. The zero option offered the Estonians no concrete possibilities in building the post-Second World War nation-State.

Thus, it was decided to embark on a track which would provide the 'newcomers' with basically three alternatives:

1. the persons concerned could apply for Estonian citizenship, but had to meet some conditions, in particular the knowledge of the Estonian language;
2. the persons concerned could register for Russian citizenship, and would be granted a residence permit which would enable them to continue to live in Estonia. It should be pointed out that it concerns 'registration' and not 'application', between which there is a minor, and yet important difference. The Russians provided the possibility for the former USSR citizens to register up until 31 December 2000;
3. the third alternative would be neither Estonian citizenship, nor registration for Russian nationality, but rather statelessness. The lack of nationality would not affect the right to continue to live and work in Estonia. Such stateless persons

[11] Merits ICJ Reports 1955, 4.

[12] See for example: W. Brubaker 'Citizenship Struggles in Soviet Successor States', 26 *International Migration Review* (Summer 1992) No. 98, pp. 269-291.

would be provided with ID-cards, as well as with aliens' passports, which could be used to travel abroad (including into the Russian Federation), depending on the legislation and visa regimes of the countries to be visited.

This 'triptych' of possibilities, in spite of the 'ugliness', is fully in accordance with international law, including human rights law,[13] though this does not mean that the procedures to be followed under the three above described alternatives, are transparent, nor does it mean that access to such procedures has been at all times ensured. It indeed took a couple of years to elaborate the various details regarding the procedures, which, as a consequence, resulted in some frustrations on the side of all concerned, like those without nationality in Estonia, the Estonian nationals, the diplomatic community, the human rights bodies and the human rights lobby. However, it is safe to state that by now Estonia has reached a level of 'fine-tuning' which should enable all those who over the years have shared their concerns and criticism with the Estonian authorities, to close their files. According to some sources, the OSCE High Commissioner on National Minorities has indeed concluded that Estonia has passed the (his own) test.

However, the implementation of any of the above-described options presents a challenge on its own for both the Estonian authorities and in particular for persons without Estonian nationality, be they foreigners or stateless persons. It is in particular up to the latter to make unambiguous choices in accepting some of the alternatives put forward for them. While making up their minds, these individuals will face a number of calculated and practical risks and considerations: military service, the impossibility to take up certain professions, the possibility to travel in the not too distant future to the (other) parts of Europe's 'Schengen-country', the need to be able to visit family members across the Narva bridge,[14] solidarity with the other members of the Russian community, and so on. It is therefore of great importance to make these persons aware of the existing options, or metaphorically said to launch a 'yes-campaign', in which the various alternatives will be repeatedly explained. During any such campaign, it should be stressed that Estonia has now reached a point whereby all concerns have duly been taken into account. It is now up to the 'newcomers' to respond in an adequate manner, whereas the scholars, the lobbyists and the outsiders, should be aware of the subtle differences between the rights, duties and responsibilities.

It should be pointed out that on 8 December 1998, the Estonian Parliament enacted an amendment to the Law concerned thereby making possible for 6,500 non-Estonian ethnic Russian children born after 1991 to be granted Estonian citizenship. The amendment should enter into force on 1 July 1999.

---

[13] See in particular my articles cited loc. cit. n. 6.

[14] See for example the Christmas issue of *The Economist* (1998) pp. 19-22 on 'borders.'

4.3 Integration and return

As until now attention has been paid to the need for the harmonisation of the procedures, i.e., to the need to combine procedures for determination of the status with deportation procedures, whenever relevant, it is necessary to look at the Estonian reality in the framework of the migration issue in general. This involves and requires information on several points like:

– precise statistical data on the number of foreigners and the composition of the foreign population (has the country become a target or transit country?), on the status of foreigners, on the situation of repatriation and detention, etc.;
– information on the visa policy presently being pursued, including a comparison with EC decisions/blacklisting; and
– the state of bilateral and multilateral co-operation needs to be ascertained (above all the assistance from EU Member States, international governmental and non-governmental organizations and in particular neighbouring countries).

This also includes the sensitive issue of a large group of non-Estonian population which settled in Estonia in Soviet times (and their descendants), in order to fully appreciate the issue of the integration of those asylum seekers who will be allowed to stay.

As mentioned above, until now Estonia has concluded a significant number of readmission agreements abolishing visa requirement. In addition to the bilateral agreements, of significance are some multilateral documents. In the context of the CSCE/OSCE the following should be mentioned: the Charter of Paris for the New Europe (1990), the Moscow Document (1991), the Helsinki Document (1992), the Vienna Documents 1992 and the Stockholm Document 1992, etc. From the Council of Europe should be mentioned the 1995 Framework Convention on Protection of National Minorities, ratified by Estonia in 1998 and the 1985 European Charter of Local Self-Government (ratified by Estonia in 1994).

However, of equal importance are a number of internal/national documents such as: the Aliens Act of 1993 (as amended in 1994, 1995, 1997, 1997); the Law on Cultural Autonomy for National Minorities of 1993; the Cultural Autonomy Law of 1925; the Law on Citizenship of January 1995; the Law on Language of February 1995; and the Integration of Non-Estonians into Estonian Society which is a policy-paper adopted by the Estonian Government on 10 February 1998. It should be mentioned that of certain relevance is also the Law of the Russian Federation on Russian Federation Citizenship, which lays down rules and regulations on 'registering' for citizenship (possible for all USSR citizens up to February 1993, extended until 1995 and later on until 31 December 2000), as well as for 'applying' for Russian citizenship.

The Estonian legislation includes the following documents of relevance for aliens and persons without citizenship:[15]

A) *Aliens Act of 1993*

The Aliens Act regulates the entry of aliens into Estonia, their stay, residence and employment in Estonia and the bases for the legal liability of aliens. According to this Act, an alien is a person who is a citizen of a foreign State or who is declared a stateless person; a permanent resident is an Estonian citizen residing in Estonia or an alien residing in Estonia who holds a permanent residence permit.

The Aliens Act regulates the issue of residence permits to aliens whose permanent residence is outside Estonia and to aliens who return to Estonia as their permanent place of residence. Residence permits can be divided into temporary residence permits and permanent residence permits and they shall be issued to a passport of an alien's country of citizenship or to the document replacing it or to an aliens' passport. A residence permit may be issued to an alien for employment, for study, to settle with an immediate relative permanently resident in Estonia, to marry a person permanently resident in Estonia or to sojourn for personal motives. The amendment to the Aliens Act, which came into force on October 26, 1997, stipulates that a permanent residence permit shall not be issued to an alien who has received a residence permit for studying or working in Estonia or to whom the Government of the Republic has given a residence permit on an exceptional basis.

Generally the settlement of aliens in Estonia is limited by the annual immigration quota established by the Government of the Republic which according to the law in force until the legal amendment of October 26, 1997, did not exceed 0.1% of the permanent population of Estonia. Since the above-mentioned amendment came into force, the annual immigration quota is 0.05% of the permanent population of Estonia. When the annual immigration quota has been achieved, the issue of a residence permit will be refused. The Aliens Act provides for those persons who have the right to settle in Estonia outside of the immigration quota.

The amendment of the law, which came into force on October 26, 1997, establishes the possibility to revoke a residence permit on the basis of an alien's application and where an alien has settled in another country and has not registered his or her stay outside of Estonia for a period which exceeds 183 days a year. If, according to the previous Law on Aliens, which came into force on 12. July, 1993, all aliens who wished to work in Estonia needed a work permit, then the above-mentioned amendment allows those aliens who have submitted their application for residence permits before July 12, 1995, and who are in possession of a temporary residence permit to work without a work permit. Aliens, who have received temporary residence permits on the basis of the decision of the Government of the Republic, are treated in exceptional terms. Besides that, on the basis of the above-mentioned amendment nationals of the European Union, Norway, Iceland and Switzerland have the right to receive a residence permit outside the immigration quota.

[15] The documents included have been provided with the courtesy of the Estonian authorities.

B) *Draft-amendment and replenishment law of the Aliens Act*

At present the draft of the amendment and replenishment law of the Aliens Act has been prepared regulating the issue of residence permits outside the annual immigration quota as well as to Estonians, to nationals of the European Union, Norway, Iceland and Switzerland, also to a spouse of a European Union national and under-aged children who are not nationals of the European Union if they arrive in Estonia together with a national of the European Union; to an alien who has settled in Estonia before July 1, 1990, and has not left Estonia to live in some other country; to a spouse of an Estonian citizen who applies for a residence permit to live together with his or her spouse due to marriage and to a child younger than one year who is descended from an alien who lives in Estonia on the basis of a residence permit. The draft also allows sojourn in Estonia on the basis of a business visa without a work permit. The draft provides for a working group for establishing the procedure for the Government of the Republic for organising the issue of residence and work permits.

C) *Regulation No. 368 of the Government of the Republic adopted on December 7, 1995, 'Affirmation of the procedure for the issue, extension and revocation of residence and work permits'*

The Regulation affirmed the procedure for the issue, extension and revocation of residence and work permits and the list of countries whose nationals may apply for residence and work permits at the Citizenship and Migration Board. The above-mentioned procedure establishes the rules for the issue, extension and revocation of residence and work permits.

In general, aliens should apply for residence and work permits at the diplomatic representations of the Republic of Estonia. The Regulation provides for those persons who have the right to apply for a residence permit at the Citizenship and Migration Board. It establishes the terms for applying and extending residence and work permits, the documents necessary for the application for residence and work permits as well as the basis for the revocation of residence and work permits.

D) *State Fee Act*

The State Fee Act and Regulation No. 54 of the Government of the Republic adopted on March 17, 1997, 'Application of sections 171 and 182 of the State Fee Act' regulate matters related to the State fee.

The State Fee Act determines the proceedings for imposing the State fee; establishes the procedure for the calculation and payment of the State fee, the rates of the State fee and the controls over imposing the State fee.

The State Fee Act provides for the amount and the procedure by which aliens have to pay the State fee to receive a residence or work permit, and in the case of a stateless person, for the proceedings related to the application for and the issue of an Alien's passport. According to the State Fee Act the Director General of the Citizenship and Migration Board and his Deputy; an ambassador, a chief consul or a consul of the Republic of Estonia have the right according to the conditions and the procedure established by the Regulation of the Government of the Republic to reduce the rate of the State fee or to exempt a person from this fee.

E) *Regulation No. 16 of January 16, 1997, which affirmed 'The conditions and the procedure for the issue of alien's passports'*

'The conditions and the procedure for the issue of alien's passports' (hereafter called 'the Procedure') affirmed by the Regulation provides for those persons to whom an alien's passport may be issued, and regulates the application for a passport. This passport does not guarantee to its holder the protection of the diplomatic and consular representations of the Republic of Estonia.

According to the Procedure an alien's passport is valid for a term of up to five years depending on the term of validity of a residence permit, issued to an alien, who has the right to a residence permit in Estonia and if he or her is not in possession of a valid identity document or if he, or she, has no possibility to obtain one. An alien's passport is valid only if a residence permit has been entered in it. In the case of need a work permit shall be entered in an alien's passport.

According to point 14 of the Procedure affirmed by the Regulation an alien's passport shall not be issued to an alien who has received a temporary residence permit to work in Estonia on a contractual basis or for any other kind of action or for studying in an educational institution of Estonia if the basis of his or her stay in Estonia has not changed.

In general, a passport shall be issued, extended or renewed within 30 days from the day of submitting an application pursuant to point 29 of the Procedure.

Point 1 of the Procedure stipulates that an alien's passport shall be issued, extended, renewed, exchanged, revoked and declared invalid by the Citizenship and Migration Board. The Citizenship and Migration Board is obliged to return the revoked passport to its holder to control its validity within a period of two months from the day of its revocation.

F) *Regulation No. 289 of the Government of the Republic adopted on September 21, 1997, concerning aliens' passports*

This Regulation affirmed the specimen of an alien's passport. The size of an alien's passport is: 88x125 mm. There are 32 pages in an alien's passport. On each page of the passport '*välismaalase pass*' in Estonian and 'alien's passport' in English is printed.

Personal data of the holder of a passport, data concerning the holder's children aged under 15, as well as the date, place and date of expiry of the passport, issuing office and the signature of an official who issued the passport, as well as the signature of the holder of the passport shall be entered in the passport.

G) *Regulation No. 211 of the Government of the Republic adopted on June 8, 1994, 'Affirmation of the basis and the procedure for the issue of a temporary travel document'*

The Law on Temporary Travel Documents, which came into force on June 19, 1994, establishes the possibility to issue a temporary travel document to an alien who is resident in Estonia and has no valid travel document for crossing the State border. The above-mentioned travel document may be issued to an alien for a single journey abroad and return or for an alien who definitively leaves Estonia. In the latter case the Citizenship and Migration Board makes the notice on the absence of the right to return to Estonia on the basis of this travel document.

H) *The Ratification Act of the Agreement between the Republic of Estonia and the Russian Federation on the withdrawal of the armed forces of the Russian Federation from the territory of the Republic of Estonia and on conditions for their temporary stay in Estonia and of the Agreement between the Republic of Estonia and the Russian Federation concerning social guarantees for the military pensioners of the Russian Federation staying on the territory of the Republic of Estonia*

The Ratification Act of the Agreement between the Republic of Estonia and the Russian Federation on the withdrawal of the armed forces of the Russian Federation from the territory of the Republic of Estonia and on conditions for their temporary stay in Estonia and of the Agreement between the Republic of Estonia and the Russian Federation concerning the social guarantees for the military pensioners of the Russian Federation staying on the territory of the Republic of Estonia (hereafter called 'the Ratification Act') declares that the conclusion of an agreement between the Republic of Estonia and the Russian Federation on the withdrawal of armed forces of the Russian Federation from the territory of the Republic of Estonia and on the conditions of their temporary stay here, cannot be interpreted as the creation of a lawful basis for the stay of the armed forces of the USSR and the Russian Federation in Estonia and concerns only the withdrawal of armed forces within the period from 26 July 1994 to 31 August 1994. The above-mentioned Agreement applies only to the territory subject to the jurisdiction of the Republic of Estonia on July 26, 1994.

The Ratification Act ratifies 'The Agreement between the Republic of Estonia and the Russian Federation concerning social guarantees for military pensioners of the Russian Federation on the territory of the Republic of Estonia' which was signed on July 26, 1994, in Moscow. The Ratification Act declares that the Republic of Estonia regards those persons as military pensioners who resided on the territory of the Republic of Estonia, were retired and received a subsidy and a pension from the Russian Federation before the conclusion of the Agreement defined in section 1 of the Ratification Act, i.e., before June 26, 1994, and, according to the agreement, did not have to leave Estonia.

The Ratification Act guarantees to military pensioners and their family members, including invalids and participants of the war from 1941 to 1945 on the territory of the Republic of Estonia, all civil and political rights and freedoms as well as social, economic and cultural rights pursuant to commonly recognised norms of international law.

I) *Regulation No. 130 of the Government of the Republic adopted on May 14, 1996, 'Affirmation of the procedure for the issue of residence permits to aliens who have served as professional members of the armed forces of a foreign State'*

The procedure for the issue of residence permits to aliens who have served as professional members of the armed forces of a foreign State (hereafter called the Procedure) affirmed by the Regulation regulates the issue or refusal to issue residence permits to aliens listed in the Procedure.

According to point 2 of the Procedure a residence permit shall be issued to those aliens and their family members who resided on the territory of the Republic of Estonia, were sent into retirement and received a subsidy and a pension from the Russian Federation before June 26, 1994, and, did not have to leave Estonia according to 'The Agreement between the Republic of Estonia and the Russian Federation on the withdrawal of the armed forces of the Russian Federation from the territory of the Republic of Estonia and on conditions for their temporary stay in Estonia' and are therefore included in the list set out in point 3 of Article 2 of the Agreement between the Republic of Estonia and the Russian Federation concerning social guarantees for military pensioners of the Russian Federation on the territory of the Republic of Estonia (hereafter called 'the Agreement') which has been specified and accepted by Estonia. The above-mentioned aliens received a residence permit on the basis of a personal application.

Members of the family of professional members of the armed forces receive residence permits on the same basis and conditions as professional members of the armed forces.

According to point 11 of the Procedure an application submitted by a professional member of the armed forces and their family members shall be examined by a special committee formed by the Government of the Republic. This committee makes a proposition to the Government of the Republic to issue or to refuse to issue a residence permit to a professional member of the armed forces and to the members of his or her family. Besides that, the above-mentioned committee makes a proposition to revoke residence permits of a professional member of the armed forces and the members of his or her family.

The Citizenship and Migration Board submits applications for residence permits of professional members of the armed forces and their family members to the above-mentioned committee. The Citizenship and Migration Board also issues and revokes residence permits of aliens on the basis of a decision of the Government of the Republic.

J) *Draft of the Identity Documents Act*

The draft establishes the obligations concerning documentation and regulates the issue of identity documents to Estonian citizens and aliens by the Republic of Estonia.

The above-mentioned draft provides for the issue of the following documents:

a) Estonian passport – a travel document of a citizen of Estonia which shall be issued to an Estonian citizen who is at least 15 years old on the basis of his or her personal application or to an Estonian citizen who is under 15, or incapable, on the basis of an application of his or her legal representative.
b) Diplomatic passport – a travel document of a citizen of Estonia which shall be issued to the President of the Republic of Estonia, members of the Board and chairmen of the committees of the *Riigikogu*, the Secretary of State, the chairman of the Supreme Court, the Chancellor of Law, the head of the State Audit Office, civil servants of the Ministry of Foreign Affairs belonging to the diplomatic corps or working at diplomatic or consular representations of the Republic of Estonia.
c) Sailor's service passport – a travel document of an Estonian citizen who works, or starts to work on a boat of a foreign country.
d) Alien's passport – a travel document of an alien resident of Estonia who does not have a travel document and who cannot obtain it. It shall be issued to aliens who are at least 15 years old on the basis of their personal applications and to aliens under 15, or incapable aliens older than 15, on the basis of a written application of their legal representative.
e) Temporary travel document – a travel document of an alien staying in Estonia which shall be issued for his or her departure from Estonia.
f) Travel document of a refugee – a travel document of a refugee who has been granted asylum in Estonia.

g) Identity document – a document which shall be issued to an Estonian citizen and an alien who is in possession of a residence permit in Estonia.
h) Certificate to return – a document which shall be issued to an Estonian citizen whose travel document has become unusable or ruined while sojourning abroad or to an alien who is in possession of a residence permit in Estonia and who does not have a travel document, or who cannot obtain it and to whom according to an international agreement, the Republic of Estonia has to guarantee entry to its territory.

K) *Draft-Regulation of the Government of the Republic: 'Conditions and the procedure of application for a permanent residence permit'*

The conditions and the procedure and the form of application for a permanent residence permit have been prepared.

The purpose of the draft is to establish the conditions and the procedure for the application for a permanent residence permit by those aliens who have applied for temporary residence permits before July 12, 1995, and to whom residence permits have been issued and who do not belong among the aliens defined in subsection 4 of section 12 of the Aliens Act.

According to this draft an alien shall submit personally, by post or via his or her representative, on the basis of a letter of authorisation an application for a permanent residence permit. If the application and the enclosed documents meet the established requirements, the Citizenship and Migration Board shall process it within a month from the day of the submission of the application.

The draft also includes the circumstances forming the basis for processing an application or for stopping its processing. The Citizenship and Migration Board may submit requests to the State and local government authorities and to legal, as well as physical, persons and to invite the applicant to an interview in the Board to review data presented in an application and documents enclosed with it.

L) *The Draft-Regulation of the Government of the Republic on conditions and the procedure for registering aliens staying away from Estonia*

Pursuant to subsection 2 of section 14 of the Aliens Act a residence permit of an alien shall be revoked if an alien has settled in a foreign country and stays outside Estonia for more than 183 days a year and has not registered his or her absence from Estonia according to the conditions and the procedures established by the Government of the Republic of Estonia.

The draft of the Regulation of the Government of the Republic: 'Conditions and procedure for registering aliens' absence from Estonia' has been prepared.

According to the draft this Regulation shall establish the conditions and the procedures for the absence from Estonia of an alien who is in possession of a residence permit in Estonia and who has settled in a foreign country and stays outside of Estonia for more than 183 days a year.

According to the established procedure an alien, or his or her representative shall submit an application for registering his or her absence including data listed in the Regulation to the Citizenship and Migration Board or to the representations of the Republic of Estonia. An application for absence shall be registered if it meets the requirements established in point 2 of the above-mentioned draft. The revocation of registering the absence shall be implemented according to the same procedure.

M) *The Draft-Regulation of the Government of the Republic: 'Affirmation of the procedure for the issue of a residence permit on exceptional terms', and the Order of the Government of the Republic on the 'Formation of the Governmental Committee'*

This draft of the Regulation of the Government of the Republic has been developed following subsection 5 of section 12 of the Aliens Act according to which exceptions may be made for aliens as set out in subsection 4 of section 12 of the Aliens Act upon issuing their residence permits. According to the above-mentioned subsection a residence permit shall not be issued to aliens who have submitted false information upon application for a visa, residence permit or work permit, who do not observe the constitutional order and laws of Estonia; whose activities have been directed against the Estonian State and its security; who have committed a criminal offence for which they have been sentenced to imprisonment for a term of more than one year and whose punishment is not completed or determined; who are, or have been, employed by the intelligence or security service of a foreign State; who are in the active service of the armed forces of a foreign State, nor to their family members; who have served as professional members of the armed forces of a foreign State or have been assigned to the reserve forces thereof or have retired therefrom, nor to their family members who entered Estonia due to a member of the armed forces being sent into service, the reserve or into retirement.

According to the draft of the Regulation of the Government of the Republic the Minister of the Interior shall decide on the issue of a residence permit as an exception or on the refusal to issue a residence permit. Where the refusal to issue a residence permit is based on the submission of false information upon application for a visa, residence or work permit, the exceptional issue of a residence permit, or the refusal to issue it shall be decided by the Director General of the Citizenship and Migration Board.

To decide on the issue, or refusal to issue, a residence permit on exceptional terms an applicant may be invited to discuss the matter of the application and additional evidence may be gathered if it is necessary for making a decision on the issue or the refusal to issue a residence permit.

In general the issue, or refusal to issue, a residence permit on exceptional terms shall be decided within the same calendar year that the application was given for processing. If an application has been submitted 2 months before the end of a calendar year, the decision shall be made during the next calendar year.

From the above overview of the relevant provisions, it is obvious that the issue regarding aliens, non-citizens and/or stateless persons has to be seen against the background of population movements in the period 1945-1989. The EU on a number of occasions appears to have expressed its agreement with activities and proposals of the OSCE High Commissioner on National Minorities, it being noted that these proposals in general are in accordance with, and sometimes over and above minimum international human rights standards for non-citizens. Where it concerns the recommendations submitted by the High Commissioner there is an impression of the sincerity and seriousness with which the Estonian authorities deal with these issues. Until now all but one of the recommendations concerned have been fully adopted; the final one (on citizenship for children born in Estonia since March 1990) is currently awaiting a second reading in Parliament and by the end of 1998 was in its very final stage.

4.4 **Activities**

In the past various and numerous measures have been undertaken aimed at assisting the authorities in carrying out the fairly ambitious integration programme. Language training is only one such activity which deserves mentioning, though it appears to receive funding from various sources. (Though coordination and transparency among the donors might be considered to be at times somewhat problematic). The Government's policy paper on the Integration of Non-Estonians into Estonian Society, adopted in February 1998, contains a number of ideas which deserve attention and support.

It seems, as indicated above, that efforts now need to be intensified towards reaching out to the non-Estonians concerned. It is quite remarkable that many groups representing national minorities and working together under the banner of the Estonian Union of National Minorities would appear to fully appreciate the subtleties of Estonia's nation-building process. More than ever, the Russian speaking non-Estonians should be confronted with, on the one hand, a 'yes-campaign' (yes towards applying for Estonian citizenship, and thereby in the not too distant future possibly, amongst other things, visa-free travel to a 'Schengen country'), a campaign which should be launched with the use of all modern technology and commercial experience. On the other hand, an information campaign should be launched on human rights and the contents of minority rights, in order to get the message across that Estonia is duly fulfilling its obligations under the international human rights regime. Moreover, the issue of responsibilities and duties (cf., Article 29 of the Universal Declaration on Human Rights) may also be raised.

Various actors, and donors in particular, should hence shift their attention from governmental activities to working directly with the non-Estonians concerned.

The fact that the Minister without Portfolio, who is at the same time the coordinator of ethnic and population affairs, has a very limited staff is of practical relevance which can affect efficiency in dealing with the implementation of State documents and policy.

Besides, it still remains to be seen which institutions should implement the February 1998 policy paper on integration. NGOs and/or various institutions may be involved or will (have to) be set up to implement a full-strength integration policy. In due time a study needs to be made with respect to the issue of institution-building and staffing too, which plays a role in the field of implementation.

5. CONCLUSION

Any integration policy is bound to fail, if it is not intertwined with an effective migration policy, in particular where it concerns mutual cooperatioin and *mutua fides*, on the one hand, and the return of those who are not allowed to stay, on the other. Estonia deserves the necessary assistance to be able to cope with both, particularly as the issues of newcomers and non-nationals are intertwined. Both groups deserve to be properly considered, as both groups deserve to know which rights they have and can expect to have and which facilities they can use. At the same time, both groups should also be made aware of their responsibilities and obligations. There are no rights without responsibilities, and vice versa, there are no duties without rights. In the case of Estonia, the authorities supported by the 'native' population have gone a long way to transform ideas and plans based on the 1949 Geneva (Red Cross) Conventions into modern legislation and attitudes which fall well within the realm of the modern 'European House'.

The Estonian Government and people deserve praise with respect to the efforts they have been taking at integration. It is now up to the potential beneficiaries of the fairly ambitious legislation and integration efforts to respond. Europe may wish to assist them, to make sure that the response is adequate. Chagall's work is about trust and communication amongst people. One day Chagall's atelier in Narva may be reopened. Artists from all over the world will want to work in that constructive environment. And they will smile at Estonia's 5 krooni banknote: it will be a global sun all right!

NON-CITIZENS AND MINORITIES IN ESTONIA AND THEIR ECONOMIC AND SOCIAL OPPORTUNITIES

by Fernand de Varennes

1. INTRODUCTION

This article does not attempt to provide a comprehensive description of how Estonia's various minorities are faring economically since that country's return to independence. It will, however, try to outline why and how the situation in this Baltic country involves a number of issues in international law and human rights.

A large segment of the population of Estonia which happens to be mainly composed of members of linguistic or ethnic minorities would seem to find itself in disadvantaged economic positions because of a series of restrictions or prohibitions due either to their status as non-citizens or because of language requirements.

Although these restrictions or results are sometimes described in political and other circles as unfortunate or undesirable, this fails to appreciate that the situation in Estonia (as well as Latvia and a number of other countries) also involves potential violations of international law.

What will be considered more specifically is whether the various exclusions and restrictions which large numbers of individuals belonging to linguistic or ethnic minorities have to endure in the economic field could constitute a prohibited form of discrimination under international treaties such as the International Covenant on Civil and Political Rights,[1] which Estonia acceded to on 21 October 1991.

Although an attempt has been made to ensure that references to the situation in Estonia are up to date, it must be pointed out that there may have been recent legislative or administrative changes.

---

[1] Adopted by UN General Assembly Resolution 2200A (XXI) which entered into force on 23 March 1976 (999 UNTS 171).

S. Trifunovska (Ed.), Minorities in Europe – Croatia, Estonia and Slovakia

2. PRELIMINARY HUMAN RIGHTS ISSUES

2.1 Naturalization, denial of citizenship and discrimination in international law

There is not in international law or European law a 'right to a specific citizenship' as such, although statelessness must be avoided. But it is no longer true that in international law citizenship is an absolutely sovereign matter to the exclusion of any 'outside' interference. While such a position is still maintained in some circles, in legal terms it is more appropriate to say that the adoption of rules and regulations concerning nationality is a matter which is subject to the sovereignty of individual States, as is the decision whether or not to even have a naturalisation process, but subject to any applicable international norms, including international human rights. Somehow, many experts seem to have forgotten that such limitations on the exercise of such sovereignty have been recognised in international law since before the Second World War, and even before the creation of the United Nations' predecessor, the League of Nations. This is demonstrated, for example, by Article 1 of the Convention on Certain Questions relating to the Conflict of Nationality Laws:

> 'It is for each state to determine under its own law who are its nationals. This law shall be recognised by other States in so far as it is consistent with international conventions, international custom, and principles of law generally recognised with regard to nationality.'

As the First Committee for the Codification of International Law indicated in its Report on Nationality, it was clearly understood almost 70 years ago that the naturalisation and citizenship rules or laws of a State must conform with any applicable international law, including a State's human rights obligations under treaty or customary law:

> '... although nationality is primarily a matter for the municipal law of each state, it is nevertheless governed to a large extent by principles of international law.'[2]

While States obviously have a great deal of latitude in the rules they adopt for naturalisation purposes, there are nevertheless international human rights that may be applicable and which would restrict a State's conduct in these matters. More precisely, non-discrimination under Article 26 of the International Covenant on Civil and Political Rights affects all areas of State activity, including

[2] League of Nations, Acts of the Conference for the Codification of International law, V.I. Plenary Meetings, 1930, p. 69.

naturalisation.[3] There is also under the Convention on the Reduction of Statelessness an obligation on signatory States to avoid creating situations of statelessness.

Furthermore, there is now a fairly strong legal consensus that children born in Estonia who would otherwise become stateless must be granted Estonian citizenship under Article 7(2) of the Convention on the Rights of the Child which reads:

> '1. The child shall be registered immediately after birth and shall have the right from birth to a name, the right to acquire a nationality and, as far as possible, the right to know and be cared for by his or her parents.
> 2. State Parties shall ensure the implementation of these rights in accordance with their national law and their obligations under the relevant international instruments in this field, in particular when the child would otherwise be stateless.'

The observations of Special Rapporteur Garretón on the situation in former Zaire is also arguably applicable to other situations of persons belonging to specific minorities being denied citizenship *en masse*:

> '129. Deputy Prime Minister Kamanda is right in maintaining, in a letter to the United Nations Security Council dated 24 October, that the adoption of rules and regulations concerning nationality is a matter subject to the sovereignty of individual States. Nevertheless, the Special Rapporteur considers that international human rights norms place limitations on the exercise of such sovereignty. The Convention on Certain Questions relating to the Conflict of Nationality Laws (The Hague, 12 April 1930) requires States Parties to recognize the laws of other States "in so far as (they are) consistent with (the) conventions" and principles of international law.
> 130. The first limitation concerns the principle of non-discrimination, which is the basis for all international human rights law and is exemplified by article 55 of the Charter of the United Nations, article 2 of the Universal Declaration of Human Rights, article 2.1 of the International Covenant on Civil and Political Rights, article 5 of the International Convention on the Elimination of All Forms of Racial Discrimination and article 2 of the African Charter on Human and Peoples' Rights.
> 131. It is discriminatory to deprive a person of his nationality for any cause other than treason or to do so only in respect of the members of two tribes because of events that occurred over 100 years ago.
> 132. The second limitation is to be found in article 12 of the International Covenant on Civil and Political Rights and article 12.2 of the African Charter on Human and Peoples' Rights, which establish the right to reside in and return to one's own country. Since this right may be invoked only by the nationals of a country, revocation of nationality implies loss of the exercise of that right. Normally – and the case of Zaire is

[3] This observation does not apply to Europe. The Convention for the Protection of Human Rights and Fundamental Freedoms (213 UNTS 222) is more restrictive than international law in its prohibition of discrimination since it does not have a general non-discrimination clause as does the ICCPR. Nor does it recognise a right to nationality to which its more restrictive non-discrimination clause (Art. 14) could apply, as is the case under the American Convention on Human Rights (OAS Treaty Series No. 36, 1144 UNTS 123, entered into force July 18, 1978).

> an obvious example – persons deprived of their nationality neither have, nor acquire, another; as a result, such persons are left without the protection of any State.
> 133. The third limitation stems from articles 1 and 8 of the 1961 Convention on the Reduction of Statelessness, the principles of which may be considered as customary international law and under which Zaire has the obligation to recognize as Zairian anyone born in its territory...'[4]

It is not suggested here that international law such as the one prohibiting discrimination automatically prevents a State from imposing certain types of naturalisation criteria. That is obviously not possible, nor even desirable. However, any naturalisation rule or requirement that would constitute discrimination in international law, or which would result in situations of statelessness as proscribed in the Convention on the Reduction of Statelessness, is quite clearly prohibited.

In practical terms, one would say for example that international law does not in every situation prohibit naturalisation criteria requiring some degree of knowledge of a State's official language. However, there may be circumstances in a State where only permitting naturalisation if an individual knows the official language could be discriminatory if it 'operates in a vacuum' in relation to the social reality of the State.

Those last words were used in an international judicial decision delivered by the Inter-American Court of Human Rights where it was suggested that linguistic requirements for naturalisation can in some situations be discriminatory, if they are 'unreasonable'. It would seem that if large numbers of people living in a country do not know the official language, then the naturalisation rules should also reflect this reality and permit the acquisition of citizenship with knowledge of the other main languages spoken in the country.[5] In other words, if large numbers of people in a State speak a language other than the official language, it may be necessary to permit naturalisation in one or more additional languages, as is the case in the UK, where knowledge of Gaelic or Welsh can be a 'substitute' for knowledge of English.

The current handling of the naturalisation, or rather the 'non-naturalisation', process of many members of the Russian-speaking minority in countries such as Estonia is obviously causing unease in international circles. In a letter to the Estonian Government dated 6 April 1993, the High Commissioner for National Minorities of the OSCE, Max van der Stoel, invoked a number of international legal instruments to urge Estonia to reduce statelessness. A similar letter was sent on the same date to the Government of Latvia. In other words, there is the suggestion that the refusal to grant citizenship to individuals belonging to linguistic or ethnic minorities who were born in these countries but who are stateless mainly

---

[4] UN Doc. E/CN.4/1997/6/Add.2 (2 April 1997) – Report on the situation of human rights in Zaire.

[5] *Costa Rican Naturalisation* case (No. OC-4/84 Advisory Opinion of 19 January 1984).

because of the language requirements is probably contrary to international law.[6]

The 1993 UNHCR report on 'Nationality Laws in former USSR Republics' also concludes that, pursuant to the Convention on the Reduction of Statelessness, Estonia must grant its citizenship to those stateless residents born on its territory.[7]

In 1995 the United Nations Human Rights Committee regarded as intolerable the non-citizenship of 28 per cent of the population and their exclusion from holding public office.

2.2 Non-citizenship and breaches of international human rights law: root causes of economic handicaps and hardships

It is important to raise the issue of citizenship in order to better appreciate that the various economic impediments and disadvantages encountered by many members of linguistic or ethnic minorities in Estonia are not simply 'unfortunate'.

To a large degree, the restrictions or obstacles that non-citizens are subjected to in the economic field could arguably be said to flow from Estonia's breaches of international law dealing with non-discrimination and/or statelessness. It is the failure to uphold these human rights, more than anything else, that can be said to be responsible for the unfortunate situation described in section 3 of this paper. As one author points out, one of the simplest ways of denying social and economic benefits to a group of individuals is to deny them citizenship, since 'full-fledged citizenship affords the most reliable surety of the enjoyment of the ensemble of social rights practiced in a particular community.'[8]

2.3 Can differences of treatment between citizens and non-citizens in economic activities constitute discrimination in international law?

There is no doubt that governments can validly make distinctions between its own citizens and non-citizens in a number of areas (as is indirectly acknowledged, for example, in the wording of Article 25 of the International Covenant on Civil and Political Rights: 'Every citizen shall have the right to vote . . .'). This does not mean, however, that any or all such distinctions will be valid in international law. As indicated earlier, there is now under international law a general

---

[6] The High Commissioner recommended that children born in Estonia who would otherwise become stateless should be granted Estonian citizenship, also taking into account Article 3, paragraph 6, of the Estonian Citizenship Act, Article 24, paragraph 3, of the International Covenant on Civil and Political Rights, and Article 7, paragraph 2, of the Convention on the Rights of the Child.

[7] On 14 April 1992, Latvia acceded to the Convention on the Reduction of Statelessness.

[8] G. Ginsburgs, 'The Citizenship in the Baltic Republics', 21 *Journal of Baltic Studies* (1990) No. 1, at p. 14.

non-discrimination principle which must be respected in all areas of State activities or involvement, and this non-discrimination principle now also applies to distinctions between citizens and non-citizens.

This is the conclusion reached by the United Nations Human Rights Committee in a series of recent decisions involving non-citizens and the Czech Republic. In that case, only citizens who were permanent residents of the Czech Republic were entitled to restitution of property or compensation for its loss following confiscation by the Czechoslovak Government in 1949.[9]

The Human Rights Committee concluded, after considering all the relevant factors, that the difference of treatment between non-citizens and citizens in those particular cases was unreasonable, given the historical context of the events involved. In other words, it was discriminatory to restrict the advantages and benefits of compensation or restitution of property to citizens, as well as incompatible with the international human rights recognised in the International Covenant on Civil and Political Rights to require Czech citizenship in order for these individuals to receive the confiscated property or compensation.

There are also other national decisions indicating, for example, that limiting certain types of employment to individuals who are citizens of a State could also be a form of discrimination in some cases, such as those involving permanent residents.[10]

The same conclusions seem generally to have been reached in the European context:

> 'Both national and international law attribute certain rights and duties to the citizenship of a person which have become more clearly defined through international conventions and the development of international case law.
> As a result, certain minimum-standards concerning the treatment of non-citizens have developed which now form part of conventions and international standards.
> An important objective in the development of international law in terms of non-citizen and minority populations has been to promote integration and democratic processes through participation in public life based on the principles of non-discrimination. In this sense, international law is based on the assumption that it is in the interest of both citizens and non-citizens that discriminatory measures towards non-citizens are as few as possible in order to facilitate harmonious coexistence among residents and peaceful coexistence between neighboring countries.

---

[9] *Simunek, Hastings, Tuzilova and Prochazka* v. *The Czech Republic*, Communication No. 516/1992, UN Doc. CCPR/C/54/D/516/1992 (1995) and *Josef Frank Adam* v. *The Czech Republic*, Communication No. 586/1994, UN Doc. CCPR/C/57/D/586/1994 (1996).

[10] See for example *Andrews* v. *Law Society of British Columbia*, (1989) 1 S.C.R, where the Canadian Supreme Court concluded that it was unjustified, and therefore it amounted to discrimination, to require citizenship for admission to the bar to practice law with respect to qualified Canadian permanent residents who are not citizens, as well as generally the Annex III of the June 1996-June 1997 Annual Report of the Commissioner of the Council of the Baltic States on Democratic Institutions and Human Rights, Including the Rights of Persons belonging to Minorities.

Principles of non-discrimination have been laid down in various international conventions as legally binding rules, and important standards have been established, e.g. within the UN, the Council of Europe, the OSCE and the European Union.'[11]

2.4 Use of minority languages in private economic activities

The issue of government measures affecting the use of a minority language in private business activities is largely unexplored in international law, although there are a number of decisions and comments at the United Nations and European levels, as well as in national decisions.

Commenting on the Language Law of the Estonian Soviet Socialist Republic adopted in 1989, Special Rapporteurs Raimo Pekkanen and Hans Danelius indicated that they had grave reservations as to provisions which seemed to make it possible for the Government to restrict the private use of language in business affairs:

> '. . . the legislator ought to be more cautious in imposing language requirements in private relationships, including private business. It may be assumed that the private persons or institutions concerned are best suited to decide themselves in what language they should conduct their mutual communications and the legislator should not, as a rule, interfere with their freedom in this regard . . . '[12]

More to the point in terms of actual legal standards, the United Nations Human Rights Committee unambiguously linked freedom of expression with the right to conduct private business activities in the language of one's choice in *Ballantyne, Davidson and McIntyre* v. *Canada.*[13]

At issue were provisions of the Quebec *Charte de la langue française*, which, in most situations, made French the exclusive language of outdoor commercial signs. In *Ballantyne, Davidson and McIntyre* v. *Canada,*[14] the authors were English-speaking residents of the Province of Quebec who claimed that the prohibition against using any language other than French on outdoor commercial signs or in a firm's name infringed upon their freedom of expression, guaranteed by Article 19 of the International Covenant on Civil and Political Rights.

---

[11] The Commissioner of the Council of the Baltic Sea States on Democratic Institutions and Human Rights, including the Rights of Persons belonging to Minorities, 'Rights of Non-citizens Residing Legally in the Member States of the CBSS – Part 2, Right of Association, Access to Civil Service and to other special posts or work', March 1998, Survey results reproduced at http://www.cbss-commissioner.org/surveys/survey9.htm.

[12] Raimo Pekkanen and Hans Danelius, Special Rapporteurs, 'Human Rights in the Republic of Estonia', 13 *Human Rights Law Journal* (1991), No. 5-6, pp. 236-256, at p. 241.

[13] Communication Nos. 359/1989 and 385/1989, 31 March 1993.

[14] *Supra.*

The Committee rejected Quebec's attempts to restrict the authors' freedom of expression. The Committee stated that Article 19(2) of the Covenant applies not only to ideas and subjective opinions which can be transmitted to others,[15] but also to any news or information, any expression, any commercial publicity or signs, and to any work of art. In other words, the Committee squarely rejected any attempt at limiting freedom of expression to a narrow field of activity such as political, cultural or artistic expression. The Committee also rejected the argument that commercial expression was somehow less worthy of protection under the Covenant, and that in such cases governments should have wider discretion in deciding what restrictions were appropriate or necessary in their country.

The Government of Quebec also contended that its provisions were necessary and reasonable in order to protect the French language in the province. In response, the Committee pointed out that Article 19 of the Covenant only permits restrictions on freedom of expression which are provided by law and necessary either to respect the reputations of others, or to protect national security, public order, health or morals. Although clearly 'provided by law', the language restrictions relating to outdoor commercial signs in Quebec were unnecessary, according to the Committee, because they protected neither the rights of other individuals, nor public order, health or morals. Furthermore, even if the restrictions were valid based upon Article 19(2)(a) or (b), the Government would have had to establish that they were justified. The Government of Quebec had made no attempt to do so as regards the provisions of the *Charte de la langue française*, beyond claiming that they were simply reasonable.

Although it was not strictly required in order to support its decision, the Committee acknowledged that the Government could validly seek to protect the French language in Quebec. It recognised that whilst a State may choose one or more official languages, it may not simply ban the use of non-official languages, at least as it relates to non-governmental services or activities. In essence, the Committee recognised that in an entirely non-governmental realm, any attempt at restricting an individual's language choice clearly violates that individual's freedom of expression.

There have also been other decisions at the national level that are relevant when discussing the use of language in private economic activities. The United States Supreme Court concluded in *Yu Cong Eng* v. *Trinidad*[16] that the government requirement that all merchants – regardless of their situation – keep their

---

[15] The Human Rights Committee added that the ideas and subjective opinions that Art. 19(2) protects must not contravene the provisions of Art. 20 of the Covenant which permit restrictions on the right to freedom of expression when it advocates violence, hatred or war. Art. 20 states:

'1. Any propaganda for war shall be prohibited by law.

2. Any advocacy of national, racial or religious hatred that constitutes incitement to discrimination, hostility or violence shall be prohibited by law.'

[16] 271 U.S. 500 (1926).

books in English, Spanish, or in a local dialect, in some cases prevented the use of the Chinese language for the conduct of private business activities and constituted a denial of the equal protection of the laws, in other words it was a form of prohibited discrimination.

In Canada, the Supreme Court also commented that it is not a violation of freedom of expression nor is it (in that particular case) unreasonable and discriminatory for the Quebec Government to require the joint use of French and one's preferred language in private business activities and administration. Canada's highest court reviewed Articles 52 and 57 of the *Charte de la langue française* in *Devine* v. *Québec*.[17] Those provisions required that business documents and reports be maintained in French, in addition to any other language chosen by private parties. Although individuals were all subjected to the same legislation, the Supreme Court of Canada pointed out that different individuals would be facing differential treatment on the ground of language, as those having French as their primary language would continue to use a single language in their affairs, whereas other individuals having another primary language would likely find themselves obliged to keep documents in two languages. However, because the latter were entitled to use their own language, in addition to French, the Supreme Court concluded that the measure, although constituting a minor violation of the right to non-discrimination, was not an unjustified, nor unreasonable, legislation:

> 'En veillant à ce que les non-francophones puissent rédiger des formulaires de demandes d'emploi, des bons de commandes, des factures, des reçus et des quittances dans la langue de leur choix, de pair avec le français, l'article 57 interprété conjointement avec l'article 89, crée, tout au plus, une atteinte minimale aux droits à l'égalité. Bien que, comme l'appelante l'a soutenu, l'exigence de l'usage concurrent du français puisse créer un fardeau additionnel pour les marchands et les commerçants non francophones, il n'y a rien qui porte atteinte à leur capacité d'utiliser également une autre langue. Par conséquent, notre conclusion concernant l'application de l'article premier demeure même si, à première vue, la violation en cause de la Charte canadienne est une violation de l'article 15.'[18]

From all of the above, a number of general observations can be made as to the status of relevant international law provisions dealing with the use of a minority language in private business activities:

1. The absolute prohibition of the use of any language in private activities such as in business would constitute a breach of freedom of expression and could probably be discriminatory.

---

[17] (1988) 2 S.C.R. 790 (Canada).

[18] Ibid., at p. 820.

2. The prohibition of the use of a minority language in private activities such as business would in addition constitute a breach of Article 27 of the International Covenant on Civil and Political Rights and similar provisions if private business activities involve the use of a minority language 'with other members of their community'.

3. Public authorities may legitimately require the use of the official language in the administration of private businesses jointly with the preferred language(s) of the individual or enterprise.

4. The preceding statement does not permit State authorities to impose the use of an official language that would in practice be too onerous or otherwise frustrate the private use of a non-official language in the administration of private business. If the requirements of the public authorities are unreasonable or arbitrary,[19] or would render the joint use of the official and minority language not possible or practical, these could be deemed to be discriminatory, or in the latter situation a breach of freedom of expression.

A State may have a variety of legitimate reasons for promoting the use of the official or national language: to ensure that it serves as a unifying bond within the State, to give the official language the appropriate standing and recognition it deserves in the private and public spheres, or even perhaps to correct some of the unjust and oppressive policies that were in place in the past and which affected the use of the official language in a negative way. All of these are legitimate considerations, but they do not permit 'restrictions' on the private use of language in the business sphere that amount to breaches of freedom of expression or non-discrimination, or the right of members of linguistic minorities to use their language amongst themselves.

[19] For example, one could argue that if public authorities required that the administration of a private business composed of only one or two individuals such as a 'mom and pop' store be required to operate in the official language, in essence meaning that its owners must be fluent in the official language or else hire an employee who is, this would be a very heavy burden in financial terms given the size of the enterprise. Such a policy would be clearly strongly disadvantageous for small private businesses, but no serious hardship for larger companies. The former could be seen as discriminatory in the case of the small business because of the unreasonable demands, but a quite reasonable requirement for larger businesses. In short, as is the case in many jurisdictions such as Quebec which has adopted legislation in the area of language use in the administration of private businesses, 'practicality' requires a policy that takes such factors into consideration. A non-discriminatory approach could require, for example, that private businesses with more than fifty employees must be administered in the official language and any other language(s) of preference. Most of the requirements involving the joint use of French in Quebec in the administration of private businesses only applies where there are more than 50, or even 100 employees under the *Charte de la langue française*. In Finland, legislation is silent as to any such requirements, except for Art. 11 of the Act on Cooperation in Business Enterprises (1969) which requires that employers in bilingual districts must provide to the delegate of their employees information on certain aspects of the affairs of the business in the minority language if there are at least 10 employees or 10% of the personnel who are members of the linguistic minority.

As long as not excluding or restricting the use of other languages in the administration of private businesses, nor requiring the use of the official language to such an extent as to amount to an unreasonable burden which would constitute discrimination or a breach of freedom of expression, official language and minority language can coexist peacefully under present existing standards.[20] The proper balance seems to be the one expressed in one document where it is stated:

> '12. All persons, including persons belonging to national minorities, have the right to operate private enterprises in the language or languages of their choice. The State may require the additional use of the official language or languages of the State only where a legitimate public interest can be demonstrated, such as interests relating to the protection of workers or consumers, or in dealings between the enterprise and governmental authorities.'[21]

3. THE SITUATION IN ESTONIA

It is in the interest of both citizens and non-citizens and of the countries concerned that discriminatory measures towards non-citizens are as few as possible in order to establish friendly relations between the countries and harmonious coexistence among the residents.[22]

3.1 The demographic context

In 1997 there were between 200,000 and 300,000 stateless persons residing in Estonia, representing about 20 or 25% of the population living in this country. These are for the most part individuals who are also members of a linguistic or ethnic minority, many of which have been born in Estonia. Most of them do not qualify for citizenship because they do no have a sufficient mastery of the official language, Estonian. There are also another 100,000 or so who are not citizens of

---

[20] To illustrate this point further, a government may have valid goals and legitimate interests in promoting and protecting the official language in the private and public spheres of society. The requirement of using the official language in a number of areas of the administration of a private business in mid to large-sized commercial activities (50 employees or more) would not be discriminatory or in breach of freedom of expression if the use of other languages is not forbidden. Nevertheless, the same type of legislation, whilst not in breach of freedom of expression, could be discriminatory if it also applied to the administration of smaller commercial businesses because it would be an unreasonable burden for them in financial or human terms, despite the legitimate goal of promoting and protecting the official language.

[21] The Oslo Recommendations Regarding the Linguistic Rights of National Minorities, Foundation on Inter-Ethnic Relations, The Hague, February 1998. The Foundation prepared the recommendations at the request of the OSCE High Commissioner for National Minorities.

[22] Annual Report May 1995-June 1996, The Commissioner of the Council of the Baltic Sea States on Democratic Institutions and Human Rights, including the Rights of Persons belonging to Minorities, Section 2.6.

Estonia but hold Russian or Ukrainian citizenship. Once again, many have been born in Estonia but cannot become citizens because of the country's language requirement. This represents more than a third of the population of Estonia, mainly composed of members of the Russian-speaking or Ukrainian minorities.

3.2 Discrimination affecting mainly minorities through denial of access to employment and labour markets to non-citizens residing legally in Estonia

3.2.1 *Employment in the public sphere*

Legally speaking, it appears that all positions in State and local government must be filled by Estonian citizens, although the Estonian Constitution under Article 30 allows such positions to be filled by citizens of foreign States or stateless persons in exceptional situations. The Law on Public Service apparently does not foresee the possibility for non-citizens to be employed as civil servants (Articles 14 and 15), although some temporary exceptions still exist (Article 169).

Precise information on what has actually occurred is difficult to obtain. One source states that in a number of key sectors, the deadlines set by the Law on Public Service were extended when it became apparent that many non-citizens would be dismissed if they did not obtain citizenship. There were situations such as in the town of Ida-Virumaa where most of the police and many local government officials should have been dismissed from their jobs.

Unfortunately, there have been few press reports about the actual outcome of this situation. Some individuals must have received citizenship, but it seems likely because of the relatively low levels of naturalization (mainly due to the inability to satisfy the naturalization language requirements) that most have not complied, even when new rules extended the deadlines to 1998.

The economic consequences of these restrictions can of course be quite serious. Although there may undoubtedly be individual exceptions, it means that about 25% of the population which are residents of Estonia are essentially excluded from certain types of employment which they may be eminently qualified to occupy, and may have occupied until recently.

Economically speaking, this suggests an increase in State-induced unemployment of individuals who would have been civil servants until the Law on Public Service comes into effect, possibly sometime this year. There appears to be confirmation from a number of independent and reliable sources confirming that unemployment rates are higher for individuals who are members of the Russian-speaking minority. The United Nations Development Programme's 1996 Estonian Human Development Report indicates, for example, that 'Unemployment rates among men and women of Russian ancestry was decidedly higher than among native Estonians.'

Furthermore, the 1995 Law on Language establishes three levels of Estonian-language proficiency for public service jobs, according to the degree of responsibility and contact with the public that each position requires. According to the law, a civil servant who did not attend an Estonian-language middle school or high school must take an examination to determine if his level of fluency meets the language requirements for the position he holds. The law also establishes a language inspectorate to check on public servants with suspect language skills and to fine employers who hire Russian-speaking individuals who speak Estonian only haltingly.

In economic terms, this means that even members of the Russian minority who have passed the citizenship hurdle can find themselves excluded from employment opportunities. In 1997 there were reports of a Russian-speaking judge and other justice officials who were not only dismissed from their positions but also prosecuted for having certificates which exaggerated their Estonian language proficiency.

3.2.2 *Employment in the private sphere*

There is anecdotal information that because resident non-citizens are being excluded from civil service jobs, many are concentrating, and are becoming more successful than citizens, in the area of private commercial ventures. However, at the same time another recent report suggested that there are still high levels of unemployment among resident non-citizens, who are of course mainly members of the Russian-speaking minority:

> 'Non-possession of Estonian citizenship makes the Russian-speaking population perceive constant insecurity. 70% of stateless non-Estonians and almost half of Russian citizens claim it [to be] the underlying reason why they experience greater difficulties in finding a job. Furthermore, they are more worried about their children's future, with their own being equally problematic.'[23]

Until just a few months ago, members of minorities who were not citizens could not work as seamen, or had difficulty in continuing their jobs because of a decree adopted in November 1994 which made it more difficult for non-citizens to obtain 'seaman's passports'. The Constitutional Review Tribunal of Estonia ruled this May that the decree was unconstitutional on a narrow constitutional basis (i.e., that the type of restriction required a legislative act rather than a decree), but it is possible that the Government could adopt a law to circumvent the constitutional argument. If that occurs, this will of course impact on the economic oppor-

[23] Tartu University Market Research Team, Estonia's Experiment – The Possibilities to Integrate Non-Citizens Into the Estonian Society, Tallinn 1997. The report can be found at http://www.oef.org.ee/.

tunities of seamen who are mainly members of minorities.

But it is not only the absence of citizenship which may result in economic difficulties for members of linguistic or ethnic minorities. In addition, since many if not most members of the Russian-speaking minority have little or no fluency in the Estonian language, they will also be excluded from other employment opportunities, with consequent economic difficulties associated with periodic or long-term unemployment. The 1989 Language Law of Estonia, and guidelines for its implementation, required a certain degree of fluency in Estonian in order to occupy or maintain most retail and service jobs.

Statistics that are available, although incomplete, do appear to suggest that there may be an ominous economic effect caused by the exclusion from or increased difficulty in obtaining certain categories of jobs for non-citizens and those with limited or no knowledge of Estonian. A 1993 UN report indicated:

> 'Unemployment has been increasing, particularly in the north-east, where the ethnic Russian minority is predominant. Apparently 20 to 25 percent of the workforce in the north-east are unemployed. Owing to the limited resources of the state and local authorities, no retraining programme for the unemployed appears to have been organised.'[24]

According to another UN document, the official national unemployment rate (recipients of unemployment benefits/population of working age) in Estonia as of 1 May 1993 was only 2.4%.[25] However, it would seem reasonable to assume that much of the unemployment in the north-east of Estonia may be due to its large concentration of heavy industry, mostly linked to the recession of the former all-Union enterprises, which has experienced major difficulties since the break-up of the Soviet Union. Other reports suggest that in addition to higher unemployment, or perhaps because of it, regions with a larger Russian-speaking population also have higher crime rates.[26] Despite this, it seems government policies in the language area has also been a factor in increasing the unemployment rates of some ethnic minority members as has admitted a UNDP report:

---

[24] *Situation of Human Rights in Estonia and Latvia*, Report of the Secretary-General, UN Doc. A/48/511, 26 October 1993, at para. 77. One should note that much of this increased unemployment in the north-east may be due to closures and reduced workforces in certain industrial sectors.

[25] Core document forming part of the reports of States Parties: Estonia 09/11/94. HRI/CORE/1/Add.50.

[26] Ethnopolicy Working Group, *Population Development and Ethnic Composition*, Institute of International and Social Studies, Tallinn Pedagogical University, available at http://www.ciesin.ee/undp/nhdr/Box81.html.

> 'The cultural-religious influence on the developmental differences and the degree of economic initiative should also be pointed out. The Eastern counties bordering Lake Peipsi and the North-eastern industrial zone, where the population is overwhelmingly non-Estonian and adheres to the Russian Orthodox religion, are also the areas which manifest a considerable amount of illegal activity, distanced from official structures. . .'

> 'Unemployment is also much higher in the single-factory towns, which have failed to reorient towards new markets, due to the incompetence in management or other factors. High unemployment can also be noticed in the cities of Narva, Sillamäe and Maardu. One of the obvious factors, besides adjustment problems of local enterprises, is the limited competitiveness of the local population in the labour market due to their inadequate command of the Estonian language. They subsist on welfare and unemployed benefits. Ethno-cultural differences are also a factor in contributing to unemployment in these towns, where the majority of residents are members of ethnic minorities.'[27]

In June 1996, the Estonian Government also defined the duties of the National Language Board (Keeleamet), including the power to fine State institutions as well as private companies for having employees whose language is not up to par. Language proficiency requirements have also been incorporated into Estonia's labour legislation, making it an offence to hire people for a whole range of jobs without proper language credentials. Fines can range from approximately US $20 for companies to $100 for State institutions. While it is too early to objectively assess the economic consequences of these measures, they suggest other obstacles which would tend to increase the economic costs and difficulties, as well as employment opportunities for non-Estonian speaking minorities, and especially those who are Russian-speaking.

3.3 **Other forms of exclusions**

In a 1993 United Nations report on the situation of human rights in Estonia, it was pointed out that the Russian Orthodox Church of Estonia was prohibited by the Estonian Department of Religious Affairs from engaging in commercial activities. It is not known at this time whether this restriction is still in place.[28]

With regard to property rights, Article 32 of the Constitution of Estonia states that the law may establish, in the public interest, categories of property in Estonia which are reserved for ownership by Estonian citizens. In practice, this would seem to have permitted the adoption of legislation that excludes mainly members of the Russian-speaking minority who happen to be mainly non-citizens. The UN Human Rights Committee recently noted that numerous rights and prerogatives, such as the right to participate in the process of land privatisation, as well as the previously noted right to occupy certain posts or practise some occupations, were granted solely to Estonian citizens. The Committee was of the opinion that permanent residents who are non-citizens were thus deprived of a number of rights under the Covenant, presumably because it probably involved discriminatory treatment, the Committee emphasising that 'all provisions in domestic law dis-

---

[27] UNDP Report 1996 at http://www.ciesin.ee/undp/nhdr96/eng/chap4.html.

[28] *Situation of Human Rights in Estonia and Latvia*, Report of the Secretary General, UN Doc. A/48/511, 26 October 1993.

criminating against non-citizens be systematically reviewed and brought into line with articles 2 and 26 of the Covenant'.[29]

There are apparently 'administrative' difficulties where individuals may also find it difficult to obtain the status of permanent resident which subsequently leads to a number of other problems. There are reports of refusals, for example, in the case of students who have returned after their studies abroad and who had been discharged of their residence permit in Estonia temporarily for the period of their study, those who came to Estonia before the introduction of visas and the Law on Aliens, and those who have a place of residence but not a residence registration in the former Estonian Soviet Socialist Republic in their passport, i.e., the so-called 'illegals'.

For these and others, difficulties or refusals affecting their status may lead to serious economic and other consequences. People who might not have been granted a permanent residence permit are likely to encounter hardships in getting employment permits, welfare benefits, loans, medical insurance and privatising their living premises.

The Legal Information Centre for Human Rights based in Tallinn has reported that it had received a number of requests for assistance in relation to difficulties in obtaining residence permits, social benefits, employment, welfare, loans, etc., connected to the determination of residency status which, of course, involves almost exclusively those who are members of certain minorities.

In November 1997, the Estonian Parliament had even passed amendments which would have allowed government officials to regulate the use of Estonian in the private sector, including economic activities such as private businesses. Quite clearly, such language restrictions would have led to limitations of opportunities for non-Estonians (even if they were citizens) in private businesses and other economic activities. Fortunately, President Lennart Meri refused to sign the amendments.

President Meri referred the issue of whether the amendments violated the Constitution of Estonia to the National Court, which ruled in 1998 that the amendments were unconstitutional. Nevertheless, it is likely that the issue will resurface, given the strong showing of the nationalist parties in the 3 October 1998 elections.

On 13 February 1999 amendments to the State language and other laws were promulgated which require proficiency in the Estonian language for many categories of employment in the services sector – both private and public. They further increase the economic disadvantages for members of minorities, regardless of their citizenship status. According to a IOM-UNDP survey of November 1996 which included a question regarding knowledge of the Estonian language, only

---

[29] Annual Report of the Human Rights Committee, 13 April 1997, UN Doc. A/51/40, paras. 111 and 124.

9% of those polled stated that their knowledge of Estonian is excellent; 16.4% that it is very good or good. But 36.4% stated that their knowledge is poor and 18.2% admitted that they have no knowledge at all; 28% consider their knowledge to be fair.

4. CONCLUSIONS

> 'Citizenship has not received the publicity of other changes in the post-Communist world, such as economic transition or the development and evolution of ruling institutions. Yet, citizenship can affect voting, occupation and residence, and can create tensions between those who receive it and those who do not.'[30]

The economic situation of individuals who belong to linguistic minorities in Estonia clearly appears to be worse than that of so-called 'ethnic' Estonians. Although there are a number of factors which undoubtedly contribute to the situation, it would seem that the Estonian Government's language and citizenship policies and requirements are contributing directly to the higher levels of unemployment amongst Russian-speaking individuals. While in a general sense citizenship or language requirements do not automatically involve breaches of international law standards, it is more than likely that some of Estonia's measures and requirements which impose barriers in terms of eligibility for certain categories of employment, or restrictions affecting private business activities may be discriminatory or contrary to freedom of expression, to name but a few human rights that are relevant.

---

[30] Barrington and Lowell, 'Nations, States and Citizens: An Explanation of the Citizenship Policies in Estonia and Lithuania', 21 *Review of Central and Eastern European Law* (1995), p. 103.

Part Three – Minorities in Slovakia

MINORITIES AND POLITICS IN THE SLOVAK REPUBLIC

by Karen Henderson

1. INTRODUCTION

Many analyses of the situation of minorities in the Slovak Republic are based on a discussion of legal criteria. The reason for this is simple: when arguing about minority rights, a State's legal framework, and its implementation in practice, can be evaluated by objective criteria which allow for comparison between different countries. When the international community criticises a State's attitude towards minorities, it is very difficult to proceed on any other basis.[1] However, such a legalistic approach presents considerable problems when dealing with the Slovak case.

The first difficulty stems from the fact that Slovakia is one of the two successor States of Czechoslovakia, which was a rather exceptional country in the two most protracted periods of its existence. As an interwar democracy from 1918 to 1938, it provided one of the era's more enlightened regimes towards minorities. As a communist State from 1948 to 1989, it also had for much of the period a good record for tolerance of minority cultures when judged by the standards prevalent within the Soviet bloc. For example, both regimes in the main permitted members of the Hungarian minority to be educated in their own language and had systems which represented Hungarian-speakers in Parliament in approximate parity to their proportion of the overall population (although in the communist case this was not genuine interest representation).[2] As a consequence of this, while in many States contemporary

---

[1] The most fateful – though not the most severe – criticism of Slovak democracy, including Slovakia's treatment of minorities, came in the European Commission's opinion on Slovakia's application for membership of the European Union, which led in December 1997 to the temporary exclusion of Slovakia from the first group of countries to embark on detailed entry negotiations. See European Commission, 'Agenda 2000: Commission Opinion on Slovakia's Application for Membership of the European Union', *Bulletin of the European Union*, Supplement 9 (1997) pp. 15-20.

[2] For details of the education system in Slovakia, see Owen V. Johnson, *Slovakia 1918-1938: Education and the Making of a Nation*, New York: Columbia University Press (1985) (for the interwar period) and Edwin Bakker, *Minority Conflicts in Slovakia and Hungary?*, Capelle a/d IJssel, Netherlands: Labyrint (1997) pp. 72-5; for details on parliamentary representation in the interwar period, see Joseph Rothschild, *East Central Europe between the Two World Wars*, Seattle and London: University of Washington Press (1977) pp. 73-135, Oskar Krejčí, *Kniha o volbách*, Prague: Victoria Publishing (1994) pp. 134-155, and Eva Broklová, *Československá demokracie: politický systém ČSR 1918-1938*, Prague: Slon (1992).

S. Trifunovska (Ed.), Minorities in Europe – Croatia, Estonia and Slovakia

disputes over the treatment of minorities focus on aspirations to improve minority rights, in the Slovak Republic the major struggle has been to formalise, and prevent the erosion of, existing rights.

The second difficulty is directly linked to the first. Because the international community emphasises legal rights and legal norms, the Slovak Governments led by Vladimír Mečiar – and especially the third Mečiar Government from 1994 to 1998 – responded to this agenda and demanded that their stances towards minorities be judged by (often elusive) international 'standards' rather than by local factors determined by the aspirations of the largest, Hungarian minority. Consequently, the concept of *nadštandardné práva* (above-standard rights) was officially promoted: the situation in Slovakia could be defended if international norms were used as a yardstick simply because Slovakia's starting point was fairly respectable in international comparison. Slovaks therefore often counter-attacked against foreign criticism by claiming that the rights of minorities in their country were better than in many other democratic States – 'above standard' – and they could usually find examples to support this contention.

The final problem of employing legal norms in the Slovak case is that they make it hard to accommodate more intangible factors such as the general political climate and issues of trust within a State's political community. The focus of this contribution is not, therefore, so much an examination of the legal status and rights of minority communities, but rather the way that different interpretations of Slovak/minority relationships led to the often highly emotive disagreements which became a prominent item on the political agenda in the Slovakia of the 1990s. While international pressure has impacted on, and will continue to influence, political decision-making in Slovakia, the key factor in determining how well Slovakia functions as a multinational State will be relationships within Slovakia's own political community.

2. MINORITIES IN SLOVAKIA

Before examining the issue of national minorities in Slovakia, it is necessary to define which communities are the subject of discussion. Four major groups can be distinguished: the Hungarian minority; the Roma minority; ethnic Slovaks in southern Slovakia who are in a minority within the communities in which they live; and other minorities (e.g., Czech, Ruthene, German, Polish).

Since this paper concentrates on the political debates surrounding minority issues, it will concentrate on the first three categories, which have been the focus of such discussion. The position of the Hungarian minority, which is the largest, and also the most politically organised and articulate group, has attracted by far the most attention domestically and internationally. The Roma, who are numerically the second largest minority even in official statistics which are generally considered to under-represent them numerically, appear in a more diffuse fashion in political debate. They lack strong political representation able to articulate coherent communal demands through official channels in the parliamentary arena, but they appear prominently in domestic political debate, where they are portrayed almost exclusively as a social problem. They are also increasingly gaining in profile in international debate, because of both measured concern about their ability to exercise civil rights, and the enforced attention to the problems of their domestic situation occasioned by increasing emigration and asylum applications from the Roma since 1997.[3] The difficulties of Slovaks living in Hungarian communities, on the other hand, have been articulated almost entirely within domestic political debate, led by spokespeople of the more nationally oriented Slovak political parties. However, the emphasis placed on their situation by part of the Slovak political spectrum is sufficient to justify their inclusion in any discussion of minority issues in Slovakia. The issue is little discussed in the international arena, and yet critical to Slovak debates on minority issues. In the case of the fourth group listed – the smaller national minorities within Slovakia – their role in political debate has only been peripheral, both in terms of the organised articulation of community demands, and of general discussion by other domestic political actors, and of concern expressed by the international community. They appear in political debate largely in lists of minorities.

Table 1 *National composition of Slovakia.*

	1992		1996	
	Total at 31.12	%	Total at 31.12	%
Slovak	4,552,220	85.66	4,608,245	85.67
Hungarian	568,218	10.69	568,444	10.57
Roma	80,949	1.52	86,383	1.61
Czech, Moravian, Silesian	58,870	1.11	58,652	1.09
Ruthenian & Ukrainian	30,875	0.58	32,165	0.60
German	5,396	0.10	5,373	0.10
Polish	2,882	0.05	3,147	0.06
Russian	1,508	0.03	1,863	0.03
Other, not given	13,228	0.25	14,660	0.27
Total	5,314,155	100.00	5,378,932	100.00

Source: Štatistický úrad SR, *Štatistická ročenka Slovenskej republiky 1997*, Bratislava: VEDA vydavatelstvo Slovenskej akadémie vied (1997) p. 159.

[3] It could in fact be argued, in Hirschman's terminology, that Hungarians have exercised the 'voice' option, while Roma increasingly prefer 'exit'. See Albert O. Hirschman, 'Exit, Voice, and the Fate of the German Democratic Republic: An Essay in Conceptual History', 45 *World Politics* (1993) No. 2, pp. 173-202.

Basic data about the size of nationalities within Slovakia in the 1990s from the Statistical Office of the Slovak Republic (ŠÚ SR) are shown in Table 1. They suffer from a problem present in statistics throughout East-Central Europe in that they clearly underestimate the size of the Roma community. While there is little dispute about the fact that many Roma do not declare their nationality as such in official censuses and surveys, their real number is unclear. The European Commission's July 1997 opinion on Slovakia's application to join the European Union estimated that the Roma made up between 4.8% and 10% of the Slovak population,[4] while the Mečiar Government, in its official response to the Commission opinion, suggested that they comprised about 5% of the population.[5] The real argument, however, related to the total number of non-Slovaks in the country. The Commission stated that 'Minorities in Slovakia make up between 18% and 23% of the population',[6] since it had added the estimated real number of Roma to the officials figures for the other minorities (of which the Hungarians are by far the largest). The Slovak Government contested this, in part by misquoting the Commission:

> 'In the Opinion it is erroneously claimed that 18-23% of the population claim affiliation to an ethnic minority, of which the Roma constitute 4.8-10% of the population. This claim does not fit with reality. According to the last census, in the Slovak Republic 14.8% of citizens claim affiliation to an ethnic minority. At the last census 83,000 citizens claimed affiliation to Romany nationality, which is less than 1.5%. Of the almost 11% Hungarian ethnic minority, a large percentage belongs to the Romany minority.
> It is thought that within the Slovak Republic there are currently 280,000 persons of Romany ethnic origin, of which a large part currently claims affiliation to the Hungarian national minority and a smaller part to Slovak or Romany nationality.'[7]

The problem with the Slovak Government statement was threefold. First, the Commission had actually made no reference to the number of Slovak citizens who 'claimed' a certain affiliation (i.e., declared it in a census), but rather to the actual makeup of the country's population, which even the Slovak Government admitted to be different from census results. Secondly, no evidence was produced in support of the argument that a large part of Slovakia's 'undeclared' Roma had stated their nationality as Hungarian in censuses. Other statistics tend to suggest that, while some Roma certainly are Hungarian-speaking, this fact does not significantly affect the 'Hungarianness' of Slovakia. The 1991 Czechoslovak census showed that 10.8 per cent of the population of Slovakia claimed to be Hungarian

---

[4] European Commission, loc. cit. n. 1, p. 19.

[5] Ministry of Foreign Affairs of the Slovak Republic, *Slovak View on the Commission's Opinion on Slovakia's Application for Membership of the European Union* (28 August 1997) p. 13.

[6] European Commission, loc. cit. n. 1, p. 19.

[7] Ministry of Foreign Affairs of the Slovak Republic, op. cit. n. 5, p. 13.

and 1.4% Roma, while 11.5% gave Hungarian as their mother tongue and 1.5% Roma.[8] Coalitions of Hungarian parties have also tended to receive around 9% of the vote in Slovak elections throughout the 1990s.[9]

Thirdly, and perhaps most significantly, the Mečiar Government paid more attention to quantitative arguments about numbers than to the qualitative issues which caused what the European Commission termed 'tensions between the government and the Hungarian minority'.[10] It exploited the existence of a substantial Romany minority in Slovakia in order both to reduce the statistical size of the Hungarian community, and to conflate the Hungarian and Roma questions. The actual size of the minorities is less important to this study than the way statistics are politicised in public discourse. As with many contentions of nationally-minded Slovaks, the argument about the coincidence of Hungarian and Roma identity is particularly potent because it contains a portion of truth. It is likely that estimates of the percentage of Slovak citizens belonging to minorities which merely add the suspected number of Slovak Roma to the number of citizens declaring other minority membership do indeed overestimate the total size of the minority community by several percentage points.

The geographic distribution of members of national minorities is politically as important as their total numbers. The Hungarian minority in Slovakia is fairly compactly located in three areas in southern Slovakia proximate to Hungary, which is crucial to some of the Slovak fears relating to Hungarian demands for autonomy. Some 77.7% of the Slovak Hungarians live in 435 municipalities where Hungarians make up more than 50% of the population, and 90% of Hungarians live in 502 municipalities where they comprise at least 20% of the population,[11] which was the traditional 'benchmark' for a mixed area used in Czechoslovakia. In a country with a relatively low level of urbanisation, the Hungarians are especially concentrated in rural areas, with 59.5% of Hungarians (compared to 42.0% of Slovaks) living in municipalities with less than 5,000 inhabitants. Just 6.0% of Hungarians, compared to 27.2% of Slovaks, live in municipalities with more than 50,000 inhabitants.[12] This inevitably means that Hungarians live in communities with an above-average unemployment rate and a below-average income.[13] The precise location of the Roma minority is far more difficult to calculate given the inaccuracy of census data in

---

[8] Český statistický úrad, *Statistická ročenka České republiky*, Prague: Český spisovatel (1993) pp. 412-413.

[9] Ibid., p. 441; Štatistický úrad SR, *Voỳby do Národnej rady Slovenskej republiky konané 30.9. a 1.10.1994*, Bratislava: Štatistický úrad SR (1994), p. 17; Štatistický úrad SR, *Výsledky hlasovania vo volbách do Národnej rady Slovenskej republiky 25 – 26 September 1998*, Bratislava: Štatistický úrad SR (1998), p. 15.

[10] European Commission, loc. cit. n. 1, p. 19.

[11] Bakker, op. cit. n. 2, p. 43.

[12] Ibid., p. 46.

[13] For the income of areas with substantial Hungarian populations, see Information Centre of the Hungarian Coalition in Slovakia, *The Hungarians in Slovakia*, Bratislava (1997) p. 15.

identifying the Roma, but there are known to be heavy concentrations in Eastern Slovakia, which is also an economically depressed area.

3. POLITICAL CLEAVAGES IN SLOVAKIA

One reason why the national composition of Slovakia is significant is that as soon as the first elections took place in post-communist Czechoslovakia in June 1990, it became clear that the electorate tended to allot its support to parties along national lines. The most immediately obvious split was that between Czechs and Slovaks. Czechoslovakia was a federation of two republics, and from the earliest days of the Velvet Revolution the Czechs and Slovaks formed their own citizens movements, Civic Forum and Public Against Violence. The division of the party system into Czech and Slovak parties was encouraged by the electoral system adopted in 1990, which, even for the Federal Assembly, divided the State into two electoral territories, each of which had its own five per cent threshold which a party had to cross in order to enter Parliament. Hence there was little electoral advantage for a party to stand in both the Czech and Slovak Republics.[14]

Another notable feature was the general prominence of nationally defined parties. In June 1990, elections were held not only for the Federal Assembly, but also for the separate Parliaments of Czechoslovakia's two constituent republics. In the election to the 150-seat Slovak National Council (renamed after independence the National Council of the Slovak Republic), a coalition of the largely-Hungarian party Coexistence and the Hungarian Christian Democratic Movement obtained 8.66% of the vote and 14 seats, and the Slovak National Party 13.94% of the vote and 22 seats. Moravians and Silesians were also elected to the Czech National Council until the 1996 Czech elections. Hungarians were represented in the first Slovak Government by the Hungarian Independent Initiative (later the Hungarian Civic Party), which was part of Public Against Violence.[15] In the June 1992 elections, a coalition of Coexistence, the Hungarian Christian Democratic Movement and the Hungarian People's Party obtained 7.42% of the vote and, once again, 14 seats, while the Hungarian Civic Party stood alone and obtained 2.29% of the vote and no seats.[16] The Slovak National Party vote declined to 7.93%, in part because Slovak national interests were now being represented by Mečiar's Movement for a Democratic Slovakia, which had broken away from Public Against Violence. In 1994, the three major Hungarian parties stood

---

[14] For analysis of effects of such technical factors on the division of Czechoslovakia, see Karen Henderson, 'Czechoslovakia: The Failure of Consensus Politics and the Break-up of the Federation', 5 *Regional & Federal Studies* (1995) No. 2, pp. 111-133.

[15] For the Slovak National Council, a 3% threshold operated in 1990 and 1992. For the 1990 election results, see *Statistická ročenka České a slovenské federativní republiky*, Prague: FSÚ/ČSÚ/SŠÚ/SEVT (1991), p. 630; Gordon Wightman, 'Czechoslovakia', in Bogdan Szajkowski (Ed.), *New Political Parties of Eastern Europe and the Soviet Union*, Harlow: Longman (1991), pp. 53-92.

[16] Český statistický úrad, op. cit., n. 8, p. 441.

together as the Hungarian Coalition and obtained 10.18% of the vote and 17 seats.[17] In 1998, the Hungarian Coalition – now transformed into the Party of the Hungarian Coalition in response to a new election law passed in May 1998 – obtained 9.12% of the vote and 15 seats.[18] It would thus appear that a stable 9% or 10% of Slovak citizens regularly vote for Hungarian political parties. The founding parties of the Party of Hungarian Coalition, which formed 'wings' within it, have a centre-right orientation – Christian Democrats, Liberals (Hungarian Civic Party), and National-Liberal (Coexistence) – so it is likely that most of the remaining Hungarians in Slovakia vote for various left of centre Slovak parties such as the post-communist Party of the Democratic Left or to a lesser extent the non-parliamentary, and more extreme, Communist Party of Slovakia.

However, in order to understand the dynamics of Slovak political life with respect to minorities, a second cleavage is just as important as the division of the electorate between Hungarian and Slovak parties. This is the cleavage which exists within the ethnically Slovak political community according to the strength of national orientation. There are indications that this division already existed in the inter-war period, and that the nationalists' electoral strongholds have remained in geographically similar locations.[19] The major battle between the different sides of the Slovak political divide are finally being openly played out during the 1990s, when independence in a democratic environment has for the first time allowed the Slovaks space to settle their own disputes with little outside interference. This has led to an extreme contestation of politics which has impacted badly on relations with the Hungarian community.

Domestic political surveys carried out within Slovakia, most notably by FOCUS and later by the Institute for Public Affairs (IVO), have repeatedly shown that Slovak political parties are differentiated by views on national and ethnic issues rather than by the left-right divide.[20] Parties in Slovakia are positioned not within a single left-

---

[17] Štatistický úrad SR (1994), op. cit. n. 9, pp. 17, 97; Karen Henderson, 'The Slovak Republic', in Bogdan Szajkowski (Ed.), *Political Parties of Eastern Europe, Russia & the Successor States*, Harlow: Longman (1994), pp. 525-543.

[18] Štatistický úrad SR (1998), op. cit. n. 9. It is worth noting that the allegiance of ethnic Hungarians to the major Hungarian election force had not necessarily decreased between the 1994 and 1998 elections. The number of votes the Hungarian Coalition received actually went up from 292,936 to 306,623. The decrease in their percentage of the total vote was due in some part to the overall turnout increasing from 75.65 to 84.24%. Since Hungarian voters had traditionally had a high participation rate, the highly politicised atmosphere in Slovakia in 1998 could not increase their turnout as much as among the Slovak electorate.

[19] See Vladimír Krivý, Viera Feglová and Daniel Balko, *Slovensko a jeho regióny: Sociolkultúrne súvislosti volebného správania*, Bratislava: Nadácia Média (1996), pp. 343-352, 365-375.

[20] See, for example, the extensive data in *Aktuálne problémy Slovenska December 1994*, Bratislava: FOCUS (1994), and Zora Bútorová, Oľga Gyarfášová and Vladimír Krivý, 'Parties, Institutions and Politicians', in Zora Bútorová (Ed.), *Democracy and Discontent in Slovakia: A Public Opinion Profile of a Country in Transition*, Bratislava: Institute for Public Affairs (1998), pp. 84-85. Slovak Radio research produced similar findings: see Ondrej Dostal, 'Dve kritéria delenia slovenských volicov', *Sme*, (13 September 1994) p. 4.

right spectrum, but within three separate left-right spectra distinguished by views on national issues. The temporary Moravcík Government, which ruled from April to December 1994, comprised the centre-right Christian Democratic Movement, the liberal Democratic Union and the centre-left Party of the Democratic Left. It was replaced from December 1994 to October 1998 by Mečiar's third Government, which was a nationally-oriented left-right coalition, comprising the Slovak National Party, which was far right in nationalist rhetoric but centrist in economic orientation; the large but rather amorphous Movement for a Democratic Slovakia, which was by self-definition 'centre', in terms of its supporters' views leftist, but with regard to its nationalism and its declared – and fulfilled – promise to create a 'stratum of rich people' in Slovakia actually rather right-wing; and the far-left Workers' Association of Slovakia. Finally, the Hungarian Coalition itself also contained a third left-right spectrum of voters, since it comprised an economic cross-section of society united by ethnicity. Insofar as its supporters have slightly left-wing views, this correlates with the fact that most Hungarians live in the south of Slovakia, where there are often high rates of unemployment.

An even more revealing 1994 survey analysed by two British academics, Geoffrey Evans and Stephen Whitefield, differentiated between attitudes of Slovak and Czech respondents towards ethnic rights, gypsies, and nationalism, which all tend to be included in the same battery of questions in Slovak surveys. This confirmed that the Czech party system was largely defined by differences in attitudes to economic liberalism, whereas in Slovakia, the best predictor of partisanship was the issue of ethnic rights.[21] However, it also discovered that – contrary to the conclusions of some Czecho-Slovak surveys – 'the existence of distinct issue bases to politics in the two countries does not appear to derive from distinct, pre-existing political cultures. Despite the political salience of ethnic issues, Slovaks do not express particularly illiberal or nationalist sentiments . . . '[22] The survey also highlighted that ethnic (il)liberalism correlates with attitudes towards gypsies far more strongly in the Czech Republic than in Slovakia. In other words, Slovaks are not particularly nationalist, but what distinguishes them is the role of nationalism in determining party support. Furthermore, it is not so much nationalism in general as attitudes towards the Hungarian minority which define the cleavages in Slovak politics. It would appear that part of the Slovak political community strongly defines both its nationhood and its political identity in contradistinction to everything Hungarian – both the imperial legacy of oppression, and the perceived threat from the Hungarian minority within its own State borders. This is the background to the disputes which have emerged between the majority and largest minority community in Slovakia since democratisation first allowed such conflicts to be aired publicly.

---

[21] Geoffrey Evans and Stephen Whitefield, 'The Structuring of Political Cleavages in Post-Communist Societies: the Case of the Czech Republic and Slovakia', 46 *Political Studies* (1998) No. 1, pp. 115-139.

[22] Ibid., p. 134.

4. THE EMOTIVE ISSUES IN MINORITY RELATIONS

Since nationalism and attitudes towards Hungarians are so important in Slovak political choice, it is necessary to examine why these are such salient factors. As in much of East-Central Europe, history looms large in the consciousness of ethnic groups in Slovakia. Many Slovaks tend to recall 1,000 years of Hungarian rule, the concerted Hungarian attempts to assimilate Slovaks totally during the last fifty years of the Austro-Hungarian empire (including the termination of all Slovak-language education above primary level), and the fact that Hungary invaded Slovakia four times during the twentieth century,[23] with further concerted attempts at assimilation in the southern Slovak territories annexed by Hungary during World War Two. Frequent reference is also made to the large-scale assimilation of ethnic Slovaks in post-World War Two Hungary. Historical Slovak Hungarian grievances against the Slovaks, on the other hand, concentrate heavily on the period immediately after World War Two, where they were hit badly both by the post-war reprisals embodied in the Beneš decrees of the democratic Czechoslovak Government, and the appalling Stalinist repression after the communist takeover of 1948.[24]

Since 1989, a variety of emotionally-laden issues have underlain the political disputes within Slovakia. The major concern of the Hungarian community is the preservation of their Hungarian language. Although, on the level of legislative controversies, there have been publicised disputes about the use of bilingual signs denoting village names in areas with Hungarian-speaking citizens, about whether Hungarian women should be forced to add the *-ová* ending dictated by Slovak grammar to their surnames, and more generally about the use of Hungarian as a language of official communication, these are in part symbolic battles: the key issue is Hungarian language education. Although there are demands for more tertiary education in Hungarian, the major concern is the continuing provision of Hungarian-language – rather than bilingual – education in schools. This is rational, since preserving the dominance of the Hungarian language in the schools which most Slovak Hungarians attend will determine whether Hungarian continues to be the normal language of communication among the Hungarian community at large, and thereby lead to a continuity in its Hungarian cultural identity.

A logical consequence of the Hungarian emphasis on language and education are demands for a cultural autonomy which allows Hungarians control over this sphere of their lives, and thereby also the guarantee that Slovak governments cannot impinge

[23] A booklet with a distinctly nationalist tone containing '100 questions and 99 answers about Slovaks and Hungarians', which succinctly outlines most of the emotive issues in Slovak/Hungarian relations, lists June 1919, November 1938, March 1939 and August 1968. See Viliam Fábry, *O Slovákoch a maďaroch: 100 otázok a 99 odpovedí*, Bratislava: Kubko-Goral (1997), p. 31. The booklet was financed by the Ministry of Culture of the Slovak Republic.

[24] See, for example, Information Centre of the Hungarian Coalition in Slovakia, op. cit. n. 13, pp. 9-11.

on current rights. Demands for territorial autonomy, which receive more limited support among Hungarians, take this thinking a clear stage further, and seek Hungarian control over most spheres of everyday life in areas where ethnic Hungarians predominate.

Among the majority Slovak population, concerns about the Hungarian minority in some respects bear a similarity to Hungarian preoccupations: they relate predominantly to a fear that their own current situation might be eroded, rather than presenting a clear programme for changing the status quo. They differ, however, in that there is less consensus and communal unity in Slovak fears: the Slovak political community lacks cohesion, and is less clearly focused on ethnic issues. It is internally markedly differentiated according to the salience of fears about the Hungarian minority, so that the issues listed below are of deep concern only for some Slovaks, namely those that are more nationally oriented. This accords with the major political cleavages among Slovak political parties. As a consequence, the Slovak agenda is more diffuse, and less easily summarised by a small number of points.

The deepest Slovak fear is of Hungarian irredentism, namely that the integrity of the Slovak State might be threatened by an underlying desire of the Hungarian minority to attach the south of the country to Hungary. This is fuelled when their Hungarian fellow-citizens talk of territorial autonomy, because historically, autonomy is associated with being a prelude to border changes.[25] Expressions of concern about the fate of Hungarians in neighbouring countries on the part of any Hungarian government in Budapest are also interpreted as a desire to assert power over Slovak territory, and are therefore viewed with hostility. Even Hungarian desires for European unity are sometimes regarded as a back-door attempt to recreate 'Greater Hungary' by removing rather than moving borders,[26] and also as a development which would open the way for Hungarian economic control over southern Slovakia.

A related fear is that the Slovaks living in southern Slovakia are being assimilated by the vibrant and well-organised Hungarian community which surrounds them. This was expressed in its most extreme form in a Slovak National Party election broadcast in September 1998 in which the party's deputy chair talked of stopping Slovaks becoming 'a ninety per cent minority in their own country'. It is assumed by some that territorial autonomy would massively accelerate such a process. It is

---

[25] See, for example, Miroslav Kusý, 'Autonómia neznamená odtrhnutie, autonómia je legálny postup', *Domino Forum* (1.3-7.3.1996) p. 4, reprinted in Miroslav Kusý, *Čo s našimi maďarmi*, Bratislava: Kalligram (1998) pp. 116-123. Official Hungarian minority views on autonomy fluctuate, but it is clearly on the agenda for discussion: Information Centre of the Hungarian Coalition in Slovakia, op. cit. n. 13, p. 12 italicises the view that 'attention should also focus on forms of self-government which are based on the principle of territorial autonomy'.

[26] This is not necessarily a misinterpretation of Hungarian views: Information Centre of the Hungarian Coalition in Slovakia, op. cit. n. 13 on p. 20 italicises the sentence 'Therefore, members of the Hungarian community in Slovakia do not see the solution in a revision of borders; instead, they await the perspective disappearance of these borders.'

claimed – for example, by the nationalist daily *Slovenská republika*[27] – that there is statistical evidence of assimilation of Slovaks by Hungarians. The suggestion is that assimilation of Slovaks is leading to a rise in the number of Hungarians in Slovakia despite the low Hungarian birth-rate. Yet this contention is contradicted by another Slovak nationalist argument discussed earlier: namely that the large number of Hungarians in official statistics overestimates the size of the Hungarian community because most Roma declare themselves to be Hungarian. A linked notion is that the Roma mainly declare themselves to be Hungarian in censuses because they think it more elevated to be regarded as Hungarians rather than Slovaks. This is indicative of a Slovak inferiority complex which assumes that Hungarians look down on them culturally.[28]

Another contested area relates to whether or not Hungarians in Slovakia are able to speak Slovak. The contention that many Slovak citizens from the Hungarian community do not have an adequate grasp of the State language is pursued on two different levels in Slovak nationalist discourse. First, the demand that there should be more teaching in Slovak, and better teaching of the Slovak language in Hungarian-language schools, is presented as a philanthropic act which will ensure that all Slovak citizens have the possibility to advance professionally throughout the country. Secondly, the failure of Hungarians to speak Slovak is considered to be a sign that they lack loyalty to the Slovak Republic.

A final Slovak nationalist demand is that the treatment of the Slovak minority in Hungary should be used as a yardstick for determining Slovak treatment of the Hungarian minority.[29] Much is made of the Hungarian failure to ensure parliamentary representation of the Slovak minority, whereas less is said of the 1993 Hungarian legislation on minority self-government. However, reciprocity is a problematic demand even from a Slovak nationalist standpoint, since earlier Hungarian successes in assimilating the Slovak minority in Hungary mean that the contemporary Hungarian State can afford to be generous to those that remain.[30] From the point of view of the

---

[27] See, for examples, *Slovenská republika* (21 August 1996) p. 5; (26 August 1996) pp. 1, 5. This argument is presented with the use of extensive data in a book published by the Ministry of Culture of the Slovak Republic: see Michal Gáfrik, 'Changes in the National Structure of Southern Slovakia's Population', in *Slovaks and Magyars: Slovak-Magyar Relations in Central Europe (1961-1991)*, Bratislava: Správa kultúrnych zariadení MK SR (1995) pp. 85-100.

[28] In the early 1990s, sociological data suggested that about three quarters of Slovaks believed Hungarians thought they were better than Slovaks, while about half Hungarians thought that Slovaks considered themselves superior. See Pavol Frič, Fedor Gál, Peter Hunčík and Christopher Lord, *Maďarská menšina*, Prague: EGEM (1993) pp. 65-66. It may also be argued that Roma declare themselves as Hungarians purely because they identify with the Hungarians as another minority.

[29] See, for example, Fábry, op. cit. n. 23, pp. 34-35; the 1994 Slovak National Party programme (p. 11) also demands 'In solving the minority question in the Slovak Republic, also taking into consideration the position of Slovaks in those national states, whose minorities live on the territory of Slovakia'.

[30] For details of the Slovaks in Hungary, see Bakker, op. cit. n. 2, pp. 139-203; for a nationalist account, see Fábry, op. cit. n. 23, pp. 49-55.

Hungarian minority in Slovakia, it is understandably completely unacceptable that their rights might be restricted by actions of a Government (in Budapest) over which their political representatives have no democratic control.

The agenda of ethnic concerns affecting Slovak-Roma relations is less developed than that of Hungarian-Slovak relations, and has emerged largely in the second half of the 1990s. A major reason for this is that the political structures of the Roma community are poles apart from those of the Hungarians: articulation of political demands is weak, and the community is internally highly fragmented, containing a little understood complexity of internal disputes which is markedly different from the unified front which the Hungarians have managed to construct. Roma parties which stood in the elections of 1990, 1992 and 1994 never obtained more than one per cent of the vote in Slovakia, and could not claim to represent all the Roma. None stood in the 1998 parliamentary elections, although Romany representatives appeared on the lists of several Slovak parties. Discontent among the Roma focuses around economic issues, particularly discrimination in employment practices which has led to high unemployment rates, and racism, most notably skinhead attacks on the Roma, but there has also been concern about sporadic attempts by local mayors to discriminate against the Roma collectively within their communities. Lacking strong political leadership, the Roma's most effective means of protest has so far been the cumulative consequence of individual protest in the form of emigration to the UK. This led to little positive response from the Mečiar Slovak Government, and the consequent imposition in October 1998 of a visa regime for all Slovak citizens travelling to Britain.

On the Slovak side, the Roma issue increased in salience between the 1994 and 1998 elections, as witnessed by the content of Slovak parties' election manifestos. In the popular mind, the Roma are regarded by Slovaks as a social rather than a political threat. Major concerns are the high level of criminality among the Roma, and resentment about the amount paid in social security benefits to the large families of unemployed Roma.[31] There are signs that Slovak political leaders are still 'feeling their way' in their responses to these issues, and that the desire to exploit popular anti-Roma sentiment is tempered by a realisation that this may merely exacerbate the solution of real problems. No party has exploited anti-Roma racism in the direct fashion employed by the Republicans in the 1998 Czech elections, and when the Slovak National Party entered the final stage of the 1998 election campaign with posters demanding a 'Slovakia without parasites', the major outcry its party leaders raised was through including Slovak Hungarians as parasites. This provided interesting

---

[31] A March 1995 survey found that the 'Roma characteristics' which most bothered Slovaks were 'criminality' and 'avoiding honest work', followed by 'low level of hygiene, lack of cleanliness', all of which were mentioned by over half of the respondents. See ÚVVM, *Rasizmus, xenofóbia, antisemitizmus a intolerancia vo vedomí obyvateľov Slovenskej republiky*, Bratislava, Štatistický úrad SR (1995) p. 35.

confirmation of the fact that it is the issue of the Hungarian minority which plays most potently on some Slovaks' emotions.

5. POLITICAL CONTROVERSIES IN RELATIONS WITH MINORITIES

The major political controversies which have marred the relationship between the Slovak majority and minorities in the post-1989 democratic period in the main reflect the emotive issues among the Slovak and Hungarian communities. There is no space here to deal in detail with all the issues which have erupted in the last eight years, but a brief summary will be given of the most salient ones.[32]

5.1 **Slovak independence**

Most Hungarians were opposed to the establishment of an independent Slovak State at the end of 1992, and Slovak nationalists resent this in the same way that they refuse to forget precisely which Slovak politicians opposed independence in 1992. On a rational level, Hungarian resistance to living in an independent Slovak Republic was based on a fear that a Slovak Government would be more likely to restrict Hungarian rights than a Czechoslovak one – which was borne out by the actions of the second and third Mečiar Governments that ruled for more than five of the first six years of Slovak independence. On an emotive level, Slovak independence also created a new situation for Hungarians because it meant that for the first time ever they were directly subordinate to Slovaks, who had been an inferior nation not even acknowledged as such prior to 1918, rather than to a Czechoslovak State which was predominantly Czech. Hungarian Slovaks faced a double problem: first, they were emerging from the communist period where formal representation of Hungarians through Hungarian communists co-opted into the 'system' was guaranteed into a democratic society where political power had to be contested openly without quotas; and secondly, they were now being thrust into a newly-independent State where they suspected that they were more likely systematically to be deprived of such power on ethnic grounds. Hungarian discomfort at living in the new Slovak Republic was compounded by the unfortunate wording of the 1992 Constitution of the Slovak Republic, the preamble of which begins 'We, the Slovak nation'.

---

[32] For further details of these and other issues, see Bakker, op. cit. n. 2; Kieran Williams, 'The Magyar Minority in Slovakia', 6 *Regional and Federal Studies* (1996) No. 1, pp. 1-20; also relevant chapters in the annual publications *Slovensko 1995 (1996/1997): Súhrnna správa o stave spolocnosti a trendoch na rok 1996 (1997/1998)*, which are now published in Bratislava by the Institute for Public Affairs. For an English version, see Martin Bútora and Peter Hunčík (Eds.), *Global Report on Slovakia: Comprehensive Analyses from 1995 and Trends from 1996*, Bratislava: Sándor Márai Foundation (1997).

5.2 Language laws

This issue first erupted in the autumn of 1990, when attempts to pass a language law formalising the use of minority languages were made. It reoccurred under the third Mečiar Government when a new law on the State language was passed, and continued with controversy about the failure to pass a law on the use of minority languages, which greatly damaged Slovakia's relationship with the EU, since a Slovak undertaking to pass such a law was broken. The EU's 1998 Accession Partnership with Slovakia highlighted this as one of the key short-term political priorities (issues to be pursued by the end of the year).[33] There has been extreme difficulty in escaping from criteria established at the time of the Treaty of Trianon of 1920, namely that minorities should have a right to use their mother tongue as an official language in areas where their number exceeds 20%. This is inherently problematic, since it deprives minorities of the opportunity to feel equally at home throughout the State in which they are citizens. It also defines part of Slovak territory as fundamentally different, which actually facilitates the demands for autonomy which Slovak nationalists find so objectionable. Later draft language laws suggested by members of the Hungarian Coalition have suggested changing this percentage barrier – for example, by reducing it to 10%, which would be of assistance predominantly to non-Hungarian minorities.[34]

5.3 Alternative schooling

This proposal of the third Mečiar Government, introduced by the Slovak National Party Education Minister, Eva Slavkovská, essentially promoted bilingual education, with the aim both of improving knowledge of Slovak among Hungarians, and making education alongside Hungarian children in mixed regions more acceptable to the parents of Slovak children. It had to be abandoned because of the stiff resistance of Hungarians, who utterly refused to accept it voluntarily because of fears of creeping assimilation attempts. Hungarian-language education was generally made more tense because of strong central control of education at the local level. This finally erupted in arguments over the banning of bilingual school reports in favour of Slovak-only reports – a highly retrograde step given the lack of bilingual official communication in Slovakia as a whole.

---

[33] The EU's short-term priorities for 1998 were 'free and fair Presidential, national and local elections in 1998; ensuring effective opposition participation in parliamentary oversight committees and supervisory boards; the adoption of legislative provisions on minority language use and related implementing measures'. See European Commission DG 1A, *Accession Partnership Slovakia*, Brussels: European Commission (1998) p. 3.

[34] See Information Centre of the Hungarian Coalition in Slovakia, op. cit. n. 13.

5.4 **Support for minority culture**

The budget for this was steadily decreased by the Mečiar Government, and part of it was channelled to pro-Government publications almost never read by Hungarians – for example, minority language supplements to the pro-Government daily *Slovenská republika*. Government publications in the mid-1990s also concentrated on emphasising the quantity of publications and institutions supporting minority languages, while ignoring the crucial question of whether they were increasing or decreasing in number.

5.5 **The Slovak-Hungarian Basic Treaty**

The Slovak and Hungarian Prime Ministers signed a bilateral treaty on good neighbourly relations in March 1995, just before the OSCE Paris Conference on Stability in Europe. This was largely a response to pressure from the EU and NATO, who insisted that aspiring members should not have disputes with their neighbours. Although it appeared a positive development, the Slovak Government later attempted to backtrack from the treaty's mention of the Council of Europe's Recommendation 1201 by denying that it implied recognition of collective rights.[35] The Slovak National Party delayed ratification until March 1996, and first demanded the approval of the 1995 State language law and the law on the protection of the republic.

5.6 **Reform of State administrative boundaries**

These were finally changed by the third Mečiar Government in 1996 in a way which prevented the concentration of the Hungarian minority within single regions and districts. Such devices had previously also been employed by various Czechoslovak Governments. Hungarian counter-proposals were likewise based on national criteria, and tended to arrange administrative boundaries to maximise the areas where they would form a majority. A further major problem remained the failure to reform the structure and power of local self-governments, where the Hungarian minority frequently had majority political control, but little actual control of economic resources. The Mečiar Government, while in power, favoured the State administration over self-government because it was so much more easy to control from the 'centre', with each *prednosta* (head of administration) appointed centrally. This generally hampered the devolution of power and local democracy in Slovakia.

---

[35] For further details, see Sharon Fisher, 'Treaty Fails to End Squabbles Over Hungarian Relations', 1 *Transition* (1995) No. 9, pp. 2-7.

5.7 **Komárno**

Meetings of Slovak Hungarian politicians which discussed territorial autonomy evoked ferocious counter-attacks from Slovak nationalists. The most famous assembly occurred in Komárno in January 1994, when 3,500 elected Hungarian representatives met to discuss the possibility of demanding autonomy as a reaction against initial government plans to reorganise local self-government. Although moderate Slovak Hungarian politicians successfully resisted a demand for autonomy being included in the assembly's proclamation, public discussion of the subject was sufficient to convince some Slovaks that territorial autonomy, and subsequent border revisions, were part of the Hungarian political agenda, and Komárno was thereafter cited as evidence of the Hungarians' ill-intent.[36]

5.8 **Reform of the Local Government Election Law**

The third Mečiar Government changed the election law for commune elections in the summer of 1998 to a system whereby single-party lists of candidates were likely to be elected to local councils.[37] However, in order to prevent all-Hungarian councils being elected in areas of southern Slovakia where Slovaks were in a minority, there were provisions that the national mix of candidates elected must match the population mix of the electorate as demonstrated in the last census. This was impractical, for while the law clearly stated that the national composition of the municipality derived from data in the last census, there were no stipulations about how the nationality of election candidates was to be defined. Since Slovak identity cards no longer indicate the declared national affiliation of the holder, it was theoretically possible for candidates to declare themselves whatever nationality they chose. The law was declared unconstitutional in October 1998, after the local election campaign had formally begun, and was rapidly changed by the new Government, leading to a minimal one-month delay in the holding of elections, which finally took place on 17-18 December 1998.

5.9 **Roma emigration**

Alongside all the issues focusing on the Hungarian minority, the position of the Roma did not make an impact on national politics in Slovakia until the number of asylum applications of Slovak Roma in the United Kingdom precipitated the introduction of a visa regime in October 1998. The Mečiar Government – still in power until 29 October 1998, albeit without an electoral mandate – retaliated by

---

[36] See Sharon Fisher, 'Meeting of Slovakia's Hungarians Causes Stir', 3 *RFE/RL Research Report* (1994) No. 4, pp. 42-47.

[37] For the text and commentary on the new law, see Dušan Šveda, Marcela Petrlová and Lívia Škultétyová, *Komunálne voľby*, Bratislava: Epos (1998).

claiming Slovakia was being discriminated against and treated like a Third World country and imposing visas on UK citizens visiting Slovakia. The visa regime for Britons was removed by the new Government within a week of taking office.

6. MINORITY RELATIONS IN SOCIOLOGICAL RESEARCH

Sociological surveys provide a useful guide to the overall dynamics of Slovak/minority relations. They make it possible to quantify how strong or widespread the emotive issues in minority relations are, and also how much general public concern there is about the political controversies in relations with minorities. Nationality is a standard demographic variable used by sociologists in Slovakia, but this usually consists of defining whether citizens are Slovak or Hungarian. The views of the Roma and other minorities are not normally presented separately because of their statistically low number in the censuses upon which quota samples are based, and it is suspected that the Roma are frequently under-represented in surveys. A second categorisation used in many sociological surveys about inter-ethnic relations is differentiation between Slovaks who live in ethnically mixed areas in southern Slovakia and those who live in ethnically homogeneous regions. A consistent finding has been that less tension is perceived by Slovaks who coexist alongside Hungarians. In other words, Slovak xenophobia is in part literally the fear of the unknown.

The data presented in this section are derived from surveys by FOCUS and the Institute for Public Affairs (IVO), and also from surveys of the Institute of Public Opinion Research of the Statistical Office of the Slovak Republic (ÚVVM pri ŠÚ SR).[38] Although the former were identified with the political parties in the anti-Mečiar opposition while the latter inevitably had somewhat closer official links, both provide serious sociological analyses and fairly similar results.

6.1 **General attitudes to national relations**

A most common question investigating ethnic prejudice in general asks respondents whether they would be bothered by people of various ethnic groups moving into their neighbourhood. It emerges that the most popular non-Slovak neighbours are Czechs, approved of by almost all Slovaks in 1993 and 1994 FOCUS surveys. Hungarians received over 60% approval, whereas the Roma, meeting with almost 80% disapproval, were considered the least desirable group, below Vietnamese and blacks.[39] Similar results were produced by a March 1995 ÚVVM

---

[38] For the period 1990-1993, see Fric et al., op. cit. n. 28, contains very detailed tables from ÚVVM and the Centre for Social Analysis (CSA).

[39] *Aktuálne problémy Slovenska po rozpade ČSFR*, Bratislava, FOCUS (1993), p. 75; *Aktuálne problémy Slovenska Máj 1994*, Bratislava: FOCUS (1994) p. 94; *Aktuálne problémy Slovenska December 1994* (1994), ibid., p. 119.

survey in which respondents were asked whether or not the public had friendly relations towards various national and racial groups. Again, the Czechs were judged most popular and the Roma least popular, with the Hungarians somewhere in between.[40] It is notable that only 24% of Slovaks in southern Slovakia did not want a Hungarian for a neighbour, while the percentage was 40% elsewhere in the country.[41]

Other survey data also show that the most problematic public attitudes are those towards the Roma. In a November 1994 FOCUS survey, over 60% of Slovak citizens did not even concede that the Roma were discriminated against, although the majority did concede that 'people tend to judge Roma only by the worst of them but there are some quite decent people among them'.[42] More disturbingly, over half of Slovak citizens agreed wholly or partially with the statement that 'Roma are a separate group of people, for whom more strict laws should apply',[43] thereby betraying not only racism, but also a deficient understanding of the basic principles of a State based on the rule of law.

A huge gap exists in Slovak and Hungarian perceptions of the status of the Hungarian minority as well. This is a 'watershed' question – that is, an issue where the views of the two communities are not merely different to a statistically significant degree, but actually diametrically opposed. One of the starkest differences emerges precisely on the question of legal rights. For example, when respondents were asked in February 1996 whether the policies of the Slovak Government towards the Hungarian minority were compatible with international norms, 78% of Slovaks said that they were, and 77% of Hungarians said that they were not.[44] The shifts in opinion in the mid-1990s emerge from FOCUS figures presented in Table 2 below. As can be seen, the gulf in perceptions between Slovaks and Hungarians deepened notably during the term in office of the third Mečiar Government from December 1994 onwards. The Hungarian minority's perception that its rights were limited became overwhelming, whereas amongst Slovaks, there was merely a small decline in the proportion who thought the Hungarian minority privileged.[45]

---

[40] 6 *Názory* (1995) No. 1, p. 32.

[41] ÚVVM, *Názory na vybrané problémy Slovákov a Maďarov žijúcich v národnostne zmiešaných oblastiach južného Slovenska*, Bratislava, Štatistický úrad SR (1994) p. 14.

[42] *Aktuálne problémy Slovenska December 1994*, op. cit. n. 39, p. 128.

[43] Ibid., p. 129.

[44] Zora Bútorová, Olga Gyarfášová, and Miroslav Kúska, *Aktuálne problémy Slovenska na prelome rokov 1995-1996*, Bratislava: FOCUS (1996) p. 111.

[45] This difference is also highlighted by an October 1997 question about whether the Hungarian minority's status had changed since the 1994 parliamentary elections: 80% of Hungarians but only 11% of Slovaks thought it had worsened, whereas 24% of Slovaks but only 2% of Hungarians thought it had improved. These results did not differ substantially from ÚVVM surveys in 1993 and 1996 which asked about whether specific rights of ethnic Hungarians were observed. See: Zora Bútorová, 'Opinions on Policy toward the Hungarian Minority', in Bútorová, op. cit. Table 2, pp. 153-154; Zora Bútorová, 'Verejná mienka', in *Slovensko 1997: Súhrnná správa of stave spoloïnosti a trendoch na rok 1998*, Bratislava: Inštitut pre verejné otázky (1998), p. 209.

Table 2 *'What is your opinion of the status of the Hungarian minority in Slovakia?' (in per cent) (FOCUS and IVO, 1994-1997).*

	December 1994		December 1995		January 1997	
	Slovak	Hung.	Slovak	Hung.	Slovak	Hung.
The Hungarian minority has limited rights and possibilities for its development	2	47	2	73	4	71
The Hungarian minority has good conditions for its development	63	49	65	24	68	24
The Hungarian minority has a privileged position	31	0	28	1	22	2
Don't know	4	4	5	2	6	3

Source: Zora Bútorová, 'Opinions on Policy toward the Hungarian Minority', in Zora Bútorová (Ed.), *Democracy and Discontent in Slovakia: A Public Opinion Profile of a Country in Transition*, Bratislava: Institute for Public Affairs (1998) p. 152.

Similar findings emerged when Slovak citizens were asked to characterise the Mečiar Government's policy toward ethnic Hungarians. In October 1997 – that is, a year before the end of the third Mečiar Government – 92% of Hungarians and only 30% of Slovaks thought that it was confrontational. It is interesting that 38% of Slovaks thought it was correct, and 15% even that it was too compliant, while 17% did not know.[46] Responses correlated heavily with party support, as is normally the case.[47] What is notable, however, is that the percentage of Slovaks who thought that the Mečiar Government's policies towards the Hungarians were correct or too compliant (53%) exceeded the combined vote for all the parties of the Mečiar Government in the September 1998 elections (37%). This suggests that Mečiar's confrontational style towards the Hungarians was somewhat more popular among the Slovak population than his policies as a whole.[48]

[46] Bútorová, loc. cit. n. 45, p. 208.

[47] Ibid., p. 210; Bútorová, Gyarfášová, and Krivý, loc. cit. n. 20, p. 86.

[48] It should also be noted that the policies towards the Hungarian minority of the Moravcík Government in the summer of 1994 were less approved of by Slovaks, but more acceptable to Hungarians, than those of the second Mečiar Government (June 1992-March 1994); and in December 1995, after a year in office, the third Mečiar Government's policies were rated more highly by Slovaks and more critically by Hungarians than those of the previous, Moravčík Government. See: *Aktuálne problémy Slovenska Máj 1994*, op. cit. n. 39, p. 98; Bútorová, Gyarfášová and Kúska, op. cit. n. 44, p. 110.

6.2 Political issues and public opinion

Surveys throughout the 1990s asking for popular reactions to specific government policies also show relatively negative stances among Slovaks towards issues which are important for Hungarians. In October 1993, when the issues were much publicised, demands that there should be bilingual name signs for villages or that Hungarians should be able to write their names in their own language were considered justified by over 70% of Hungarians (and partially justified by about 20% more), whereas only about half of Slovaks considered them wholly or partly justified – and mainly the latter.[49] Significantly, the demand for bilingual signs appeared more reasonable to those Slovaks who actually lived in the mixed areas affected by the provision.[50]

On the issue of loyalty towards the Slovak Republic, FOCUS's October 1993 survey showed that 84% of Hungarians thought they would have voted against the division of Czechoslovakia if there had been a referendum.[51] However, it has to be borne in mind that 56% of Slovaks produced the same response, so this cannot validly be used as proof of disloyalty after the split. Later surveys suggested that over 40% of Slovak citizens changed their mind and retrospectively approved the division of Czechoslovakia, or at least came to terms with it.[52] On another issue of 'loyalty', when Hungarian Slovaks were asked whether the Hungarian population was as concerned about the well-being of Slovakia as their Slovak fellow-citizens, an overwhelming majority (over 90%) replied positively. Yet less than half of Slovaks believed them – unless they actually live in mixed areas.[53]

In terms of deficient Hungarian knowledge of Slovak – another of the Slovak nationalist grievances – sociological surveys do not seem to confirm that this is objectively a particular problem. ÚVVM surveys in the first half of the 1990s asked Slovaks and Hungarians in mixed areas whether they could communicate well, with problems, or not at all, in the other language. Interestingly, this seemed to be an extremely subjective criterion, since ten per cent of both Slovaks and Hungarians apparently ceased being able to communicate well in the other language between 1990 and 1994, which is objectively impossible. As shown in Table 3 below, whereas

---

[49] *Aktuálne problémy Slovenska po rozpade ČSFR* (1993), op. cit. n. 39, p. 79. For earlier data on the use of bilingual signs, see Fric et al., op. cit. n. 28, pp. 59, 64, and for 1994 figures, *Aktuálne problémy Slovenska Máj 1994*, op. cit. n. 39, p. 93, *Aktuálne problémy Slovenska December 1994*, op. cit. n. 39, p. 121. See also results of *Názory na vybrané problémy Slovákov a Maďarov*, op. cit. n. 41, p. 18 for March 1994 responses to a similar question.

[50] Fric et al., op. cit. n. 28, pp. 59, 64; *Aktuálne problémy Slovenska Máj 1994*, op. cit. n. 39, p. 96.

[51] *Aktuálne problémy Slovenska po rozpade ČSFR*, op. cit. n. 39, p. 82.

[52] For FOCUS figures from December 1994, December 1995 and January 1997, see Zora Bútorová, 'Transformation Challenges in Public Perception', in Bútorová, op. cit. Table 2, p. 32.

[53] Frič et al., op. cit. n. 28, p. 67; *Aktuálne problémy Slovenska Máj 1994*, op. cit. n. 39, p. 95; Bútorová, Gyarfášová and Kúska, op. cit. n. 44, p. 114.

in 1990, 37% of Slovaks in mixed areas alleged that they spoke only Slovak, this percentage had increased to 52% by 1994. In the same period, the number of Hungarians who had problems communicating in Slovak, or who only spoke Hungarian, allegedly increased from 21% to 31%.[54]

Table 3 *Ability to communicate in Slovak and Hungarian among respondents in nationally mixed areas in percentages (ÚVVM 1990-1994).*

	Good communication in both languages	Problems with communication	Only communicates in one language
Slovaks			
1990	38	25	37
1993	29	20	51
1994	26	22	52
Hungarians			
1990	79	18	3
1993	67	28	5
1994	69	26	5

Source: ÚVVM, *Názory na vybrané problémy Slovákov a Madarov žijúcich v národnostne zmiešaných oblastiach južného Slovenska*, Bratislava, Štatistický úrad SR (1994) p. 21.

The inability of Hungarians to communicate in Slovak was strongly linked to age and education. Whereas 12% of Hungarians over 50 claimed not to speak Slovak in 1994, the percentage was only one per cent for those between 30 and 49, and 4% for those between 18 and 29. The gap according to education was even greater. Only one per cent of Hungarian graduates and those with a completed secondary education said they spoke no Slovak; among those with some secondary school education the percentage was 3%, but among those with only basic education – who are likely also to be older – the percentage was 16%, with a further 47% saying they had difficulties communicating in Slovak.[55] The implication of this is that younger Hungarians in the early 1990s were bilingual to a very high degree which would not be easy to improve. The difficulty in language usage seems to be rather a political one, namely that the sense of threat felt by the Hungarian community after Slovak independence was driving them away from wanting to be bilingual in Hungarian and Slovak. It consequently seems that coercive efforts of Slovak Governments to increase bilingualism were counter-productive.

---

[54] *Názory na vybrané problémy Slovákov a Maďarov*, op. cit. n. 41, p. 21.

[55] Ibid., p. 22.

On the highly emotive issue of the Magyarisation of Slovaks, FOCUS surveys give the most graphic evidence that it is a myth to suggest that Slovaks are being assimilated. When asked, in December 1995, whether there was a threat of Magyarisation for Slovaks in southern Slovakia, some 60% of Slovaks who lived in districts with less than one per cent of Hungarians thought there was; however, this percentage declined as the number of Hungarians increased, so that in areas where more than 50% of the population were Hungarian, only a few per cent of Slovaks thought there was a danger of Hungarians' assimilating them.[56]

A further subject of political argument that does not appear substantiated by sociological data is the issue of primary school education in the mother tongue in southern Slovakia. The Slovak National Party in particular has been vociferous in demanding that no Slovak child should be forced to attend a Hungarian-language school. However, in 1994 some 92% of Slovaks in southern Slovakia stated that they were satisfied with the possibilities for children to attend schools with teaching in their mother tongue, and only 6% were dissatisfied. Dissatisfaction was somewhat higher among Hungarians, among whom 85% were satisfied and 10% dissatisfied.[57] Given the financial limitations of the Slovak education system, the existing situation seems a fairly good compromise.[58] Political arguments about education seem therefore to be just that – political arguments without much resonance among the people directly affected.

6.3 **Autonomy and irredentism**

Major differences between the views of Slovaks and Hungarians in southern Slovakia only set in where the (political) issue of formal cultural autonomy of the area is discussed. Here, predominantly favourable Hungarian views contrast with predominantly negative Slovak views.[59] What is particularly interesting, however, is that on this issue, Slovaks living in southern Slovakia feel more negative about the Hungarian minority having autonomy in education and culture than is the case with Slovaks who live outside southern Slovakia (that is, in areas which would not be affected by the provision). Whereas 53% of Slovaks outside the affected area basically disagree with cultural autonomy, this rises to 61% among Slovaks in southern Slovakia.[60] Given the strong tendency for Slovaks in southern Slovakia generally to have more positive views on issues of Slovak/Hungar-

---

[56] Bútorová, Gyarfášová and Kúska, op. cit. n. 44, p. 115. For earlier figures, see Frič et al., op.cit. n. 28, p. 65.

[57] *Názory na vybrané problémy Slovákov a Madarov*, op. cit. n. 41, p. 25.

[58] For Slovak Government statistics on Hungarian language education, see Ministry of Education of the Slovak Republic, Department of Schools in Ethnically Diverse Areas, *Information about Training and Education of Ethnic Minorities in the Slovak Republic*; for the Hungarian account, see Information Centre of the Hungarian Coalition in Slovakia, op. cit. n. 13, pp. 26-28.

[59] *Názory na vybrané problémy Slovákov a Maďarov*, op. cit. n. 41, p. 27.

[60] Ibid., p. 28

ian coexistence than Slovaks in other parts of the country, it would appear that cultural autonomy is a genuine issue of concern, rather than a myth that has been politicised by Slovak nationalists whose electoral strongholds are in other parts of Slovakia. It can thus be viewed as a 'core issue' in Slovak/Hungarian relations – that is, one whose salience is confirmed by sociological data.

Similar findings emerged in a February 1996 FOCUS survey when questions about territorial autonomy were asked, although the authors point out that there may have been confusion among respondents about the precise meaning of the term. While the Party of the Hungarian Coalition denied that it aimed for territorial autonomy during the 1998 election campaign (in part perhaps for fear of increasing support for Mečiar), in 1996 the demand appears to have been supported, fully or partly, by 45% of Hungarians, whereas it was largely rejected by only 35%. This contrasted with 5% support among Slovaks, and 82% opposition. The number of 'don't knows' among the Slovaks was lower than among the Hungarians, who were more divided on the issue.[61] Also interesting, however, are ÚVVM surveys which in 1994 divided responses according to whether Slovak respondents lived in mixed areas, as shown in Table 4.

Table 4 *Views (in percentages) about the demand that in districts of Slovakia where Hungarians are a majority of the population they should have the right to territorial autonomy (ÚVVM 1994).*

	Hungarians	Slovaks in southern Slovakia	Other Slovaks
Agree entirely	33	1	2
Agree rather than disagree	25	3	5
Disagree rather than agree	17	13	20
Disagree entirely	10	77	67
Don't know	15	6	6

Source: ÚVVM, *Názory na vybrané problémy Slovákov a Maďarov žijúcich v národnostne zmiešaných oblastiach južného Slovenska*, Bratislava, Štatistický úrad SR (1994) pp. 29-30.

While, generally, views are in line with those in FOCUS surveys, Hungarian support for territorial autonomy in this earlier survey is higher, as is also Slovak opposition. But crucially, once again the opposition among Slovaks living in the affected areas is higher than among those outside. As with cultural autonomy, this issue does not seem to have been invented by Slovak nationalist politicians. It is a 'core issue' of genuine concern to the Slovaks most affected.

[61] Bútorová, Gyarfášová and Kúska, op. cit. n. 44, p. 124.

Views on the even thornier issue of border revisions are dependent on the precise slant of questions. FOCUS surveys have presented respondents with the statements that 'the majority of Hungarians reject changing borders and annexing the southern regions of Slovakia to Hungary' and 'the hidden goal of the majority of Hungarians living in Slovakia is changing the borders and annexing the southern regions of Slovakia to Hungary'. Such statements elicited the finding that some 34% of Slovaks thought the Hungarians wanted border changes, while 30% thought they did not and the remainder did not know. The fear of Hungarian irredentism is thus clearly alive in the minds of a third of Slovaks. Hungarians, on the other hand, overwhelmingly rejected the notion that Hungarians wanted border changes; 92% stated that they did not, while only 3% thought they did.[62]

ÚVVM surveys, on the other hand, did not ask about whether borders should be changed, but posed the subtly different question of whether the border between Slovakia and Hungary was just. Here, Hungarian responses were more ambivalent, as shown in Table 5 below. This indicates that there was some justification for the Slovak suspicion that substantial numbers of Hungarians did not really like the border as it was, even if they did not perceive a desire to change it. Certainly, the Hungarians of Slovakia lack the strong conviction that borders are in the right place which is enjoyed by their Slovak fellow citizens.

Table 5 *Responses of Hungarians, Slovaks in the southern regions of Slovakia and Slovaks elsewhere about the border between Slovakia and Hungary (ÚVVM March 1994).*

	Hungarians	Slovaks in southern Slovakia	Other Slovaks
Just for Slovaks and Hungarians	40	88	81
Unjust for Slovaks	1	2	7
Unjust for Hungarians	25	0	0
Unjust for Slovaks and Hungarians	14	2	4
Don't know	20	8	8

Source: ÚVVM, *Názory na vybrané problémy Slovákov a Maďarov žijúcich v národnostne zmiešaných oblastiach južného Slovenska*, Bratislava, Štatistický úrad SR (1994) p. 20.

The conclusion that can be reached from comparing the demands of Slovak political leaders with sociological data is that the genuine issues among Slovaks are

[62] Ibid., pp. 124-125. For earlier findings, see Frič et al., op. cit. n. 28, p. 65. In the earlier CSA surveys, up to 19% of Hungarians (in 1992) thought that the Hungarian minority would like to annex southern Slovakia to Hungary.

fears about Hungarian demands for cultural or territorial autonomy, with an underlying fear that border changes have not been entirely banished from the Hungarian political agenda. Other issues, such as the Hungarian ability to speak Slovak, the use of bilingual signs, provision of mother tongue schooling and assimilation of Slovaks by Hungarians could be omitted from the Slovak political agenda. On the Hungarian side, it appears that Slovak nationalist demands at the level of the political elites merely fuel the Hungarian fears which lead to the demands for autonomy so unacceptable to the Slovaks with whom they coexist, on the whole, rather well.

7. THE 1998 ELECTIONS AND BEYOND

During 1997 and 1998, there were some signs that the prominence of political disputes between Slovaks and Hungarians was diminishing, or rather that they were being overwhelmed by the acerbity of the divisions within the Slovak community in the run-up to the September 1998 parliamentary elections. International concerns about Slovak democracy, which had previously concentrated very heavily on minority questions, also became more strongly focused on whether the elections would be fair, as witnessed by the EU's 1998 Accession Partnership for Slovakia.[63] The Slovak parties increasingly concentrated their attacks on each other, and appeared studiously to avoid the minorities question. By early 1998, the pro-Mečiar daily newspaper *Slovenská republika* was printing fewer cartoons with negative portraits of Hungarians, and tended to replace them by cartoons attacking President Kovác (who was to leave office on 1 March 1998 and could not be replaced because no other candidate could obtain 60% support in Parliament), or the Slovak Democratic Coalition (a group of five opposition parties which had higher support in public opinion polls than Mečiar's Movement for a Democratic Slovakia in the early months of 1998).

The reduction in prominence of the Hungarian issue was reflected in the election manifesto of Mečiar's Movement for a Democratic Slovakia, which avoided specifically mentioning Hungarians. There was reference to the Roma under several headings, and while the message appeared generally liberal and tolerant, its pledge to 'prevent the creation of hotbeds of tension, manifestations of intolerance and racially motivated attacks, especially in areas with a higher concentration of citizens of Romany ethnicity'[64] was open to dual interpretation. The manifesto also repeated the nationalist message that Slovaks in mixed (that is, largely Hungarian) areas were being assimilated, since it pledged 'to support the culture of Slovaks living in linguistically mixed areas with the aim of eliminating tenden-

---

[63] See n. 33.

[64] Hnutie za Demokratické Slovensko, *Zmluva na 3. tisícročie medzi HZDS a občanmi SR Volby* (1998) p. 45

cies towards cultural assimilation'.[65] This was followed by a pledge 'to raise the national consciousness of citizens of Roma ethnicity so that they are able freely to declare their affiliation within the framework of the census', which was consistent with the nationalist claim that the Roma currently fortify the statistical ranks of the Hungarian minority. The Slovak National Party did not issue an election manifesto, but rather a lengthy party programme full of patriotic declarations based on the Slovak nation rather than Slovakia as a multinational State.[66] Its statements of tolerance and respect for minorities were in marked contrast to the pronouncements of its leadership.

The opposition manifestos appeared equally reticent to mention the word 'Hungarian'. This omission was most extraordinary in the programme of the Slovak Democratic Coalition, which contained no section on minorities despite the programme's inordinate length.[67] The Party of the Democratic Left contained an appropriately sized section on nationality policy, but succeeded in making specific reference to the Roma as Slovakia's second largest minority without mentioning the name of the largest. It conceded some of the demands of the Hungarian minority, but also contained statements focused on Slovak nationalist fears, such as promising to endeavour 'to create such conditions in areas where national minorities predominate so that every citizen considers it essential to learn Slovak in their own interest of broader fulfilment' and to strive 'that not a single community should lack a school with Slovak as the language of instruction'.[68] The Party of Civic Understanding, first formed in the spring of 1998, gave its section on 'minority policy' a more prominent place at the beginning of the manifesto, and even mentioned the minority issue in relation to foreign policy as well. However, it paid attention to Slovak nationalist fears, too. Whereas the first highlighted point in its section on minorities hit a key issue by emphasising 'not lowering the existing standard of minority rights in the Slovak Republic', it also emphasised 'support for regular teaching of the Slovak language to members of national minorities' and 'promoting the preservation of the language and cultural identity of Slovak minorities abroad'. It further explicitly rejected demands for territorial autonomy.[69] As for the programme of the Party of the Hungarian Coalition itself, its introduction stated that 'improving the situation of the

---

[65] Ibid., p. 31.

[66] *Program Slovenskej národnej strany*, Bratislava (1998).

[67] See the 135-page Slovenská Demokratická Koalícia, *Volebný program Spolu za lepšie Slovensko*. For comment on this, see Miroslav Kusý, 'Národnostná politika', in Grigorij Mesežnikov (Ed.), *Voľby 1998: Analýza volebných programov politických strán a hnutí*, Bratislava: Inštitút pre verejné otázky (1998) pp. 45-61. Professor Kusý did discover the adjectives 'minority' and 'national' (*národnostná*) used on a total of four occasions, which I had overlooked due to their lack of prominence.

[68] Strana demokratickej lavice, *Volebný program Lepší život pre cestného a pracovitého človeka*, pp. 64-66.

[69] Strana obcianského porozumenia, *Cesta k obcianskému zmiereniu a prosperite Slovenska*, pp. 6-7, p. 37.

citizen depends on the development of democracy and the creation of a State of prosperity',[70] and much of the programme emphasised the need to create a democratic State based on the rule of law, and the checking and decentralisation of power. The taboo subject of autonomy was not mentioned. It is notable, however, that whereas the sections on education and culture deal in detail with the concerns of the Hungarian community, the Roma are specifically mentioned only in the final paragraph of the section on social policy.[71]

The attempts of political parties in Slovakia to downplay the issue of the Hungarian minority in 1998 may seem extraordinary in light of the attention paid to their position in international critiques of Slovak Government policy, yet it had a clear rationale for all sides involved domestically. For Mečiar, it would have been unwise to attack the Hungarians given his party's desire not to be definitively excluded from the EU accession process; and the tactic of displaying concern about the situation of the Roma (even if at odds with the unconstructive approach to the issue demonstrated to the British Foreign Office in response to their concerns about the wave of Roma asylum applications) was a creative attempt to deflect criticism of the country's general attitude to minorities. The evasion of the Hungarian question by the opposition was likewise rational, since they were aware of the need to attract support from the 'middle ground' of the Slovak political spectrum, whose views on this particular issue were nearer to Mečiar's than on many others. The opposition parties were acutely aware that sympathy towards Hungarian demands might be heavily exploited by the Government. Finally, that the Hungarians themselves colluded in the glossing over of minority policy disputes in the election campaign was a wise move. It had been clear for several years that it was almost impossible in terms of electoral arithmetic for Mečiar to form a government after the 1998 elections, so they could not afford to risk making comments which would allow the 'Hungarian card' suddenly to be exploited at the last moment to secure an otherwise impossible victory for the more nationally-minded Slovak parties. In view of the high level of historical aversion to Hungarians among parts of the Slovak population, it is undoubtedly positive that debate should be focused on the general strengthening of civic rights rather than 'Hungarians' as such.

The results of the 1998 elections give very positive signs for the development of inter-ethnic relations in Slovakia. Mečiar's support has declined slowly but steadily since 1992; the nationalist heartland has been reduced to the areas around the Váh valley in the Trencín and Žilina regions; and the age structure of the Movement for a Democratic Slovakia vote suggests that demographic factors will lead to a continuation of its decline.[72] Furthermore, the participation of the Party of the

---

[70] Strana madarskej koalície, *Volebný program*, p. 1.

[71] Ibid., p. 19.

[72] See, for example, exit poll data from the International Republican Institute/FOCUS, *Volebný výskum*, (25-26 September 1998).

Hungarian Coalition in the four-party Government formed in late October 1998 should send positive signals to the international community, as well as integrating the Hungarian political leadership into national decision-making in the Slovak Republic. The Government programme approved by Parliament on 2 December 1998 contained a number of provisions securing the cultural and language rights of minorities and promised to ratify the European Charter of Local Self-Government,[73] and the coalition agreement between the Government's constituent parties had undertaken that none of them would pursue such contentious questions as territorial autonomy or alternative bilingual education.[74]

There are, however, a few pitfalls awaiting the post-Mečiar Slovak Government. The most commonly voiced international concern has been that it might be short-lived because of internal tensions without the coalition, and there have been some early disputes between the Party of the Democratic Left and the Party of the Hungarian Coalition. The fate of the opposition is, however, of equal importance. While Mečiar's Movement for a Democratic Slovakia appeared to be declining sharply after its election defeat, once shorn of governmental responsibility for getting Slovakia into the European Union and NATO, it may also resort to whipping up nationalist feeling against membership of Western organisations. The Slovak television and nationalist press campaign against the OSCE observation mission to the 1998 elections demonstrate that such attacks (in that case, against an organisation of which Slovakia was actually already a member) are clearly possible. Finally, the Roma question will not be as amenable of simple solutions as Slovak-Hungarian relations, and the European Commission's *Agenda 2000* reports of July 1997 contained strong indications that it is deeply concerned about the situation of the Roma throughout the candidate States. Applying to join the EU has been described as attempting to 'jump on to a moving train' because its political agenda constantly progresses, and Slovakia may therefore find that a backward-looking programme of repairing the damage to Slovak-Hungarian relations wrought by the past Mečiar Governments is no longer sufficient to satisfy the fears of EU Member States who are already concerned about their own difficulties with far smaller Roma communities than those in Central and Eastern Europe. Nevertheless, the general trend in Slovak political life at the end of the 1990s was towards seeking constructive solutions to minority problems in line with internationally acceptable standards, and the reduction in tension witnessed in late 1998 seems likely to continue.

8. CONCLUSION

Deficiencies in the treatment of minorities in Slovakia were one of the reasons why the European Commission negatively evaluated the state of Slovak democ-

[73] For the draft Government programme, see *Národná obroda* (20/21 November 1998).

[74] See *Sme* (29 October 1999) p. 1.

racy in its July 1997 opinion. The Mečiar Government accused the Commission of 'lack of objectivity' because it had 'praised' Romania, where minority rights were no better than Slovakia, and decided that there were 'no great problems' in Estonia,[75] where basic minority rights could be regarded as inferior to those in Slovakia because nearly a quarter of the population lacked citizenship. Such Slovak protests are not easy to refute, and it therefore seems clear that, although this was never explicitly stated by the Commission, what really worried them in Slovakia were the negative trends in developments. The Romanian and Estonian Governments were striving to do something about minority rights, while under Mečiar, they were slowly being eroded. In this respect, the installation of the new Slovak Government in October 1998 marked a 180-degree change in direction.

However, while legal rights are important, what is crucial for the Slovak Republic are not legislative changes but the establishment of trust between Slovaks, Hungarians and the Roma. Whereas the 1998 election programmes of many of the opposition parties emphasised Slovakia's paramount need to create trust on the part of Slovakia within the international community with a view to integration into European structures such as the EU and NATO, little was said of the need to build trust between the majority and minority populations.

The distrust of the Slovak Hungarians towards the Slovaks intensified after 1993, as the second and third Mečiar Governments pursued policies on language, education and local government which were hostile to Hungarian interests. Just as important, however, was the deterioration of the general political atmosphere. The racism of the newspaper *Slovenská republika*, which had editorial links with Mečiar's Movement for a Democratic Slovakia, created a climate where no rational Hungarian could help but suspect that even apparently reasonable legislative proposals, such as the introduction of bilingual alternative schooling, had actually been framed with the intention of attacking the Hungarian community. By Western standards, the anti-Hungarian rhetoric of the Mečiar Governments was more reprehensible in what was ostensibly a democratic country striving for fair representation and rights of minorities than the state of Slovakia's legislation and educational provision for minorities.

Slovak distrust of the Hungarians, on the other hand, remained firmly anchored in past grievances relating to the lamentable way Slovaks were treated under Hungarian rule in the twentieth century. For this reason, fears of the Hungarian minority only have overwhelming importance and immediacy for part of the Slovak community, and are predominantly backward-looking. Other Slovaks look to the future, trust in the international acceptance of Slovak independence and are primarily concerned with the resolution of other problems, such as the state of the economy, social welfare and European integration. In the Hungarian community, on the other hand, recent events serve to create a more united front.

---

[75] Ministry of Foreign Affairs of the Slovak Republic, op. cit. n. 5, p. 13.

The future resolution of outstanding problems depends largely on whether minority rights are seen as a 'zero-sum game', in which gains by one community represent a loss by another. The sporadically endorsed, and often denied, Hungarian demands for cultural and territorial autonomy appear particularly dangerous because a majority of Slovaks – and more particularly those in the area concerned – regard this as meaning a loss for Slovaks. On the other hand, a carefully drafted law on the use of minority languages could be accepted merely as representing a gain for Hungarians.

Many problems are also posed by the legacy of communism. This appears in several guises. First, there is a lack of enthusiasm for bilingualism among both Slovaks and to some extent also Hungarians. This derives in part from the failure of communist societies to admit to the paramount need for a State to communicate with its citizens: if a State is not used to explaining itself to citizens in one language, it is unlikely to occur to it to do it in two. Secondly, there is a residual tendency to seek monolithic solutions: the nationalist part of the Slovak community is prone to the view that there is one Slovak interest, and that people can therefore be divided into the 'pro-Slovak' and 'anti-Slovak', on the lines that they who are not with us are against us. The merging of the Hungarian electorate into one Party of the Hungarian Coalition is also slightly problematic in that – despite the institutionalisation of wings within the party – it allows limited articulation of differing views among Slovak Hungarians on general political issues. Thirdly, the notion of collective rights, in which citizens are defined by nationality and not as individuals, has a certain resonance of communist thinking. Yet while the Hungarians are accused by Slovak nationalists of pursuing collective rather than individual rights, in fact it was the third Mečiar Government's 1998 law on local elections which went to extremes in trying to define citizens by their ethnic affiliation: it did not allow a candidate to have a mixed or complex identity. Many of the fears of discrimination felt by both the Slovak Hungarians and – more particularly – the Roma would diminish if Slovakia were able to adopt the Western standards of equal opportunities endorsed by the European Union. Unfortunately, in communist societies jobs were allocated largely according to political criteria or the personal criteria of informal contacts. The establishment of real transparency, openness and competition in distributing power and responsibility would automatically reduce the salience of ethnicity as a selection criteria. However, until such an ideal state can be approached, the legal protection of minority rights is essential.

The fundamental problem of the Mečiar Governments was that they demanded loyalty from non-Slovak minorities while pursuing policies that meant it was impossible for such allegiance to become stronger. Hungarian demands therefore automatically focused on attaining more power within the territories in which they lived, rather than increasing their voice in Slovak politics as a whole. The inclusion of Hungarians in the Slovak Government is thus a wholly positive development. A far greater future challenge to Slovak governments will probably prove to be relations with the Roma, who have so far remained outside Slovak national politics, and in some cases chose also physically to leave the country.

Ultimately, civic nationalism needs to replace ethnic nationalism among all groups of the population. A precondition for this is the recognition of the fact that the Slovak Republic is a multinational State, and that this is a positive quality rather than a minority problem.

THE LEGAL SITUATION OF SLOVAKIA'S MINORITIES

by Marcia Rooker

1. INTRODUCTION – DEMOGRAPHIC SPECIFICATIONS

Like in other Central and Eastern European States a considerable part of the population of Slovakia identify themselves as members of a minority. Almost 15% of the 5.4 million Slovaks belong to a minority. According to the data in Slovakia's State report to the UN Human Rights Committee in 1996, based on information gathered in 1994, Hungarians are by far the largest minority: 568,714 persons or 10.6% of the population.[1] There is reason to believe that this number includes about 150,000 Hungarian-speaking Roma who prefer to be identified as Hungarians.[2] The Hungarians are concentrated in southern Slovakia, where the border between Hungary and Slovakia cuts through ethnically mixed areas. In the thirteen mixed Slovak-Hungarian districts the percentage of Hungarians varies from 4.1% to 87.9%.[3]

The second largest minority is constituted by Roma, 83,988 persons or 1.6% of the population according to the census; they are concentrated in the eastern part of the country. Here the number of Roma may be as high as 15%-18%.[4] It is acknowledged by the Slovak authorities that the number of 83,988 Roma is not accurate, the real number must be higher; between 250,000 and 500,000 according to the Slovak Government.[5] In a Minority Rights Group report their number is estimated between 480,000 and 520,000.[6] But in a more recent publication of this organisation the estimate number is 'up to 350,000'.[7] Absence of exact information on the number of Roma is common in most, if not all European states. A reason for unreliable figures is that Roma may not identify themselves as Roma

---

[1] UN Doc. CCPR/C/81/Add. 9, 1996, p. 20.

[2] US Department of State, Slovak Republic Country Report on Human Rights Practices for 1997 (1998), section 5.

[3] S. Pufflerova, 'National Minorities in Slovakia', 5 *Helsinki Monitor* (1994) No. 1, pp. 52-63, at p. 56.

[4] Pufflerova, loc. cit., p. 57.

[5] UN Doc. CCPR/C/SR. 1598, 1997, p. 7.

[6] J.P. Liégois and N. Gheorghe, *Roma/Gypsies, A European Minority*, Minority Rights Group (1995) p. 7.

[7] Minority Rights Group, *World Directory of Minorities* (1997) p. 245.

S. Trifunovska (Ed.), Minorities in Europe – Croatia, Estonia and Slovakia

during a census, because they are afraid to do so. Or they do identify themselves as a member of the majority or another minority, while this identity may not be accepted by outsiders. Furthermore, the still often used term 'gypsies' is not interchangeable with 'Roma', counting Gypsies may have another outcome than counting Roma, and counting those who have Romany as a mother tongue has yet another outcome.

More reliable are the percentages of the small minorities. The Czechs account for 1 % of the population. All other minorities constitute less than one percent of the population: Ruthenians, Ukrainians, Germans, Moravians or Silesians and Poles.[8] Not mentioned in the 1994 figures were Jews. In the 1991 census only 134 persons identified themselves as Jews.[9] According to the Minority Rights Group the Jewish community in Slovakia actually counts about 3,000-5,000 persons.[10]

This article will mainly focus on Hungarians and Roma, the two most numerous minorities and who are, incidentally, poles apart. But first a more general framework.

2. INTERNAL LEGAL POSITION

2.1 **Constitutional rights**

The Slovak Constitution was adopted on 1 September 1992. The preamble acknowledges the presence of minorities. In its so-called 'Fundamental Provision', it says:

> 'We, the Slovak Nation, mindful of the political and cultural heritage of our forefathers and of hundreds of years of experience in the struggle for our national existence and statehood . . . together with the members of national minorities and ethnic groups living in the territory of the Slovak Republic . . . establish this Constitution.'

This provision reflects the fact that Slovakia is a young nation in search of a national identity. The preamble emphasises Slovak identity, thus giving members of minorities a supporting role as citizens of the Slovak Republic.

A separate Chapter 4 of the Constitution is devoted to minorities, while some other provisions are also of a certain relevance for minorities. Articles 33 and 34 guarantee certain rights like the right to development of minority cultures and to use minority languages, as well as the right to participate in decision making in

---

[8] UN Doc. CCPR/C/81/Add. 9, 1996, p. 20.

[9] M. Olejnik and S. Gabzdilova, 'Minorities and Foreign Policy: the Case of Slovakia', in: *Minorities and Foreign Policy, Harmonie Papers* (1998) p. 92.

[10] Minority Rights Group, op. cit. n. 7, p. 245.

matters that affect minorities. Further, membership of a national minority or an ethnic group should not be detrimental to anyone, and the exercise of minority rights should not lead to a breach of integrity of the Slovak Republic or to discrimination against other citizens.

The Constitution does not make clear what makes a minority a minority. It does not give criteria to decide on that question, nor does it enumerate the minorities to which these constitutional provisions apply. And although minorities may have certain rights with respect to the use of their languages, the Slovak language is the State language in the territory of the Slovak Republic, according to Article 6(2) of the Constitution.

The UN Human Rights Committee has shown concern about the fact that no legislation to implement Article 6(b) (the use of languages other than Slovak ought to be regulated by law) and Article 34, para. 2b (the right of members of national minorities to use their mother tongue in administrative relations) has been adopted and '. . . recommends that legislation be rapidly adopted to secure language rights for minorities . . .'[11]

Other relevant constitutional provisions which deserve mentioning are Article 12 and Article 47. Article 12 includes a non-discrimination clause and the freedom to opt for a minority identity. Article 47 is part of the section on the right to judicial and other legal protection and guarantees that a person who does not speak the language used in court is entitled to an interpreter.

The heart of the debate on the Constitution is that constitutionally guaranteed freedoms and rights can be modified by a simple parliamentary majority, as that simple majority can adopt laws contradicting the Constitution.[12] The Constitution itself needs a two-thirds majority in order to be amended. Such a qualified majority is necessary to protect the fundaments of a State against decisions swayed by the issues of the day. If necessary the Constitutional Court can declare laws unconstitutional. And so it did with parts of the law on the State language that was adopted in 1996.[13] Although the Mečiar regime seemed to have ignored decisions by the Constitutional Court that it did not like,[14] the Ministry of Culture is preparing an amendment to the Law on the State Language.[15] That brings us to laws on the national level.

---

[11] UN Doc. CCPR/C/79/Add. 79.

[12] UNHCR Report, 1998, p. 10 with reference to several disputes.

[13] ECRI's country by country approach, Vol. III, 1998, p. 60.

[14] UNHCR Report, 1998, p. 10 with reference to disputes concerning NATO and the reinstatement of MP Gaulieder to the Slovak Parliament – Gaulieder was involved in the kidnapping of the President's son.

[15] ECRI Report, ibid., n. 13, p. 60.

2.2 Other national laws

The Constitution provides for a number of national laws with respect to minorities, like a law on minority languages (Article 6.2 of the Constitution) and laws guaranteeing certain rights for minorities (Article 34.1 of the Constitution). But these provisions have not been implemented, or – like the Law on the State Language adopted in 1995 – have been implemented in a way which violates the Constitution. This Law on the State Language affirms that the State language is Slovak and has to be used in official government matters, while the status of minority languages is not yet decided on in a law implementing the Constitutional obligation.[16]

A new Law on Name and Surname, adopted by the Slovak Parliament on 24 September 1993 and welcomed by minorities, introduces important changes. However, the most important change compared to the old law is that female citizens are no longer obliged to use the Slovak suffix '*-ova*' when they have a non-Slovak name.[17] This suffix often resulted in unpronounceable names.

Another significant regulation is the Decree on Vertical Road Signs, issued in 1993. With this Decree the Government tried to eliminate bilingual road signs, as part of a policy of elimination of all bilingual designations. Due to protests especially from the Hungarian minority the proposal was altered and it now allows the use of bilingual signposts in communities where the minority population exceeds 20%.[18]

The main achievement of the Mečiar Government with respect to minorities is subsidising cultural, broadcasting and publishing activities for minorities. Although it seems some of these subsidies have been severely cut. Especially the Hungarian minority complains about the elimination of the funding of their cultural organisations.[19]

Substantial measures to improve minority participation in political life or strengthening their position on the labour market have not been adopted during the Mečiar era.

3. INTERNATIONAL LEGAL RULES APPLICABLE TO SLOVAKIA'S MINORITIES

Slovakia has ratified the major international human rights instruments and documents combating racism and intolerance, including the UN Covenant on Civil and Political Rights (CCPR) and the UN Convention on the Elimination of All

---

16 Minority Rights Group, op. cit. n. 7, p. 246.
17 Pufflerova, loc. cit. n. 3, p. 54.
18 Minority Rights Group, op. cit., n. 7, p. 246.
19 US State Report, ibid., n. 2, section 5.

Forms of Racial Discrimination (CERD). For the position of minorities Articles 26 and 27 of the CCPR are most important, as is the CERD. According to the Human Rights Committee's General Comment on Article 27, belonging to a minority is a human right and is therefore inalienable and does not depend on recognition by a State. Article 27 is linked to Article 26: non-discrimination is not enough, a State has to take additional measures to guarantee to members of minorities not only equality by law but also equality in fact. 'States are obliged to ensure the survival and continued development of . . . the minorities concerned.'[20]

Slovakia submitted a report in accordance with Article 40 CCPR in 1996.[21] This report has been the object of constructive dialogue between Slovak State representatives and the UN Human Rights Committee during a session in July 1997. In its Concluding Observations[22] the Committee states that it is pleased with certain developments but at the same time concerned about remnants of the former totalitarian rule, both in institutions, rules and political and social attitudes. For example, the establishment of the Commission for Minorities is welcomed but concern is expressed about Roma falling victim to racist attacks and not being adequately protected. The Committee recommends that '(a) priority be given to addressing discrimination, in particular through training and education campaigns; and (b) mechanisms to monitor non-discrimination laws and to receive and investigate complaints from victims urgently be established'.[23] The Committee also noted with concern that the use of minority languages in official communications is not secure, and recommends 'that legislation be rapidly adopted to secure language rights for minorities'.[24] The Committee is also concerned 'that insufficient provision, in particular in relation to allocation of resources, is made in the field of educational and cultural rights for the benefit of the Hungarian population.'[25] Recommendations from UN Committees may not immediately be implemented by an unwilling government. Thus it may seem a rather powerless mechanism. But the recommendations and the promises made by the governments can be used by national organisations in their dialogue with the government concerned.

CERD contains a catalogue of rights which people should enjoy without discrimination. Of course these rights are most important to members of minorities. Slovakia has not yet fulfilled its reporting obligations under Article 9. No use has been made up to now of the possibility to lodge an individual complaint against Slovakia either under article 14 of CERD or the First Optional Protocol to the CCPR.

---

20 General Comment 23, UN Doc. A/49/40, 1994.
21 UN Doc. CCPR/C/81/Add. 9.
22 UN Doc. CCPR/C/79/Add. 79.
23 UN Doc. CCPR/C/79/Add. 79, paras. 14 and 15.
24 UN Doc. CCPR/C/79/Add. 79, para. 24.
25 UN Doc. CCPR/C/79/Add. 79, para. 24.

Of course, Slovakia is also Member State of the Council of Europe and a party to the European Convention on Human Rights and Fundamental Freedoms. Besides, it has ratified the European Framework Convention for the Protection of National Minorities. The ECRI (The Council of Europe Commission on Racism and Intolerance) has published a country report on Slovakia in April 1998.[26] These country reports review the situation in each Member State in order to provide governments with helpful and concrete proposals. According to ECRI the democratisation process in Slovakia has not yet been completed. All key areas identified by ECRI as meriting particular attention are minority issues: problems of the national minorities, especially Hungarians; the situation of the Roma; the restrictive nature of the Law on the State Language; and the absence of a reliable system of data collection with respect to minorities, racism and discrimination. The ECRI report also contains some recommendations. With respect to international legal instruments it advises Slovakia to consider ratifying the European Charter for Regional or Minority Languages and the European Social Charter.

The OSCE bodies have also expressed their concern about minorities in Slovakia. Hungarian-Slovak relations are a recurring item on the agenda of the OSCE High Commissioner on National Minorities. Among other things, the High Commissioner suggested setting up a committee of experts to monitor the Hungarian and Slovak minorities for two years.[27]

On a bilateral level a Treaty on Good-Neighbourly Relations and Friendly Co-operation was concluded between Hungary and Slovakia in March 1995. Slovakia ratified this Treaty in March 1996.[28] It applies to the Slovak minority in Hungary and the Hungarian minority in Slovakia. The Treaty, on the one hand, declares as 'guiding principles' rights already enshrined in treaties like the European Convention and the CCPR. On the other hand, it obliges Slovakia and Hungary to apply as 'legal obligations' the norms and political commitments contained in the OSCE Copenhagen Final Document, the UN Declaration on the Rights of Persons belonging to National or Ethnic, Religious and Linguistic Minorities, and Recommendation 1201 of the Parliamentary Assembly of the Council of Europe.[29] The implementation of these international standards has not come about during the Mečiar regime.

---

[26] ECRI, 1998, pp. 59-67.

[27] Pufflerova, loc. cit. n. 3, pp. 52-63.

[28] This is remarkable as Hungary and Slovakia at that time were involved in a procedure before the International Court of Justice with respect to the dispute concerning the Gabčikovo-Nagymaros Project, which is a Slovak-Hungarian initiative to realise a system of locks in the Danube.

[29] I. Pogany, 'International Human Rights Standards and the New Constitutions: Minority Rights in Central and Eastern Europe', in: *Constitutional Reform and International Law in Central and Eastern Europe* (1998) pp. 156-159.

4. EQUAL TREATMENT AND PROTECTION AGAINST DISCRIMINATION

4.1 **Hungarians**

The presence of a Hungarian minority in Slovakia is a result of the disintegration of the Austrian-Habsburg Empire when three hundred years of Hungarian rule had come to an end. Out of the chaos after the First World War the democratic republic of Czechoslovakia emerged with Tomás Masaryk as President. Many Hungarians lived on the Slovak side of the newly established border between Hungary and Slovakia and thus became citizens of the new republic and the second largest minority with 5.57% of the population in 1921, only outnumbered by the Germans: 23.36% of the population.[30] The position of the Hungarians had changed from members of the ruling majority to members of an ethnic minority. Although part of the population was worried about the future conduct of the once dominant Hungarians, Czechoslovakia had a rather positive attitude towards the League of Nations minority protection system.[31] With respect to language rights for minorities Czechoslovakia was at the time more liberal than neighbouring countries.[32]

The democratic Czechoslovak Republic lasted until 1938. On 29 September 1938 the Munich Treaty was concluded between Germany, the United Kingdom, France and Italy. With the false hope of maintaining peace, Sudetenland – until then Czechoslovak territory – was ceded to Hitler's Germany. A few weeks later, on 2 November 1938, the Vienna Arbitration by Germany and Italy brought the southern part of Slovakia once again under Hungarian rule; the Slovaks living there were badly treated. After WW II this territory became once more Czechoslovakian.[33]

After the War anti-Hungarian feelings were common and the Czechoslovak Government, on the other hand, made several attempts to reduce the Hungarian minority by expulsion and expropriation,[34] forced resettlement in the Czech lands and by assimilation. All these attempts were not successful as the Hungarian minority continued to exist in these territories.[35]

During the communist era ethnic tensions were suppressed, only to re-emerge after the collapse of the totalitarian regime. The 1968 Prague Spring held promises for a better position for minorities; Hungarians, Poles and Ukrainians gained minority status, but in the end nothing changed. In 1989 the Velvet Revolution

[30] D. Crowe, *A History of Gypsies of Eastern Europe and Russia* (1995) pp. 44-45.
[31] J. Robinson, *Were the Minorities Treaties a Failure* (1943) p. 169.
[32] Robinson, ibid., p. 209.
[33] Olejnik and Gabzdilova, loc. cit. n. 9, p. 93.
[34] Crowe, op. cit. n. 30, p. 54.
[35] Olejnik and Gabzdilova, loc. cit. n. 9, p. 93.

gave new hope for democracy, respect for human rights and a recognition of minority rights. The first changes were promising, but both Slovak and Hungarian nationalist sentiments influenced Slovak policies after the dissolution of Czechoslovakia in 1992.[36] It manifested itself in the above mentioned Law on the State Language adopted in November 1995. This Law limits the use of minority languages and strengthens the position of the Slovak language, as all official publications and all dealings with State authorities have to take place in Slovak. The Hungarian coalition has appealed to the Constitutional Court. As stated above, parts of the Law were declared unconstitutional. The Ministry of Education interpreted the Law by no longer allowing bilingual schoolcards. Principals and teachers ignoring this interpretation met with disciplinary measures. More successful was the Hungarian protests against a proposed law to expand the use of Slovak in Hungarian schools. The law never came about. But a law on the use of minority languages was not presented to Parliament either, despite the advice of the OSCE High Commissioner on National Minorities to do so.[37] Hungarian organisations also protested against a cut in Government support for their cultural activities.

A factor not to be ignored in the position of the Hungarian minority is the influence of Hungary. Hungary has an proactive policy with respect to the 3.5 million Hungarians living outside the kin-State. Leaders of the Hungarian organisations in Slovakia are in close contact with the Hungarian Government. At first the Hungarian Government, like the Slovak, emphasized the nationality issue, with the statement of the Prime Minister Jozsef Antall that Hungary had the right to interfere with other States on behalf of the Hungarian minority living in that State.[38]

From 1994 onwards the Hungarian Prime Minister Gyula Horn has developed another policy, aiming at good neighbourly relations with a bilateral treaty as a means. The aspiration of both Hungary and Slovakia to qualify as Member States of NATO and the European Union will have contributed to this more co-operative way of thinking.[39]

4.2 **Roma**

Presumably the Roma entered the Slovak lands sometime during the fifteenth century, although some writers state they were present as early as the thirteenth or even the eleventh century. They were portrayed as castle musicians and metal workers. Later they served in the royal Hungarian army. But in the sixteenth century when the Turks defeated the Hungarians, a negative attitude towards the Roma developed. They were isolated from the rest of the population, only al-

---

[36] Olejnik and Gabzdilova, loc. cit. n. 9, p. 94.
[37] US State Report, ibid., n. 2, section 5.
[38] Olejnik and Gabzdilova, loc. cit. n. 9, p. 104.
[39] Olejnik and Gabzdilova, loc. cit. n. 9, pp. 105-106.

lowed to live in special settlements, denied profitable work and they were looked upon as pagans and spies.

In following centuries wars and armed conflicts continued to destabilise the area. Roma were denied both the possibility to settle and to live a nomadic life. Like elsewhere in Europe, the Roma were outlawed in the sixteenth century. This lasted until the reign of Maria Theresia (1740-1780) who introduced her infamous assimilation policy when Roma were no longer called 'gypsies' but 'new Hungarians'. Her son and successor Joseph II (1780-1790) retained this policy. After the death of Joseph II a new era of wars and revolutions began, only to end after the Revolutions of 1848. Then serfdom was abolished and illiterate Slovaks, including Roma, were to be educated. Even special Roma schools were established. But this was not to last. In 1867 a new policy was introduced: Magyarisation. No more Roma schools but poverty and discrimination was the fate which the Roma shared with Slovak peasants. Statistical data from the end of the last century reveal that the majority of Roma in Slovakia were illiterate. Only Roma musicians could make a reasonable living as could some craftsmen, but the majority must have lived in depressing circumstances, poor, without basic provisions, isolated, illiterate and with no prospects. The situation hardly improved after the First World War when the League of Nations minorities protection system guaranteed them equality. Significant is the quote from a Slovak local official from those days: 'The penalty of imprisonment has no effect on them, because imprisonment only improves their living conditions. It often happens a Gypsy without resources commits a crime only to escape the pangs of hunger.'[40] In those years even pogroms against the Roma took place in Czechoslovakia. But at the same time efforts were made to improve their situation. Again, some Roma schools were opened. But again, it was not to last. The 1938 Munich and Vienna accords put an end to these developments.

During the Second World War most Czech Roma fell victim to Nazi persecution, while most Slovak Roma survived the war. Only in 1944 when the Nazis decided to occupy the Slovak puppet-State were massacres of the Roma carried out as retaliation for their role in the uprising, the Slovak National Insurrection in September and October 1944.

After the War many Slovak Roma were forced to resettle in the Czech lands where a lack of labour force was created with the expulsion of Germans from the Sudetenland. After the communist take-over the government aimed at the integration of the Roma. Nomadism was outlawed. Settled Roma did in general live in very poor conditions, not much better than what they were used to before the War.

The Prague Spring promised some improvements and Roma nationalism flourished for the first time in history. But in the seventies a new assimilation campaign was introduced including a programme to persuade Roma women to be

[40] Crowe, op. cit. n. 30, p. 45.

sterilised[41] and attempts to reduce illiteracy among the Roma by sending Roma children to schools for the mentally retarded because of their lack of knowledge of the Czech or Slovak languages.[42]

Their situation has not improved since the Velvet Revolution or the dissolution of Czechoslovakia. Now the Roma fall victim to skinhead attacks. At least one person has died as a result of such violence.[43] The European Roma Rights Centre in Budapest has documented cases of violence against Roma where the Slovak Government denied the crime, or denied the racist dimension in a crime, reversed the charges or denied community violence. Thus the Government tries to trivialise the scale of the problem.[44]

The racist violence against Roma is one of the principle subjects of concern to the UN Human Rights Committee. The Government's attitude to qualify Roma as 'socially unadaptable' and other racist remarks are not very helpful in changing the climate. Roma children are still referred to schools for the mentally handicapped. The lack of education will not be solved in this way. Unemployment, poor housing, low life expectancy, high infant mortality, hardly any access to State services all await new generations of Roma. All this is entangled with the many age-old prejudices against this minority. To give just one example: private employment offices publish lists of job vacancies with the note: 'no Roma'.[45]

The ECRI recommends free legal aid to any victim of discrimination without sufficient means to bring a case to court. The European Roma Rights Centre has funds to pay lawyers defending Roma whose fundamental rights have been violated. They have a hard job finding lawyers to do the job. Defending Roma is bad for business.

One positive development is the fact that the Slovak Government has adopted 'Principles of the Government Policy Towards the Roma'. This document was prepared by the Czechoslovak Government in 1991. The principles for this comprehensive approach include the equality of the Roma with other national communities; equal treatment in the social sphere and transferring powers and responsibilities from Central Government to city councils.[46] Further, the Government has appointed someone to monitor the problems of violence against Roma and all other problems encountered by 'disadvantaged citizens'.[47] But for the moment that is all paper.

---

[41] P. Oefner and B. de Rooy, *Het afkopen van vruchtbaarheid* (1990).

[42] Most of the information in this paragraph comes from the chapter on Czechoslovakia in Crowe, op. cit. n. 30.

[43] US State Report 1998, ibid., n. 2, section 5.

[44] ERRC Report, January 1997.

[45] ECRI Report, 1998, p. 62.

[46] UNHCR Report, 1998, p. 11.

[47] ECRI Report, 1998, p. 62.

5. SPECIFIC RIGHTS

5.1 **Citizenship**

One of the examples illustrating the negative effects of certain national laws on the position of minorities is the Slovak Law on Citizenship of 19 January 1993, whose negative impact is felt especially by the Roma minority. In fact, after the dissolution of Czechoslovakia both the Czech Republic and Slovakia had to adopt a new law on citizenship. The Czech Law was criticised as many Roma, among whom were even those who had lived in the Czech lands all their lives, were denied Czech citizenship. They either had to move to Slovakia or remain in the Czech Republic as stateless inhabitants deprived of civil rights they had enjoyed until the dissolution of Czechoslovakia.[48] The Council of Europe had an expert group visit the country to advise on how to change the law and to mitigate the undesired effect of statelessness among former Czechoslovak citizens.[49] Still, an unknown number of Roma have become *de jure* or *de facto* stateless as a result of the dissolution of Czechoslovakia and the Czech citizenship law.

The Slovak Law seems less draconian. It is not so problematic to acquire Slovak citizenship, that is a Slovak passport to travel abroad. But such a passport is insufficient to enjoy fully the rights linked to citizenship. Therefore one needs a citizen's identity card. These identity cards are issued by the municipalities only to people who can prove that they have a legal residence in that municipality. As a consequence the few nomadic Roma in Slovakia may be deprived of an identity card. But even owning a house or renting one is not enough, the place has to have a minimum space per inhabitant. Especially the Roma often live in substandard houses. They may have a Slovak passport, but '*lack of a permanent domicile means that the citizen may be denied his civil, political, social and economic rights.* Rights affected include voting, petition, association, travel within the country, marriage, birth and death registration, employment and legal payment of taxes'.[50]

5.2 **Minority Languages**

The use of minority languages is one of the main issues concerning minorities in Slovakia. In November 1995 the Slovak Government adopted the Law on the State Language, which among other things annuls the 1990 Act on the Official Language, that gave certain rights to Hungarians in areas where they constitute more than 20% of the population. The new Law on the State Language prohibits

---

[48] M. Rooker, 'Staatloos en Rechtloos, de marginalisering van Roma in Tsjechië', *Oost Europa Verkenningen,* No. 140 (1995) pp. 11-18.

[49] Council of Europe Expert Report on Citizenship Laws, 1996.

[50] UNHCR, 1998, p. 9, emphasis not added.

the use of any other language but Slovak in official dealings, limits the use of minority languages in the media and in cultural activities, even when the target-audience is composed almost entirely of members of minority communities.[51] As mentioned above, report cards issued by Hungarian schools have to be in Slovak. Principals that continue to issue such cards bilingually face disciplinary measures.[52] And even when a patient consults a doctor the language has to be Slovak, or both Slovak and a minority language if the patient does not speak Slovak.[53]

The UN Human Rights Committee[54] and the OSCE High Commissioner on National Minorities have both recommended the adoption of legislation securing the position of minority languages. However, this obligation was declined by the Slovak Government which in September 1997 declared that it no longer saw a need for such a law.[55] All this despite: (a) the fact that Article 6(2) of the Constitution states that '[t]he use of languages other then the state language in administrative relations will be regulated by law'; and (b) the fact that Slovakia sees as legally binding with respect to the Hungarian minority the Council of Europe Parliamentary Assembly Resolution 1201, whose Article 7(3) reads: 'In the regions in which substantial numbers of a national minority are settled, the persons belonging to a national minority shall have the right to use their mother tongue in their contacts with the administrative authorities and in proceeding before the courts and legal authorities'.

An implementation of the constitutional right for minorities to use their language has indeed not been introduced. The only perhaps positive development in this respect is that parts of the Law on the State Language were declared unconstitutional, and an amendment is in the process of preparation.[56]

5.3 **Education**

Speaking in more general terms, facilities for education in the mother tongue have improved for most minorities in recent years, though it should be pointed out that the situation of Hungarians in this respect has deteriorated. Minority groups have the right to establish private educational institutes. They can use textbooks which are different from the ones on the official list. Even the Government can establish minority schools.[57] In fact three kinds of minority education could be distinguished: (a) instruction in the minority language only; (b) bilingual instruction; and (c) instruction in Slovak with the mother tongue as one of

---

[51] Pogany, loc. cit. n. 29, p. 165.
[52] US State Report, 1998, section 5.
[53] Pogany, loc. cit. n. 29, p. 184.
[54] UN Doc. A/52/40 p. 61.
[55] US State Report, 1998, section 5.
[56] ECRI Report, 1998, p. 60.
[57] ECRI Report 1998, p. 63.

the subjects. Monolingual schools only existed for Hungarians, but they have been replaced by bilingual schools.[58] Schools with bilingual instruction also exist for Germans and Ukrainians. In schools in which Slovak is the instruction language, Ukrainian, German, Ruthenian and Romany can be taught as one of the subjects. For the Roma 'zero-preparatory classes' have been introduced as a attempt to reduce the number of Roma children dropping out of school or just never attending. But what seems to be a good initiative may be severely hampered by the way in which it is carried out. The fact that this project is called 'an experiment for the linguistically disadvantaged and socially neglected children' does not give much hope that it will assist the Roma minority in a proper way in the implementation of their right to be educated in their mother tongue.[59]

5.4 **Political representation**

With the elections of October 1998 the Mečiar era came to an end. Hungarians and Roma did not hold positions in the Mečiar Government,[60] although it may be considered that Hungarians were well represented at the local level. According to some statistics they seem to be in control of 450 municipalities.[61] The new Government is established with the participation of the Hungarian Coalition Party. Three Hungarians have been appointed to ministerial posts. One of them, Pal Czáky, who is now a Deputy Prime Minister and Minister in Charge of Human Rights and Minority Rights, emphasises that his first priority is to improve the situation of the Roma.[62] The Minister of the Interior has appointed a Roma advisor.

According to the OSCE High Commissioner on National Minorities, the new Slovak Government has also announced that it is willing to co-operate with the Czech Republic and Hungary in improving the situation of the Roma.[63]

6. CONCLUDING REMARKS

Since the 1989 Velvet Revolution and the dissolution of Czechoslovakia the legal position of the Hungarian minority has deteriorated, despite international and bilateral commitments and some constitutional safeguards. But, the last elections

---

[58] ECRI Report, 1989, p. 63.

[59] UN Doc. CCPR/C/SR. 1589, p. 8.

[60] US State Report, 1998, section 3.

[61] UN Doc. CCPR/C/SR.1589, p. 7.

[62] L. Sachs, 'Five Centuries of Discrimination . . . and Still Counting', 2 *Refugees* (1998) No. 113, p. 22.

[63] Interview by Renée Postma with the OSCE High Commissioner on National Minorities, in *NRC-Handelsblad* (9 January 1999).

seem to have brought a change for the better, with a Government with an eye towards the justified wishes of minorities. The legal positions of the other minorities have improved with respect to possibilities to develop their culture, although subsidies for cultural activities have been cut. Their possibilities for mother tongue education have also improved. And the introduction of zero classes for the Roma can still be a step forward, dependent on the modes of its implementation. For the Roma, adequate protection against racial violence and hate speech, discrimination and a programme to improve living and working conditions (housing, vocational training, work) are indispensable factors for the realisation of basic human rights. As pointed out above, the new Government seems to have a much better attitude towards minorities. Its initial measures – the appointment of a Minister especially in charge of minorities and human rights and the willingness to co-operate with neighbouring countries with respect to the issues of minorities – provide hope for the future.

THE ECONOMIC SITUATION OF SLOVAKIA'S MINORITIES

by Edwin Bakker

1. INTRODUCTION

Inequalities that divide disadvantaged minorities from advantaged or dominant groups are the enduring heritage of four major historical processes: conquest, State building, migration and economic development. The role of dominant groups has been of particular importance as every people who established an empire, settled frontiers, who conquered non-believers, civilised natives, or who built a modern State, did so at the expense of weaker and less fortunate peoples. [1]

This article assesses to what extent one can speak of economically weaker and less fortunate minorities in the case of Slovakia's two largest minorities: the Hungarians and the Roma. It elaborates on the question whether these two minorities constitute economically disadvantaged groups or not, and, if so, in which areas. The paper also investigates to which extent disadvantages can be considered as a direct or indirect consequence of deliberate social policy and practice by the (Czecho-) Slovak State.

After a brief discussion on more general and theoretical notions of the economic status of minorities associated with Gurr's *Minorities at Risk Project*,[2] the article will focus on the minority situation in Slovakia, by providing an overview of the demographic situation of different ethnic, national and religious minorities within the Slovak Republic, a description of and discussion on the main issues concerning the legal status of minorities, as well as the Government's policies and practices towards these groups in the post-communist era. Before embarking on the issue of the economic situation of the two largest minority groups in Slovakia, the article explores the main specific minority issues concerning the Hungarian and Roma population and gives an outline of Slovakia's economy after the fall of the communist regime. The economic situation of the Hungarians and the Roma is illustrated with concrete examples and summarised on the basis of extensive data from the *Minorities at Risk Project*. Concluding remarks regarding economic inequality, its possible causes and solutions and a reflection on

---

[1] T.R. Gurr, *Minorities at Risk: A Global View of Ethnopolitical Conflicts*, Washington DC, US Institute for Peace Press (1993), p. 34.

S. Trifunovska (Ed.), Minorities in Europe – Croatia, Estonia and Slovakia

the possibilities of a comprehensive approach to the 'Roma question' constitute the final part of this article.

2. A GENERAL VIEW ON THE ECONOMIC STATUS OF MINORITIES

In a world in which the number of minorities is much higher than the number of dominant State-forming majorities, many national or ethnic groups face restricted access to political and economic resources. They experience differential treatment as a consequence of a widespread social practice, a deliberate government policy or of both.[3]

Many dominant State-forming groups that emerged as winners in conquest, State building, and economic development, succeeded in establishing patterns of authority. They also created various kinds of social barriers to protect their advantaged positions, including the policies and practices for which one could use the shorthand label of 'discrimination'.

Discriminatory practices towards minorities were widespread throughout the world until World War II. In the past half-century, however, the legal underpinnings of discriminatory barriers have been dismantled in many plural societies. In the same period, politics of accommodation and reform have been adopted leading toward power sharing and more equal material well-being among different national or ethnic groups.[4] These general processes did not take place in the same fashion and with the same pace in all the world's regions. In some parts of the world manifest economic differences have persisted.

The persistence or even increase of economic (and political) inequalities among groups is a consequence of their differential access to scarce positions and resources. With respect to this, a distinction can be made between historical processes and contemporary conditions: whereas the former explains the origin of inequalities, the latter contributes to their maintenance. These inequalities in the economic situation of groups are expressed in the following areas: income, land and other property, access to higher education, presence in commercial activities, presence in professions, and presence in official positions.[5]

Inter-group economic differences are also expressed in differences in regional economic development and regional unemployment levels. Some of these differences are the result of historical processes. Many autochthonous minorities origi-

---

[2] The *Minorities at Risk Project* is an independent, university-based research project that monitors and analyses the status and conflicts of minority groups around the world. The project, directed by Ted Robert Gurr, comprises a global survey, providing coded profiles of almost 300 major ethnic or national groups and data on their current concerns and involvement in conflict since 1945.

[3] Gurr, op. cit. n. 1, p. 6.

[4] Gurr, op. cit, n. 1, pp. 36-37.

[5] Gurr, op. cit., n. 1, p. 41.

nated in or were pushed into resource-poor regions which facilitated the perpetuation of their economic disadvantages and made it more difficult for them to exercise political influence on the centre. Examples of resource-pour or otherwise problematic regions are rural areas, mountain regions and/or in peripheral regions along international borders.[6]

Maintenance of cultural differences are a function of enduring traits of a group, their way of life, language, religion, and traditional region of residence. It can be argued that cultural differences cause or reinforce political and economic disadvantages because they make it difficult for minorities to operate effectively in institutions established by dominant groups. They also give dominant groups rationales for denying access to people who are 'different'. However, according to Gurr,[7] there is no general empirical basis for arguing that inequalities affecting minorities are in a function of cultural differences. They only have a moderate correlation with political and economic differentials and a weak correlation with political and economic discrimination. An exception to the general rule is the situation of most of the Roma in Europe. In their case cultural differences play a role in maintaining disparities due to values and beliefs that discourage participation in the political and economic systems of a dominant group.[8] Distinct characteristics of the Roma are also often used as rationales for discriminatory policies and practices, particularly in Central and Eastern Europe.

In general, compared to cultural differentials, past or present discrimination has a much greater impact on the extent and persistence of minorities' disadvantages. Economic inequalities have often, though not always, been created and reinforced by deliberate social practice and public policy. Since there are no universally accepted scholarly or legal standards about what constitutes discrimination, Gurr[9] uses an internal standard for comparison when judging whether discrimination is or has been present. He argues that the relevant question is whether members of a group are, or have been, deliberately restricted in their access to the conditions of material well-being, or political participation and influence, in comparison with other groups in their society. Following this way of thinking, groups are the subject of economic discrimination when their members are or have been systematically excluded from access to desirable economic goods, conditions, or positions that are open to other groups in their society.

The impact of these policies and practices on economic inequality varies greatly among world regions. It is weakest in Asia and Eastern Europe. According to Gurr,[10] the explanation lies in the distinctive political culture of each re-

[6] Cf., J. Fidrmuc, 'Ethnic Minorities and Regional Unemployment', in S. Sarpetta and A.Woetter (Eds.), *The Regional Dimension of Unemployment in Transition Economies*, Paris, OECD-Centre for Cooperation with Economies in Transition (1995) pp. 382-415.

[7] Gurr, op. cit. n. 1, p. 58.

[8] Gurr, op. cit. n. 1, p. 40.

[9] Ibid.

[10] Gurr, op. cit. n. 1, pp. 59-60.

gion. The contrast is particularly sharp between the socialist regimes of the former Soviet Union and Eastern Europe and the nationalist and sectarian regimes in, for instance, the Middle East. In contrast to the latter, the socialist regimes were committed to eliminating discrimination and to provide minorities, as equal members of the working class, with opportunities for political and economic advancement within the Communist Party and State apparatus.

3. THE DEMOGRAPHIC SITUATION IN SLOVAKIA

Like most States in Central and Eastern Europe, Slovakia's population is composed of more than one ethnic or national group. Besides the Slovaks, the young independent Republic is home to Hungarians, the Roma, Czechs, Ruthenes, Ukrainians and to a number of other smaller groups.

The autochthonous Hungarians who live in the south of the country constitute Slovakia's largest minority. According to the 1991 census of the Czech and Slovak Federal Republic, 568,000 citizens claimed Hungarian nationality within the Slovak part of the then still existing federation. This number represented 10.7% of Slovakia's total population.[11] According to the same census, 608,000 Slovak inhabitants stated Hungarian to be their mother tongue.[12] This number corresponds to almost 12% of the total population.

Slovakia's second largest minority group are the Roma. Their exact number is unclear. Unofficial estimates claim that as many as 750,000 live in Slovakia, but the 1991 census recorded only 79,000 persons who identified themselves as Roma.[13] According to estimates of the urban and communal offices of Slovakia's State administration, by 1989 about 254,000 Roma lived throughout the country, constituting 4.8% of the population.[14] It is more likely, however, that they number more than 300,000 persons.[15] This discrepancy in numbers is at least partially due to the fact that many Roma claim other nationalities, either as a result of assimilation or fear of persecution.[16]

Among other minority groups in the Slovak Republic belong 53,000 Czechs. The 1991 census also distinguishes 17,000 Ruthenes and 14,000 Ukrainians, con-

---

[11] SUSR (Statistický Úrad Slovenskej Republiky), *Národnost a nábozenské vyznanie obyvatelstva Slovenskej Republiky*, Bratislava (1994).

[12] S. Pufflerová, 'National Minorities in Slovakia', 5 *Helsinki Monitor* (1994) No. 1, pp. 52-63, at p. 62.

[13] SUSR (Statistický Úrad Slovenskej Republiky), *Statistical Yearbook of the Slovak Republic 1997*, Bratislava (1997) p. 151.

[14] K. Orgovanová, 'Roma in Slovakia', 4 *Quarterly of the East and Central Europe Program* (1994) No. 4, [www.geocities.com/Paris/5121/slovakia.htm].

[15] Minority Rights Group, *World Directory of Minorities*, London (1997) p. 246.

[16] J. Fox, 'Roma (Gypsies) in the Slovak Republic', *Minorities at Risk Project* (1995) [www.bsos.umd.edu].

sidered by many as belonging to the same ethnic group.[17] In addition, there are some 5,400 Germans and 2,800 Poles.[18]

The country's main religiously defined minorities are the small Jewish community (some 1,000 persons) and the more than 10,000 Jehova's Witnesses.[19]

The State-forming Slovaks number about 4.5 million. They make up between 80% and 85% of Slovakia's total population.

4. THE LEGAL POSITION OF MINORITIES IN SLOVAKIA

The collapse of communist rule in 1989 promised a rapid improvement to the rights of minorities in (Czecho-)Slovakia. The Charter of Fundamental Rights and Freedoms, adopted by the Czechoslovak Federal Assembly in January 1991, prohibited all forms of discrimination and reaffirmed the right to education in the mother tongue. For its part, the 1992 Slovak Constitution gave minorities the right to develop their culture, to communicate in their own language with State officials, and to be educated both in the Slovak language and in their own mother tongue. Nevertheless, there was a feeling of discontent since both these instruments seemed implicitly to deny minorities any 'State-forming' role within the new political structure. Moreover, the retention after 1992 of a government composed of nationalists and neo-communists aroused fears for the interests of minorities.[20]

Since Slovakia's independence in January 1993, the position of its minorities has gradually deteriorated. The 1993 Surname Law made compulsory the registration of names according to the rules of Slovak grammar, although some concessions to minority-language usage were made in 1994. The right of minorities to use their own language was circumscribed in 1995 by the Act on the State Language. The Act affirms Slovak as the State language, it imposes harsh financial penalties for its misuse or misspelling, and establishes that the use of minority languages shall be the subject of future legislation. However, despite international pressure by the European Union (EU) and the Organization for Security and Co-operation in Europe's (OSCE) High Commissioner on National Minorities (HCNM) to draft a minority language law, and despite initial promises to do so, in 1998 the Slovak Government issued a memorandum claiming that there was no need for such a law.[21] Besides curbing minority rights, recent Government policies include a very substantial and disproportional reduction of State subsidies for

[17] Minority Rights Group, op. cit. n. 15, p. 247.

[18] SUSR, op. cit. n. 13, p. 159.

[19] SUSR, op. cit. n. 13, p. 505.

[20] Minority Rights Group, op. cit. n. 15, p. 245.

[21] Cf., E. Bakker, 'Growing Isolation: Political and Ethnic Tensions in the Slovak Republic', 9 *Helsinki Monitor* (1998) No. 1, pp. 23-36.

minority cultural organisations. Members of the ruling parties also contributed to the stigmatisation of the Roma and the Hungarian minority by labelling them respectively as 'criminals' and 'natural enemies of the Slovak State'.[22] It should be emphasized that although the Slovak political policy towards minorities has provided the country with a bad reputation, the OSCE, EU and the Council of Europe fact-finding missions recommended only certain alterations in policy, not because of the demands of the legally binding norms of international law, but because of the fact that their implementation would prudently reduce the risk of conflict.[23]

The relationship between the Slovak Government and the Hungarian minority has been strained since Slovakia's declaration of independence following the election victory by the nationalist and neo-communist parties in the 1992 general elections.[24] Not least for historical reasons, this relationship has many aspects which are considered to be particularly sensitive in the eyes of both sides.[25] According to the OSCE High Commissioner on National Minorities, the most sensitive questions include minority claims as regards the following: teaching in their mother tongue; the use of their mother tongue in official communications; registration of their names in Hungarian; placing bilingual road signs in the areas where they reside; appropriate State assistance for cultural projects; and full participation in the political life of the country.[26]

After some delay and international pressure, some of these questions were properly addressed by the Slovak Government. Most issues, however, are still not resolved despite promises by the authorities to do so. In addition, some new disputes emerged under the Mečiar administration. The introduction of a new Law on the State Language of the Slovak Republic in 1995, the Government's refusal to introduce a law on minority languages, gerrymandering administrative districts, and the Government's reluctance to implement the 1996 bilateral Treaty between Slovakia and Hungary resulted in fierce and sometimes unbridled reactions from representatives of the Hungarian minority. These representatives claim 'fair' opportunities to preserve their national identity. To this end, they call for more legal guarantees and self-determination with regard to the expression, pro-

---

[22] Cf., United States Department of State, *Slovak Republic Country Report on Human Rights*, Czechoslovak Committee of the European Cultural Foundation, Rights Practices for 1997. Bureau of Democracy, Human Rights and Labor, Washington D.C. (1998); E. Bakker, *Minority Conflicts in Slovakia and Hungary?* Capelle a/d IJssel, Labyrint Publication (1997).

[23] Cf., K. Williams, 'The Magyar Minority in Slovakia', 6 *Regional and Federal Studies* (1995) No. 1, pp. 1-20.

[24] In the course of the 1992 election campaign, very strong anti-Hungarian sentiments were vented in Slovakia (H. Kruyzen, 'De Hongaren in Slowakije', in H. Ramkema and E. van Schaik (Eds.), *Tussen recht en repressie*, Amsterdam, Instituut voor Publiek en Politiek (1994) pp. 74-94.

[25] FIER (Foundation on Inter-Ethnic Relations, The Hague), *The Role of the High Commissioner on National Minorities in OSCE Conflict Prevention: An Introduction* (1997) p. 72.

[26] Ibid.

tection and development of the national identity of the Hungarian minority within the region they inhabit.

At this point in time the Hungarians are in conflict with the majority of the Slovak political parties. The latter often perceive the Hungarian efforts to preserve their distinct national identity as being opposed to their attempts to elevate the process of nation-building. The ruling nationalist and neo-communist parties even view the Hungarian demands for the protection of their identity as a sign of the group's disloyalty towards the young Slovak State. Particularly the Hungarian demands for territorial autonomy are regarded as a first step towards secession. Being afraid that history might repeat itself, they believe that the Government should not give in to the demands of the Hungarians. This view shared among the Slovaks was partly caused by the map of the proposed 'Hungarian' administrative region in the south of Slovakia which resembles the territories annexed by Hungary in 1938. Whether sincerely felt or simulated, the fear of secession by the regions predominantly inhabited by Hungarians was one of the arguments used by the Slovak politicians and journalists to condemn the minority's call for self-determination. The Slovak National Party, a junior member of the ruling coalition, reacted to the Hungarian call by demanding a ban on Hungarian political parties.

Such a reaction and the above-mentioned Government policies are perceived as anti-Hungarian by representatives of this minority. Some other views stress that the restrictive minority policies should be seen as part of the general pressure on the opposition groups.[27] Whether specifically anti-minority, anti-Hungarian or anti-opposition, Mečiar's restrictive and sometimes even repressive policies have resulted in a more hostile relationship between the Government and the Hungarian minority.

It should be pointed out, however, that in the south of Slovakia, Hungarians and Slovaks continue to coexist peacefully. Moreover, it appears that the average Hungarian and his or her Slovak neighbour attach greater importance to general socio-economic issues than to specific political issues dealing with ethnicity and national identity. This, however, does not detract from the fact that the Hungarians increasingly feel themselves to be treated differently from Slovaks, i.e., as second-class citizens.

Besides the Hungarians, for years the Roma have been treated as second-class citizens. They constitute Slovakia's most rejected minority who live on the margins of society. Several polls point to the wide social gap between Slovak society and the Roma. In 1992, for instance, 52% of respondents declared a hostile atti-

---

[27] Cf., M. Kusý, 'Minorities and Regionalization in Slovakia: Regionalization as a Solution for the Hungarian Minority Issue in Slovakia', 7 *Helsinki Monitor* (1996) No. 1, pp. 58-64, at p. 59.

tude towards the Roma. A 1994 survey revealed that as many as 92% of the respondents mentioned that they would not like to have a Roma neighbour.[28]

In contrast to the Hungarians, the Roma are not represented by co-operating professional political organizations that could perhaps bridge the huge gap between the Roma and the Slovak society. Instead, representatives of the 40-odd Romany parties squabble over contradictory views.[29] This complicates the possibility of a consistent representation of the social, cultural and civil interests of the Roma population.[30] The greatest obstacle to a stronger political organization is the lack of skilled persons among the Roma who are sufficiently educated for a political career.[31]

The situation of the Roma minority also differs from that of the Hungarians with regard to the absence of a 'peaceful coexistence' between the Roma and other groups. The marginal position in society or the alleged 'unadaptability' of the Roma results in severe social tensions and has led to radical and aggressive attitudes on both sides. Attacks on the Roma, mostly by skinheads, are a regular occurrence in Slovakia. These often result in serious injuries, in some cases even with fatal consequences. Human rights monitors have reported that the police remain reluctant to take action.[32] The Slovak authorities have been at best slow, and in many cases completely inactive in responding to this country-wide extremist violence.[33] Moreover, sometimes remarks by public figures and even by members of the Government incite an anti-Roma sentiment, despite the fact that the punishment for racial hatred propagation is clearly defined. Populist and nationalist politicians typically point to the problem of a high level of (petty) crime committed by some members of the Roma community against the group as a whole.[34]

Another major political issue of concern to the Roma is exclusion and discrimination with regard to housing, education and employment. This minority group often live segregated from other groups and usually have worse living conditions. The number of Roma living in unbearable conditions in rural communities and devastated central city zones is agglomerating and represents a potentially very serious social and economic problem. An equally critical problem is the extremely high level of unemployment among the Roma.

---

[28] Ministry of Labour, Social Affairs and Family of the Slovak Republic, 'Conceptual Intends of the Government of the Slovak Republic for Solutions of the Problems of Romany Population Under Current Social and Economic Conditions', Bratislava (1997) p. 32.

[29] 'Slovak Romanies: The Underclass', *Business Central Europe*, Issue IV (1998).

[30] IDC-CEU (Information and Documentation Centre of the Council of Europe), *Roma People in Slovakia and in Europe*, Bratislava, Slovak Helsinki Committee & Information and Documentation Centre of the Council of Europe (1995) p. 35.

[31] Pufflerová, loc. cit. n. 12, p. 59.

[32] US Department of State, op. cit. n. 22, p. 11.

[33] ERRC (European Roma Rights Center), *Report on Roma in Slovakia* (1997), www.osi.hu/colpi/piln.

[34] Under communist rule, the Roma were officially held responsible for 50% of robberies and 60% of petty thefts (Minority Rights Group, op. cit. n. 15, p. 246).

5. POST-COMMUNIST ECONOMIC SITUATION

5.1 **In general**

The high unemployment among the Roma and other groups, including Slovaks, is directly related to the economic transformation process following the Velvet Revolution of 1989. After the fall of the communist regime, the Czech and Slovak Federal Republic embarked on a sweeping privatization programme. The aim was to convert its almost entirely State-owned and State-controlled economy to a market system. Unlike the Czech Lands, Slovakia inherited an ineffective structure of heavy industry. Many of its products were unfit for competition on either the domestic or the international market. This industrial structure was a burden on Slovakia's transition to a market economy. Serious economic problems occurred despite the favourable macro-economic legacy it shared in the macro-economic stabilisation success of the former Czechoslovak Federation. Employment rates in the two republics have diverged sharply since the beginning of the economic transformation. Agricultural regions, such as the south of Slovakia, experienced a sharp rise in unemployment rates. In agriculture, subsidies were given to mass-production efforts by the former communist regime in order to acquire self-sufficiency in foodstuffs. After the fall of the communist regime, these subsidies were cut. This worsened the situation of many producers and led to the closure of many agricultural cooperatives. In addition, Slovakia was hit hard by the Federal Government's decision to stop arms exports, which were far more important to the Slovak than to the Czech economy. Slovakia's economy was also negatively affected by the slow growth of its private sector and the low rates of foreign investment. As a result, the Slovak unemployment rate reached 11.8% in 1991, less than three years after the Velvet Revolution.[35]

In 1992, the final year of the unified Czech and Slovak State, a partial stabilisation of Slovakia's economic situation was achieved. There were even signs of economic revival, particularly as a result of the gradual adaptation of enterprises to the new strict conditions. Nevertheless, industrial production decreased by 13.7%, and the volume of agricultural production fell by 11.9%.[36]

The positive tendencies observed by the end of 1992 were initially interrupted by the split of the Czech and Slovak Federal Republic and by a slow-down in economic reform. Unemployment started to rise sharply, reaching 14.6% by the end of 1994.[37] The most serious systematic economic problems experienced by

---

[35] The World Bank, *Slovakia: Restructuring for Recovery*, Washington (1994), p. 3.

[36] Ibid.

[37] SUSR, op. cit. n. 11, p. 196

the transformation were the slow pace of privatisation, the low influx of foreign investment, and a shortage of domestic credit and investment resources.[38]

The first half of 1994 brought some, if only relative, economic stabilisation. Inflation during the first half of the year was only 4.1%, and unemployment stabilised at just over 14.1%.[39] By 1995, an economic recovery had set in: the Slovak economy grew by 7.2% in 1995 and 6.9% in 1996.[40] Economic growth and development was particularly strong in production, productivity, wages, domestic consumption, and exports. Inflation in 1995 and 1996 remained low. The unemployment level, however, stabilised at around 13% in 1997,[41] which is a relatively high rate if compared to the unemployment rate in the Czech Republic or to the situation under the communist regime. Moreover, regional differences in economic development and unemployment continued to persist. The unemployment rates remained high in the predominantly rural districts in the south and east of Slovakia,[42] whereas, at the same time, in Slovakia's largest cities they remained below average. Economic diversification in these urban centres made them less vulnerable to plant closures than was the case in smaller municipalities, as the latter are often dominated by a single employer.

In the period from 1990 to the first half of 1997, Slovakia received more than 1 billion US dollars in foreign direct investment aimed at fostering economic development and political stability. German companies have the largest share of foreign investment in Slovakia followed by Austria and the United Kingdom.[43] The relatively low investment figures are partly a consequence of Slovakia's poor record as regards privatisation. While privatisation has been virtually completed (the private sector share of GDP is more than 85%), some of the most lucrative State-owned firms have been placed off-limits to privatisation. Moreover, the political motivation behind Slovakia's privatisation process, particularly the preference for domestic buyers and the low prices paid by most of those buyers, has ensured a lack of new capital for the country's resource-poor companies.[44]

5.2 The Hungarian minority

As a result of the 1920 Trianon Treaty, the Hungarian region in the present-day Slovakia was cut off from what continued to be the Hungarian State and was united with the far more advanced Czech Lands. This promoted limited industrial

---

[38] B. Angyal (Ed.), *Possibilities and Limitations of Development of the South-Western Slovakia*, Kolárovo, Civitas Foundation (1994) p. 7.

[39] The World Bank, op. cit. n. 35, p. 4.

[40] US Department of State, *Background Notes: Slovak Republic* (April 1998) p. 5.

[41] Ibid.

[42] OECD, *Economic Surveys: the Slovak Republic*, Paris (1996)

[43] US Department of State, op. cit. n. 40, p. 5.

[44] Ibid.

development, stimulating the economy as a whole. During the 1920s and the 1930s, most members of the Hungarian minority benefited from the new economic situation. In the predominantly rural economy of the region inhabited by Hungarians, the peasantry made up the majority (65.4%) of the Hungarian population.[45] At a first glance, it seems that a certain percentage of the peasantry was content with Czechoslovak rule, at least from the economic/financial point of view. The land reform carried out in the early 1920s had redistributed the land more equitably. Even more important was the autarchic policy of the Government, which shielded grain producers from potentially cheaper imported foodstuffs. As a result, the wheat-producing area in the south of Slovakia, mainly inhabited by Hungarians, was better off than before the war. Moreover, the southern-most region of the State, inhabited by the Czechoslovak Hungarian minority, was more suitable for the cultivation of certain products than were other parts of the country. This gave the Hungarian farmers a competitive advantage in the production of high-value agricultural products such as wine, fruits, and vegetables. Thus, a large share of the Hungarian minority were better-off economically in the new political situation compared to their fellow Hungarians on the other side of the border.

After World War Two, the overall situation of the members of the Hungarian minority deteriorated. They lost their civil rights, Hungarian schools were closed and thousands of Hungarians were expelled or fled from the re-united Czechoslovak Republic, among them many persons belonging to the Hungarian elite. In addition, many Hungarians lost their private property as part of a collective punishment for the disintegration of the first Czechoslovak Republic.

Following the communist *coup* in 1948, confiscation of private property, nationalisation of companies, several land reforms, and the establishment of farmers' cooperatives provided the necessary conditions for the planned development of a socialist economy.[46] During the communist era, employment in the agricultural sector gradually declined while more jobs were created in the industrial and services sectors.

The traditionally agricultural region inhabited by Hungarians also had its share in industrialisation. The communist regime invested in projects such as a shipyard, two chemical plants and a large paper mill in the south of Slovakia. Notwithstanding this, representatives of the Hungarian minority claimed that the economic policies of the communist regime neglected their region.[47] The heart of the

---

[45] Of the rest of the Hungarian population 16.9% worked in industry, 6.3% were merchants or worked in the financial sector, and 3.8% were civil servants or professionals (P. Magocsi, 'Magyars and Carpatho-Rusyns', in G. Skilling, (Ed.), *Czechoslovakia, 1918-1988: Seventy Years from Independence*, London, Macmillan (1991) pp. 105-129, at p. 108).

[46] Cf., Bakker, op. cit. n. 22.

[47] Együttélés, *From Minority Status to Partnership; Hungarians in Czechoslovakia/Slovakia 1918-1992*, Bratislava (1993).

Hungarian region continued to lag behind economically, certainly compared to other regions in Slovakia. For instance, whereas the economy of the West Slovak region had gone through a stage of massive industrialisation, its southern 'Hungarian' part maintained a rural character.[48] In 1988, ten districts covering the south of Slovakia with 23% of the total population, contained only 14% of the total fixed assets.[49] In general, it would be safe to say that the overall picture is one of a lack of major investments in the economy of the 'Hungarian' region throughout the communist era. However, it remains unclear whether this can be ascribed to the fact that the region is inhabited by Hungarians. The region's situation along the State border could also have played a role since many former communist governments imposed strong restrictions on economic development in border regions.[50]

In the wake of the post-communist economic reform, the unemployment rate in the Slovak Republic rose rapidly. From the outset, there were clear regional disparities. The lowest level of unemployment has been in Bratislava. The highest unemployment rates have been registered in south-central Slovakia in regions with a large percentage of both Hungarians and Roma among the population. Although there is no clear relationship between population composition and regional unemployment in the Slovak Republic, regions with a low share of Slovaks are often characterised by an unemployment rate which is above the country's average.[51] By the end of 1995, for instance, the unemployment rate in districts with a substantial Hungarian population was 5.6% higher than the average rate for the Slovak Republic (see Table 1).[52]

The relatively high unemployment rate in the south of Slovakia may, for a large part, be explained by the fact that this region is rural in character, it lacks large cities and straddles a State border: these are three factors which in general often have a negative impact on economic development in Central Europe. Especially the traditional agricultural background of the Hungarians and their regions seem to have had a negative impact on their present economic situation as they have been hit particularly hard by the collapse of the agricultural sector. Despite the loss of many jobs in this sector, the proportion of Hungarians working in agriculture is still around 20%, which is almost twice as high as among members of the Slovak majority (see Table 2).

With regard to the poor economic situation in the agricultural sector at present, and the implications for the Hungarian minority, it should be noted that the Hun-

---

[48] Cf., Bakker, op. cit. n. 22.

[49] sos Transylvania-Geneva Committee (Ed.), *The Hungarian Minority in Slovakia*, Bratislava–Komárno (1994).

[50] Cf., J. Fidrmuc, loc. cit. n. 6.

[51] Idem.

[52] Districts (as they existed up to 1996) with a substantial Hungarian population are the districts of Dunajská Streda, Komárno, Galanta, Nové Zámky, Levice, Velky Krtís, Lucenec, Rimavská Sobota, Roznava, and Trebisov.

garians had been in a somewhat favourable position under the communist regime. During the 1980s, part-time farming in privately owned gardens and greenhouses was widespread in the south of Slovakia. A relatively large part of the Hungarian minority managed to earn additional income by selling their much-wanted quality products in markets as far away as the Czech Lands.[53] At present, many of them still manage to supplement their income by producing and selling vegetables, fruit, and wine.

Table 1 *Unemployment rates in Slovakia and the districts covering the Hungarian region as of December 31, 1991-1995.*

Region	1991	1992	1993	1994	1995
Slovakia as a whole	11.8	10.4	14.4	14.8	13.1
Districts with a Hungarian majority *	13.7	14.4	21.0	20.7	17.3
Districts with more than 20% Hungarians **	14.1	14.6	20.3	21.3	18.7

* The districts of Dunajská Streda and Komárno.
** The districts of Dunajská Streda and Komárno, and the districts of Galanta, Nové Zámky, Levice, Velky Krtís, Lucenec, Rimavská Sobota, Roznava, and Trebisov.
Source: SUSR (1995), (1996); OECD (1996).

Table 2 *Employment structure of the Hungarian minority in Slovakia in percentages, 1970 and 1991*

	1970		1991	
National group	Slovaks	Hungarians	Slovaks	Hungarians
Economically active *	1,914	232	2,244	280
Primary sector	18.9	34.4	12.8	23.8
Secondary sector	46.0	36.0	43.5	35.2
Tertiary sector	33.9	28.4	39.6	36.4
Unknown	1.2	1.2	4.1	4.6
Total	100.0	100.0	100.0	100.0

* In thousands.
Source: Collegium Carolinum (1977) p 77; Együttélés, op. cit. n. 47, p. 12.

53 E. Bakker, 'Teleurstelling na euforie: de Hongaarse minderheid na de "Fluwelen Revolutie"', 3 *Geografie* (1994) No. 3, pp. 40-42.

Despite the opportunities to increase household income through small-scale private farming, the average income of members of the Hungarian minority is less than that of members of the Slovak majority.[54] This is due to lower wages in branches where the Hungarian minority is traditionally over-represented, such as agriculture, and higher wages in sectors traditionally employing very few Hungarians, such as mining, manufacturing, and the modern services industry. The higher unemployment among Hungarians also contributes to a lower average income. The same holds time for the level of educational attainment among members of the Hungarian minority, which is significantly lower than among members of the Slovak majority.[55]

Their relatively low educational level is also mentioned as one of the reasons why members of the Hungarian minority have been under-represented in higher posts within various branches of the economy. Limited fluency in the Slovak language and the widespread popular belief that Hungarians generally do not want to speak Slovak has also had a negative impact on Hungarian employability. According to Hungarian minority sources, this under-representation is also due to discrimination by (the former Czechoslovak and) Slovak authorities which have been responsible for the employment of a large part of the total working population. They also claim that Hungarians have been completely excluded from the process of privatising Slovakia's larger companies. Moreover, many Hungarian entrepreneurs have complained that certain branches of banks have declined to provide business loans.[56] Belonging to a group associated with the political opposition makes the obtaining of credit a complicated and difficult process since the banking sector is strongly interwoven with politics.

The data on the economic situation of the Hungarian minority collected by the *Minorities at Risk Project* support the above-mentioned examples of economic disadvantages of this group. With regard to employment opportunities the data reveal substantial differences in access to civil service for Hungarians and Slovaks and provide proof of economic discrimination for the period between 1990 and 1996. The data also indicate disadvantages with regard to four key indicators of the group's economic status. They confirm substantial differences with regard to income, access to higher education, the presence in professions and the presence in official positions. The Hungarians are equal to Slovaks only with regard to property ownership and the presence in commerce. Based on these observations and findings in the field of Government policies and practices, the *Minorities at Risk Project* categorises the Hungarians in Slovakia as a slightly disad-

---

[54] D. Treiman and I. Szelenyi, *Social Stratification in Eastern Europe After 1989: General Population Survey (Datafile)*, Los Angeles, University of California (1993).

[55] L. Gyurgyík, *Magyar mérleg: a szlovákiai magyarság a népszamlálási és a népmozgalmi adatok tükrében*, Bratislava, Kalligram (1994) p. 124.

[56] ICHC (Information Centre of the Hungarian Coalition in Slovakia), *The Hungarians in Slovakia*. Bratislava (1997) p. 15.

vantaged group suffering from historical neglect which does not receive any support in the form of remedial government policies.[57]

5.3 **The Roma minority**

Due to the lack of even some of the most basic economic statistics on the Roma, an analysis of the particular aspect of their economic situation is rendered both difficult and precarious. A more in-depth analysis is lacking because of the fact that most of the Roma are not registered as members of the group and because of the fact that the group is hardly integrated in the official economy at all.

Estimations of the actual unemployment rate among the Roma are very tentative since official figures relating to the size of the Roma population are underestimated. Also, collecting information about the ethnic or national origin of registered unemployed persons is generally not embarked upon in order to avoid any eventual accusation of discriminatory practices. Nonetheless, rough calculations based on the unemployment register arrive at an unemployment rate of more than 40%, while in some localities the rate is as high as 90%.[58]

The extremely high unemployment level is partly explained by the fact that Roma workers often cannot compete with other workers and they are usually the first to be laid off.[59] Very few are sufficiently qualified to take up skilled work or enter apprenticeships in industry. The overall educational level is appallingly low. There are only possibilities of obtaining traditional low-paid occupations and casual work, which increases the danger for some of falling into petty crime. As a consequence, a disproportionate number of young Roma find themselves in penal institutions.

Because of the above-mentioned the Roma population also tends to suffer unevenly from higher rates of poverty.[60] Many Roma families live on social welfare or unemployment benefits which is seldom sufficient to make both ends meet. In addition, credible reports by human rights monitors indicate that the Roma continue to suffer from discrimination in the administration of State services and housing.[61] They usually live in very poor conditions. In rural areas, they often live 2-3 kilometres outside a village in camps or settlements lacking even basic facilities.

A Government proposal to improve the socio-economic situation of the Roma was formulated in the 1991 Principles of Government Policy towards the Roma. It proposed an improvement to the situation by means of education and housing projects for less adaptable groups of citizens. Parts of these plans had already

---

[57] *Minorities at Risk Project* (1998), ibid., nn. 1 and 2. Data set, (www.bsos.umd.edu).

[58] A. Nesporová, 'Comments', in S. Scarpetta. and A. Woetter (Eds.), *The Regional Dimension of Unemployment in Transition Economies* (1995), pp. 396-397, at p. 397.

[59] IDC-CEU 1995, op. cit. n. 30, p. 36.

[60] US Department of State, *Slovak Republic Country Report*, op. cit. n. 22, p. 11.

been realized before Prime Minister Mečiar's Government of nationalists and neo-communists came into power in 1992.[62] However, since then very few Government initiatives have been taken. The Conceptual Intends of the Government of the Slovak Republic for the Solution of the Problems of the Roma Population under Current Social and Economic Conditions, approved by the Cabinet in 1997, promised 49 million US dollars to be spent on education, housing and the integration of the Roma over the next five years. But for 1998 the Government reserved only 808,000 US dollars, and postponed almost every initiative until the general elections of September 1998.[63]

Even the few measures that have gone ahead have proved double-edged. Under the Conceptual Intends, city officials in two of Slovakia's largest cities have erected cheap one-room bungalows on the outskirts of suburbs. The Roma living in the city centre and whose rent was in arrears were then evicted and forced to move to the new sites. Roma representatives claimed that such policies were aimed at segregation and were tantamount to State discrimination.[64]

There are only slight chances that the socio-economic position of the Roma can be improved by the group itself. They are very much divided politically and lack professional parties. Moreover, the few individual Roma wo do make it out of the 'Gypsy underclass' are often reluctant to risk their precarious status by helping their outcast fellow citizens.[65]

The observations by the *Minorities at Risk Project* support the very negative picture of the socio-economic situation of Slovakia's Roma. The data for the period between 1990-1996 collected by Gurr and others indicate a situation of economic inequality and discrimination. They show slight differences between the Roma and the Slovaks with regard to access to civil service, higher education, income, property, and their presence in commerce, the professions and official positions. Because of the wide range of differences between both groups, the project speaks of an overall situation of extreme economic differences. It also finds proof of economic (and political) discrimination and categorises the Roma in Slovakia as a very seriously disadvantaged group suffering from social exclusion and a group that is not supported by government policies aimed at improving its situation.[66]

---

[61] Idem.
[62] Cf., Pufflerová, loc. cit. n. 12, p. 58.
[63] Business Central Europe, op. cit. n. 29.
[64] Idem.
[65] Idem.
[66] Minorities at Risk Project, ibid, nn. 1 and 2.

6. CONCLUDING REMARKS: DISADVANTAGES, POSSIBLE CAUSES AND SOLUTIONS

Based on the above-mentioned findings, it can be concluded that both Slovakia's Hungarians and Roma are economically disadvantaged and suffer from discrimination. There are, however, considerable differences between these two minorities regarding the extent of inequality, its possible causes and solutions to overcome these inequalities.

The Hungarians are an example of an only slightly disadvantaged minority that suffers from historical neglect and that is not supported by Government policies aimed at overcoming some of the historical disadvantages. Their heritage of historical neglect seems to be mainly caused by severe discrimination in the post-war years. Particularly harmful were the 'elimination' of the pre-war Hungarian elite as a result of post-war expulsions and exile, the lack of education in the period between 1945 and the early 1950s, and the confiscation of Hungarian private property in 1945.

As regards the Hungarians, the present disadvantages are in the field of employment, income, access to higher education, their presence in the professions and their presence in official positions. This situation is partly explained by ongoing discriminatory policies and practices. There are, however, few manifest examples of discrimination, except for the clear under-representation of Hungarians in official positions. Cultural and in particular linguistic differences, also seem to have a negative impact on the economic status of the Hungarian minority. Although almost all Hungarians speak Slovak, limited proficiency in the State language makes it difficult to function effectively in the State institutions, which gives these institutions a good excuse for denying them access to official positions. However, probably a more important factor is the economic characteristics of the regions in which the Hungarians live. Especially the relatively high unemployment rate seems to be primarily a consequence of the fact that the south of Slovakia is a typical rural region that lacks large cities and straddles the State border. Therefore one could argue that the disadvantages of the Hungarian minority are not just and not primarily a minority issue.

In order to avoid a sense of grievance among members of the Hungarian minority and to secure a peaceful coexistence between the minority and the majority, it is necessary to overcome the existing economic disadvantages of ethnic Hungarians in Slovakia. A regional development policy promoting structural adjustment and economic development especially in regions with high unemployment is a possible solution to bridge the gap in material well-being and economic opportunities.

Up until now the Government has made several attempts to run regional development programmes from the capital. However, these schemes have hardly been successful. The co-ordination of regional day-to-day politics were hampered by both geographic and bureaucratic distance. A way to overcome these obstacles would be a return to the decentralisation policy of the early 1990s. To this end, with the application of the subsidiarity principle, the central Government should endow local and regional self-government with greater powers and financial means.

As mentioned earlier, the economic situation of the Roma is hardly comparable to that of the Hungarians. Whereas the situation of the latter is characterised by only limited disadvantages and few discriminatory practices, the situation of the former is, at best, poor. Slovakia's Roma suffer from miserable living conditions, extremely high unemployment, appallingly low educational achievement, downright social exclusion and blatant discrimination.

The situation of the Roma also differs from that of the Hungarians with regard to the causes of disadvantages and the persistence of discrimination. These causes are inter-dependent, multi-faceted and complex, though two clear dimensions can be distinguished. The first dimension of possible causes comprises characteristics of the Roma minority. The second dimension is composed of past and present policies and practices of governments and other ethnic or national groups.

As factors which contribute to the existence of economic disadvantages and discrimination, as well as to the persistence of this situation, the following, *inter alia*, can be listed: a lack of united professional political representation, limited (entrepreneurial) incentives, limited endeavour to achieve acceptance by the majority society, social and moral retardation and criminality, cultural differences from other groups, limited proficiency in the Slovak language, and a high demographic growth rate. These factors are directly or indirectly linked to the past and present policies and practices of the Government and other ethnic or national groups that make up the second dimension of possible causes. Examples of these policies and practices are economic and political discrimination, a lack of legal and police protection, and keeping prejudices alive and constructing new ones through the mass media.

Especially these prejudices constitute one of the main obstacles to possible solutions of the 'Roma question' as they are deep and in some cases even deepening. The negative reputation of the Roma among the Slovak voters makes the Government reluctant to initiate effective efforts to address the deep social, educational and economic problems of the Roma. Their reputation also makes it easy for the Government to ignore the problem or to characterise it as 'unresolvable'. But even a government that would attempt to improve the situation of the Roma might be frightened by the complexity of the problem and the very likely failures it will be confronted with. Some opportunities for at least partial success are related to the fact that the Roma question is not a problem centred around one specific minority, but one that concerns Slovak society as a whole. The solution of this problem involves not merely measures directed towards the Roma, but measures to make Slovakia's society as a whole more tolerant of diversity, less discriminatory and capable of ensuring equal opportunities for all. This will take a long time and any achievement is not guaranteed.

7. A REFLECTION

Until October 1998, subsequent neo-communist and nationalist coalition governments headed by Prime Minister Mečiar had more or less ignored the socio-economic problem of the Roma minority. They did very little to stop discrimination in employment, housing, and the administration of State services, including police and legal protection. Moreover, remarks by Members of Parliament belonging to the then ruling parties played to anti-Roma sentiment.

The political changes in the Slovak Republic in the autumn of 1998 might mark the beginning of a much better relationship between the Slovak State and the Roma minority. The new Government composed of four liberal-democratic parties has committed itself to improving Slovakia's record with regard to the rule of law, human rights, and the protection of minorities. It is hoped and expected that this new Government is willing to initiate a more comprehensive approach to one of the most serious and complicated socio-economic and ethnic questions in Central Europe.

Conclusion

SOLUTIONS TO THE PROBLEMS OF MINORITIES: GENERAL OR TAILOR-MADE? – SOME REFLECTIONS

by Willem van Genugten

1. INTRODUCTION

Over the years, minority issues have gained a troublesome image. In the eyes of many observers, minorities are basically nationalist movements aiming at secession – 'one nation, one State' – or at least at autonomy or a level which is more or less equivalent thereto. And while aiming at these goals, they want protection as collectivities, at the same time avoiding that their individual members have access to worldwide recognised human rights, i.e., to the rights that belong to a citizenship-based, multicultural society. Given this starting point, it is sometimes difficult to have a non-ideological, practical debate on minority issues.

The present book discusses the minority situation in three countries – Croatia, Estonia and the Slovak Republic – from the perspective of politics, law and economics. The contributions contain much data, accompanied by all kinds of analyses, recommendations and future perspectives. As such, the book illustrates that 'the' minority problem does not exist: although there are many similarities, the specifics dominate the picture in the countries discussed. This final contribution to the book serves to find out to what extent solutions to minority problems can be general, and to what extent they should be tailor-made (or a combination thereof). Needless to say the balance is mine, that is to say, it is made up by somebody working in the field of international law, who by education and present occupation tries to have an open eye for lessons to be learned from other disciplines.

Having said this, I have identified four topics which have to be dealt with: autonomy and secession; groups rights and multiculturalism; economic deprivation; and the role of the international community. They can be seen as issues which are at stake in every minority situation, on a practical or a more abstract level. The order of presentation should not be seen as a form of 'ranking'.

S. Trifunovska (Ed.), Minorities in Europe – Croatia, Estonia and Slovakia

2. AUTONOMY AND SECESSION

In many contributions, the word 'autonomy' is used, reflecting aspirations by the relevant minority. The concept of autonomy, however, should be dealt with cautiously. Autonomy as such is nothing, or – better to say – it can easily be an empty shell. Using the word means immediately clarifying what one is talking about. Autonomy can, under certain circumstances, be almost equal to secession, while it can also stand for something like the right to use one's own language 'only'. The use of the word 'autonomy' has to be linked to its contents, before it can be given a specific meaning. In addition, one can agree with Gudmundur Alfredsson that 'the label does not matter as long as the central government agrees to share power and leave local matters in the hands of group representatives' (p. 8).

In the book it is illustrated what autonomy means in the concrete minority situations of the countries under scrutiny. Snežana Trifunovska, for instance, States that the Serbs in Croatia initially asked for cultural autonomy, demands 'which were treated with a striking lack of sensitivity' (p. 24). She also notes, however, that the Serbs, when Croatia became a sovereign State, took the position that autonomy, meaning *internal* self-determination, was no longer enough, and that it had to be replaced by the right to secession for the Krajina and the Srijem regions in Croatia, as well as by the right for these regions to join their kin-State (Serbia) – *external* self-determination (p. 24). Later, however, these claims to secession by the Croatian Serbs were renounced, due to, as Trifunovska notes, their military defeat in 1995 and the normalisation of the relations between Croatia and the Federal Republic of Yugoslavia (p. 29). Trifunovska also notes that Croatia is one of the examples which prove that the change of State borders sometimes 'can be a more painful than joyful process' (p. 38):

> 'Unlike in other countries which dismembered in the post-Cold War period (USSR and Czechoslovakia), in Croatia the process of becoming a sovereign State was followed by an inter-ethnic armed conflict which not only devastated the economy, but created and in some instances increased inter-ethnic hatred especially between the ethnic Serbs and Croats' (p. 38).

It is another illustration of the need to act carefully when the issue of maximising autonomy or pleading for secession is at stake. I will return to this.

In relation to the Slovak Republic, Karen Henderson states that the major concern of the Hungarian community within this Republic is the preservation of its Hungarian language, including the right to be educated in that language, and that this logically leads to 'demands for a cultural autonomy which allows Hungarians control over this sphere of their lives' (p. 151). She also states that demands for territorial autonomy receive more limited support among Hungarians (p. 152), adding that 'the deepest Slovak fear is of Hungarian irredentism, namely that the integrity of the Slovak State might be threatened by an underlying desire of the

Hungarian minority to attach the south of the country to Hungary' (p. 152). And this fear is 'fuelled when their Hungarian fellow-citizens talk of territorial autonomy, because historically, autonomy is associated with being a prelude to border changes' (p. 152).

Analysing the present cultural autonomy situation, Henderson, *inter alia*, concludes that the Slovaks living in southern Slovakia – i.e., the region where the Hungarian minority is mainly living – feel more negative about the existing autonomy agreement than those who live outside the region. I agree with Henderson that the differences are significant, although they should not be overestimated: of those living outside the southern part of the Slovak Republic still some 53% basically disagree with cultural autonomy for the Hungarians, while 61% among the Slovaks in southern Slovakia are against (p. 161). In relation to the quest for territorial autonomy, the overall picture is more or less the same (p. 152).

In relation to Estonia, Marina Martynova states that in 1993 the Estonian State Assembly passed the Law on Cultural Autonomy for National Minorities, 'which seems to be of the utmost importance for the Russian population' (p. 98). However, due to the fact that the Law only allows Estonian citizens to profit from it, large parts of the Russian population are excluded from the application of the Law (p. 98). In addition, and consequently, Martynova notes that 'for the time being and in the absence of a concept providing for Russian autonomy, the Russian leaders in Estonia do not know in which way the autonomy could be realised' (p. 100). Further to that, there is no consensus among the Russian leaders in Estonia on aspects of a possible cultural autonomy, such as the risk that accepting cultural autonomy for Russians with Estonian citizenship only 'could make the existing split between the Russians even deeper' (Martynova, p. 100).

The logical conclusion, emerging from the foregoing 'heli-flight' above the autonomy issue, is that the concept of autonomy requires careful consideration and handling. Such a conclusion does not need further evidence. But how about the other side of the coin? Cannot autonomy requests, apart from being an approach which sometimes adds fuel to the fire, also sometimes be seen as a solution for minority problems? My answer to this question is definitely positive. Creating autonomy for well-defined areas and functions can contribute to avoiding a situation in which the parties confront each other with non-political means, like the use of arms. Using the concept of autonomy in a – from both sides – sensible way, can also lead to stability instead of the continuation of the disorder which is normally apparent in the case of minorities 'struggling for their cause'. What 'sensible' means, will be discussed later. For the moment I would like to quote Gummundur Alfredsson, who states that autonomy 'has been successfully implemented in many countries' (p. 11). There sometimes seems to be a tendency to forget this.

3. GROUP RIGHTS AND – VERSUS? – MULTICULTURALISM

The resistance against concepts such as autonomy is often based on an aversion to the underlying concept of 'collective rights' or 'group rights'. Such an aversion can often be seen on the level of States, who are afraid of being confronted with claims by entities like national minorities, but also on the level of those who strongly believe in a multicultural society, based on respect for everyone's individual human rights and the concept of citizenship. The issue is, in all its diversity, dominantly present throughout the book. As far as I am concerned, this is for good reasons, because it is a core issue in the debate on the protection of minorities. In the words of Marina Martynova, the issue can be formulated as follows:

> 'The position and rights of the non-indigenous population in Estonia are linked with the theoretical view on the essence of what is a nation. In reality the subject of discussion is the choice between the ethnic and the civic principle in State-building, though it has not been formulated in these terms. (...) An explanation for the "Estonian case" lies in the theories of the Soviet past. The Marxist-Leninist view on the concept of a nation was based on the ethnic principle. It defined members of a nation as an ethnic community and not as citizens of a State' (p. 87).

Partly due to this history, for many former communist countries it is extremely important to fully realise the notion of citizenship. The issue is touched upon by, amongst others, Marina Martynova, Peter van Krieken and Fernand de Varennes, who discuss the situation in Estonia, with special emphasis on the 1992 Law on Citizenship and its consequences for the Russian minority. And in relation to the Slovak Republic, Marcia Rooker states that 'an unknown number of Roma have become *de jure* or *de facto* stateless as a result of the dissolution of Czechoslovakia and the Czech citizenship law' (p. 185), while Snežana Trifunovska touches upon the political and economic dimensions of citizenship in Croatia, for instance as to 'the restriction of access to employment and to all subsequent rights' (p. 34).

The notion of citizenship is directly linked to such issues as the right to political participation and representation, but also to the right to use one's own language. In the words of Fernand de Varennes, it would even seem 'that if large numbers of people living in a country do not know the official language, then the naturalisation rules should also reflect this reality and permit the acquisition of citizenship with knowledge of the other main languages spoken in the country' (p. 126). Karen Henderson and others underline such aspects as the right to write one's name in one's own language, while Marcia Rooker amply discusses the 1995 Slovak Law on the State Language, which 'prohibits the use of any other language but Slovak in official dealings' and which 'limits the use of minority languages in the media and in cultural activities, even when the target-audience is composed almost entirely of members of minority communities' (p. 185-186).

These practices strongly prohibit a full realisation of the notions underlying the concept of citizenship.

A more theoretical theme, directly linked to that of citizenship, relates to the issue of multiculturalism: the need to make persons live peacefully together, whatever their ethnic background. Budislav Vukas speaks, in relation to the Serbs in Croatia, about 'the establishment of confidence and co-existence with the Serb population' as the 'major, but difficult task of the Croatian authorities and the local populace' (p. 58), while Edwin Bakker discusses the situation of the Roma in Slovakia: their alleged 'unadaptability' results 'in severe social tensions and has led to radical and aggressive attitudes on both sides' (p. 196). It brings him to the conclusion that the problems the Roma are confronted with are also problems of Slovakian society as a whole, and that one is in need of measures to make this society 'more tolerant of diversity, less discriminatory and capable of ensuring equal opportunities for all' (p. 206). Karen Henderson also strongly underlines the importance of tolerance, stating that it is a 'consistent finding' that 'less tension is perceived by Slovaks who coexist alongside Hungarians' and that, therefore, 'Slovak xenophobia is in part literally the fear of the unknown' (p. 159).

To some extent this is an open door, but an important one, with a high degre of reality. Multiculturalism is based on and characterised by trust among individuals from different backgrounds, at least – negatively formulated – to the extent of tolerating differences in colour, habits, et cetera, and preferably – positively formulated – to the extent of real intercultural exchanges, through, for instance, reading each other's newspapers or even such things as intercultural marriages.

The issue of tolerance and mutual understanding is directly linked to the way the media – and communication channels more in general – function. They can contribute in a negative as well as in a positive sense to the realisation of multiculturalism. In the former case one can think of spreading racial hatred or other one-sided information, while in the latter case one can think of articles and programmes which try to advance and build upon ideas that underlie the issue of multiculturalism. Without asking them to 'teach and preach', the media can play a significant role in that respect. In the book, the role of the media and communication more in general is discussed by, amongst others, Karen Henderson. She observes that many problems in the field of communication, including the lack of preparedness to use bilingualism as a starting point, can be traced back to the communist era (the 'legacy of communism'). This is due to 'the failure of communist societies to admit to the paramount need for a State to communicate with its citizens: if a State is not used to explaining itself to citizens in one language, it is unlikely to occur to it to do it in two' (p. 172). And:

> 'Unfortunately, in communist societies jobs were allocated largely according to political criteria or the personal criteria of informal contacts. The establishment of real transparency, openness and competition in distributing power and responsibility would automatically reduce the salience of ethnicity as a selection criteria' (p. 172)

State communication channels as well as the media can play a major role in that respect. The same can be said of education. Investing in younger generations, through educational programmes which can be considered to create tolerance for and a better understanding of 'other cultures' and which constantly fight against prejudices as to 'the other', is probably the best guarantee for a future of peaceful coexistence of different groups. This is also important from the perspective of the self-esteem of children, who can – schematically speaking – develop into basically nationalist actors or grow up as 'world citizens'. The same goes, *mutatis mutandis*, for the education of such different groups as journalists and, for instance, law students. Nevertheless, the possibilities for educational programmes in that respect should not be overestimated. Teachers (often) belong to one of the parties themselves – be it to the majority, to the minority, or to a minority within the minority – and are asked more or less to transcend themselves, and to act as the ideal person upon whom the idea of multiculturalism starts from and is based upon. Do we not all remember, however, Thomas Hobbes' negative view of the human character – as expressed in his *Leviathan* (1651) – and should we not be convinced, given recent European and African experiences, that he is still right, at least to some extent?

Anyhow, education can – and should – be seen as a means to contribute to a tolerance-based society, at the same time giving the possibility to transfer values which belong to the group. Formulating the possibilities of education in this way, one can see that in education the two lines, which are so characteristic for many minority issues, come together. In the book, the issue is illustrated by Karen Henderson, where she speaks about the proposal of the third Slovak Mečiar Government which 'essentially promoted bilangual education with the aim both of improving knowledge of Slovak among Hungarians, and making education alongside Hungarian children in mixed regions more acceptable to the parents of Slovak children' (p. 156). The proposal had to be abandoned, however, 'because of the stiff resistance of Hungarians, who utterly refused to accept it voluntarily because of fears of creeping assimilation attempts' (p. 156).

Another illustration of the sensitivity of the education issue stems from Marina Martynova, where she notes that in the 1998 Estonian language Strategy and Integration Strategy documents 'education is seen as one of the most influential tools in the process of integration', that 'knowledge of the Estonian language should remove any cultural barrier to subsequent education and employment', and that 'the State is supposed to ensure teaching in a non-Estonian language and to provide education on the history and development of the country of origin' (p. 101).

As is shown through these examples, education is linked to many aspects of society which go far beyond issues such as tolerance and multiculturalism only. It is also about such important things as access to the labour market. As Mirjana Domini notes, 'the education and qualification of minority members to a large degree determine their position in the economy and their possibilities to adapt to new, changed conditions' (p. 79). I will come back to this in the section on 'Economic Deprivation: Cause or Result?'

Before doing so, I would like to add some words on the issue of group rights versus individual rights, and on notions, linked thereto, such as multiculturalism and citizenship. They are in line with my concluding remarks on the autonomy issue. In my opinion it would be a good thing if States would fully accept – in the debates on minority issues as well as in their various national legal practices – the concept of collective rights, as a possible road towards the (beginning of the) solution of problems which otherwise might not be solved at all. This acceptance, however, should be combined with the claim that the rights of the individuals belonging to such a collectivity have to be fully respected. This 'double approach' is reflected in, for instance, the 1994 UN draft Declaration on the Rights of Indigenous Populations and is consistent with existing international law.[1] Probably, the Croatian Constitutional Law, as described by Snežana Trifunovska in the present book (pp. 27-29), can also serve as an illustration of this multi-layer approach. It is my conviction that a multiculturalist approach, based on full respect for individual human rights and on tolerance towards all kinds of ethnic backgrounds and identities, and the recognition of group rights do not have to be in conflict. Such an approach brings in the fruitfulness of thinking in terms of self-determination for minorities, as a concept which creates room for them in addition to the legal status States and individuals do have in international (human rights) law, while it also underlines that finally collective wishes can only be realised when taking individual wishes into full consideration (and when accepting 'opting out clauses' in case individuals do not want to live under the rules of the new leadership). In the words of Gudmundur Alfredsson:

> 'Group rights for minorities are necessary to guarantee a number of rights (including those to identity, culture and education), to otherwise approximate circumstances enjoyed by the majority, to allow individuals to draw on the strength of their groups, and to facilitate interaction of groups with the States in which they live and with international organizations. If group rights are rejected and preferential treatment denied, discriminatory patterns will persist and the equal enjoyment of human rights by minorities will never be realized' (p. 16).

Group rights as a prerequisite for the realisation of individual human rights. Much of the resistance against group rights can be traced back to the exclusive emphasis in the former communist countries on the rights and the interests of the collectivity, without leaving space for their individual members. One should, however, not stick to the dangers of the concept of group rights only, and develop an open and pragmatic eye for the advantages the concept is also to be associated with. On this level there is, to my mind, still a world to win over.

---

[1] See, for instance, the view of the UN Human Rights Committee in the case of the Indian woman *Sandra Lovelace* v. *Canada* (case no. 24/177).

4. ECONOMIC DEPRIVATION: CAUSE OR RESULT?

Many minority problems are directly related to an overall poor economic situation. As soon as the economic situation becomes worse, members of minorities, or minorities as a whole, belong to the first victims. This becomes apparent in less access to work, more discrimination on the job market, growing prejudices as to their economic capacities. The minorities serve as the natural scapegoat every situation automatically creates at the moment things are not going according to expectations or wishes.

The importance of economic welfare, or things like participation in society through access to the job market, should not be underestimated. In the words of Edwin Bakker, it appears, for instance, 'that the average Hungarian and his or her Slovak neighbour attach greater importance to general socio-economic issues than to specific political issues dealing with ethnicity and national identity' (p. 195). The same author links the specific economic situation in southern Slovakia to the specific qualities of the Hungarians living there.

> 'The relatively high unemployment rate in the south of Slovakia may, for a large part, be explained by the fact that this region is rural in character, it lacks large cities and straddles a State border: these are three factors which in general often have a negative impact on economic development in Central Europe. Especially the traditional agricultural background of the Hungarians and their regions seem to have had a negative impact on their present economic situation as they have been hit particularly hard by the collapse of the agricultural sector' (p. 200).

In this example, one can say, the negative consequences of the changes in the economic patterns are directly linked to the specific qualities of the Hungarians living in southern Slovakia, but not to their minority status. Other authors, however, make such linkages between economic deprivation and being a minority. Fernand de Varennes, for instance, notes that the 'economic situation of individuals who belong to linguistic minorities in Estonia clearly appears to be worse than that of so-called "ethnic" Estonians' (p. 139). And: 'Although there are a number of factors which undoubtedly contribute to the situation, it would seem that the Estonian Government's language and citizenship policies and requirements are contributing directly to the higher levels of unemployment amongst Russian-speaking individuals' (p. 139).

As to the same author, these 'restrictions or obstacles that non-citizens are subjected to in the economic field could arguably be said to flow from Estonia's breaches of international law dealing with non-discrimination and/or statelessness' (p. 127). But not all economic problems the Russian minority in Estonia is confronted with, are related to the absence of a recognised citizenship. De Varennes: '(...) even members of the Russian minority who have passed the citizenship hurdle can find themselves excluded from employment opportunities' (p. 135).

In addition, the quality of the jobs occupied by members of minorities on average varies in a negative sense in comparison to those occupied by members of the mainstream society. On that subject, it is noted by Mirjana Domini 'that in Croatia the Italian minority had the largest number of management staff, while the Roma had none' (p. 69). About the Roma she adds:

> 'The greatest losers of the changing system (the transformation of the economy and privatisation) have been the qualified, semi-skilled and auxiliary Roma workers, employed in socially-owned/State firms, who have been redundant. With the increase in the unemployment rate and the problems of retraining, as well as a difficult adaptation to changed working conditions (especially by private contractors), more and more of the Roma have been thrown out of work and income' (p. 77).

Edwin Bakker adds as to the (non-)position of the Roma on the job market that the extremely high unemployment level of the Roma can be partly explained by the fact 'that Roma workers often cannot compete with other workers' and that very few 'are sufficiently qualified to take up skilled work or apprenticeships in industry' (p. 203). The Roma are therefore extremely vulnerable to the risk of entering downward spirals, a process which they can never reverse on their own.

This brings me to the issue that minorities easily come to live in a position of *overall* misery. Again, the Roma are a case in point. In the words of Edwin Bakker, they 'suffer from miserable living conditions, extremely high unemployment, appallingly low educational achievement, downright social exclusion and blatant discrimination' (p. 206). Can it be worse? Probably not. But in many other cases there are also relations between lack of education and access to the labour market, between the non-ability to speak the majority language and access to higher-qualified labour, et cetera. Marina Martynova notes in relation to that, that the non-ethnic Estonians in Estonia face all kinds of problems in different fields, but that 'all these problems are linked to the political one' (p. 87). And Edwin Bakker reaches the same conclusion when he states that 'economic inequalities have often, though not always, been created and reinforced by deliberate social practice and public policy' (p. 191). Economic deprivation: cause or result? The answer can only be found – if ever – on the basis of a detailed tailor-made research. However, the reality is anyhow that in many situations minorities are confronted with a cumulation of problems. Saying so, however, is not yet the same as saying that the majority is the only party to be blamed for that. Sometimes it is, in other cases the answer will be more nuanced and balanced. As I will argue in the final section, it is no solution to consider minorities as victims only. Before doing so, I would like to discuss one issue which always puzzles me professionally: to what extent is international law and international organisations a helping hand in solving minority problems?

5. THE ROLE OF INTERNATIONAL ORGANISATIONS

The minorities issue is on the agenda of several international and regional organisations – see Gudmundur Alfredsson's chapter, especially section 6, for a handy overview –, sometimes already so for some decades, sometimes since only a few years. The question is, to what extent does it matter what these bodies are doing. In general, one might hope that it does, be it on the level of developing standards that can be 'translated' into national policy and legislation, of creating complaint procedures to which members of minorities have access, of organising round tables or offering mediation facilities and 'good offices', or, to mention just one other example, on the level of offering entry to an organisation upon the condition that the relevant State respects the internationally recognised rights of (the members of) its minorities.

The present book gives a series of illustrations of positive influences resulting from the activities of international organisations and their specific bodies, committees, and the like. Gudmundur Alfredsson, for instance, notes that the UN Human Rights Committee, established to monitor compliance with the International Covenant on Civil and Political Rights, 'has made major contributions to the jurisprudence on minority rights' (p. 19), and in doing so the Committee is one of the bodies 'pushing States towards compliance' (Alfredsson, p. 12). Other examples relate to, for instance, the activities of the relatively new, European Commission against Racism and Intolerance (ECRI) – see, amongst other things, Marcia Rooker's remarks on the ECRI involvement in the situation in Slovakia, p. 180 –, while Budislav Vukas touches upon the positive role the European Commission for Democracy through Law ('Venice Commission') played in Croatia. He notes that on the basis of the Commission's recommendations Croatia:

> 'undertook two measures: In January 1998 the Council of National Minorities was set up to act as an independent consultative body defining the interests of minorities and proposing actions in this respect to the Croatian Parliament and the Croatian Government. Secondly, the Croatian Constitutional Court has accepted the Venice Commission's proposal on the participation of international advisors in the work of the Court in cases dealing with minority issues' (p. 58).

Vukas is also quite positive on the role the 1991 Hague Conference and the 1992 London Conference on the former Yugoslavia have played in relation to developments in Croatia. He notes, *inter alia*, that the Croatian President Tudjman has stated that, as a result of the first Conference, the Croatian Constitutional Law 'was modelled on the Hague Draft Convention' (p. 46). Of course, one can add, President Tudjman might have had additional political reasons to say so, but nevertheless he did.

In general, States are prepared to adopt measures – and to underline the fact that they have done so – as soon as they can become members of such organisations as the Council of Europe, the European Union or the NATO. The book gives several illustrations of States being prepared to adapt their legislation and practices as soon as these memberships are to be gained. Budislav Vukas, for instance, mentions that 'in the process of its admission to the Council of Europe, Croatia was required to reconsider its suspension of some of the provisions of its Constitutional Law' (p. 58), while Snežana Trifunovska in relation to the same country notes that 'the increasing Croatian integration in all major international and European institutions [seems to contribute] positively to the internal political/ security situation' (p. 29). In addition, Karen Henderson notes that the discussions on Slovakia's language law 'greatly damaged Slovakia's relationship with the EU', while later on the issue was taken up as 'one of the key short-term political priorities' in the EU's 1998 Accession Partnership with Slovakia' (p. 156). In sum, one can say that, if used with an open eye to the sensitivities minority issues are almost always connected with, the linking of such issues to membership negotiations can sometimes lead to a breakthrough, which cannot otherwise be reached.

In the book, several examples are also given of the positive influence the High Commissioner on National Minorities of the Organisation on Security and Co-operation in Europe has had on the solution of many minority issues. To give only one example: Peter van Krieken notes that Estonia in a sincere and serious way deals with the High Commissioner's recommendations, and that it has adopted 'until now all but one of the recommendations concerned', the final one – on citizenship for children born in Estonia since March 1990 – being underway at the moment of finalisation of his text (pp. 120-121).

Apart from the international organisations and their bodies, external influences also come from the kin-States. They have, more or less by definition, an interest in finding solutions for the problems their 'co-nationals' in another, often neighbouring country, are confronted with. Such an interest sometimes leads to bilateral treaties – as in the case of Croatia and Italy (see Budislav Vukas, p. 61) and between Slovakia and Hungary (see, for instance, Karen Henderson, p. 157) – while in other situations the normalisation of the relations can lead to a situation which is less tense. In that respect, Mirjana Domini notes that 'with the normalisation of relations between the Republic of Croatia and the FR of Yugoslavia, possibilities have been created for the development of cultural and economic relations between the Serbian minority and its kin-State within the framework of accepted international standards' (p. 77). But, of course, the role of the kin-State can also be very detrimental, for instance, by supporting in an unbalanced way wishes for a far-going autonomy, or by stressing the possibilities of secession and/or the establishment of a federation with the kin-State, and so on – see, for instance, Snežana Trifunovska, p. 26, on the role of Serbia in relation to the Croatian Serbs, and Marcia Rooker, p. 182, on the role of Hungary in relation to the Hungarian minority in Slovakia. However, a thoughtful and honest assessment of the roles played by the kin-States can only be made on a case-by-case basis ('tailor-made'), carefully taking into consideration all the effects and side-effects of the kin-State's activities on the position of the 'kin-minority', in the short as well as the long term.

Looking at the issue of 'external influences' from an overall perspective, one can say that the book, not surprisingly, provides many examples illustrating that the international community, at least to some extent, is influencing the course of events, be it on the level of reminding States of what standards they have to live up to, or through active involvement in specific cases (see above). One can add that through the many channels which are available to the international community, a lot of extra attention has been given to minority problems. Generally speaking, that is a good thing in itself. In the words of Gudmundur Alfredsson: 'Governments do not welcome institutional pressure and criticism and would rather avoid it', while the debates in international fora 'put political, diplomatic and public pressure on governments to mend their ways' (p. 13). In that 'game' of creating public attention to specific governmental activities and of creating pressure on governments to change their policies, also non-governmental organisations (NGOs) and the civil society more in general can play an important, if not sometimes decisive role. The activities of many of the above-mentioned international, governmental organisations and their expert-based and governmental bodies, would in many cases not be effective without clear internal support, pushing governments in the same direction.

6. CONCLUDING REMARKS

Minority issues are often seen as a threat to peace and security, and are therefore considered to be highly sensitive. However, even in specific cases minority problems cannot be considered to contain such threatening aspects, they often rightly ask for attention. Minority protection is also about the preparedness to share economic resources, about tolerance, about intrastate good neighbourly relations, et cetera. As such, minority protection is about much more than solving potentially burning issues alone, although it cannot be denied that this is an important aspect. Minority protection is also about preventing the conflict stages that nobody wants.

In that respect the issue of group rights versus individual rights deserves special attention. As argued above, a sound mix of tolerance towards (ethnic) differences through the legal recognition of some collective claims, followed by the claim upon the minority to be tolerant towards the individual claims of its members, can serve as a sound basis for a multicultural society. For obvious reasons, group rights are often considered to be dangerous instruments, depriving individuals of their personal freedoms. One should not forget, however, that group rights can also be instrumental in a positive sense.

Minorities are often seen as pitiful and as victims of oppression by governments that do not want to listen to their justified wishes. This is, no doubt, often the case, as it is also often the case that in studies on minority issues the perspective of these victims and the solutions which are proposed by their representatives are, more or less uncritically, taken as a starting point. In that respect, it might be good to note that minorities, and especially their leaders, also have responsibilities towards society as a whole, that is to say, that one has to look at reasonable means first, without immediately using warlike language, drenched with nationalist terminology and striving to secession, as often happens. Therefore, a sense of responsibility is a first requirement for minority representatives – and others, like journalists. In the words of Peter van Krieken, 'there are no rights without responsibilities' (p. 122). Applying this to Estonia, he states that 'the Estonian Government and people deserve praise with respect to the efforts they have been taking at integration. It is now up to the potential beneficiaries of the fairly ambitious legislation and integration efforts to respond' (p. 122). Finding solutions asks for a preparedness to act responsibly, from two sides. Many minorities to my mind rightly ask for a recognition of their right to be different, while also in many situations the balance is still so much one sided, that it would be more or less unjust to speak about the responsibilities the minorities and their representatives have towards the society as a whole. Nevertheless, in many situations a turning point can be realised, be it from within and/or through assistance from the outside – governmental as well as non-governmental – world, and in that case, it can be more fruitful to accept the point reached than to strive for more. Needless to add that in many cases such a turning point has not yet been reached.

To end. Finding solutions for minority problems will always be a first responsibility for the parties themselves. However, the international community, with its standards and its implementation as well as its supervisory mechanisms, can be highly instrumental in that, as many contributions to the present book show. In the end, the solutions can only be tailor-made. They can take their inspiration from general standards for minority protection as developed by the international community, they can be based on an analysis of best practices, they can even be made in comparison to other cases in which one has found durable solutions, but finally they have to fit as a made-to-measure suit. If the character of the case involved, including its historical, economic and social specifics, is not – or not sufficiently – taken into consideration, such a lack of specificity can serve as a breeding ground for new frustrations, with the type of consequences of which recent history has provided so many shameful examples.

INDEX

ABOUT THE AUTHORS

Introduction

Prof. Dr. Gudmundur Alfredsson – Professor of the Law Faculty and Director of the Raoul Wallenberg Institute for Human Rights and Humanitarian Law at the University of Lund, Sweden

Part One – Minorities in Croatia

Dr. Snežana Trifunovska – Senior University Lecturer, Law Faculty of Nijmegen, The Netherlands, Editor-in-Chief of the *European Yearbook on Minorities*

Prof. Dr. Budislav Vukas – Professor of International Law, Law Faculty, Institute of International and Comparative Law, University of Zagreb, Croatia; Elected Member of the International Tribunal of the Law of the Sea

Mrs. Mirjana Domini – Senior Researcher at the Institute for Migration and Ethnic Studies in Zagreb, Croatia; the head of the project *Minorities and Transfrontier Cooperation*, member of the Advisory Committee on the Council of Europe Framework Convention for the Protection of National Minorities

Part Two – Minorities in Estonia

Dr. Maryna Martinova – Head of the Department of European Studies, Institute if Ethnology and Anthropology, Russian Academy of Sciences, Moscow, Russia

Dr. Peter van Krieken – Lecturer of Human Rights and International Law at the Webster University, Leiden, The Netherlands; Special Advisor on International Affairs at the IND/Ministry of Justice, The Hague, The Netherlands

Dr. Fernand de Varennes – Director, Asia-Pacific Centre for Human Rights and the Prevention of Ethnic Conflict; Editor-in-Chief of the *Asia-Pacific Journal on Human Rights and the Law*

Part Three – Minorities in Slovakia

Mrs. Karin Henderson – University Lecturer, Department of Politics, University of Leicester, Leicester, UK

Mrs. Marcia Rooker – Assistant Researcher and Junior Lecturer of the Law Faculty of Nijmegen, Centre for Migration Law, The Netherlands

Dr. Edwin Bakker – University Lecturer, Faculty of Policy Studies, Peace Research Centre, University of Nijmegen, The Netherlands

Conclusion

Prof. Dr. Willem van Genugten – Professor of International Law at Tilburg University and Professor of Human Rights at Nijmegen University, both in the Netherlands.

FSC
www.fsc.org
MIX
Papier | Fördert gute Waldnutzung
FSC® C083411

Kolibri 360 GmbH
Ferdinand-Jühlke-Straße 7
99095 Erfurt, Deutschland
produktsicherheit@kolibri360.de